When You Cook Upon a Star

Shining Recipes from Near and Far

WIMMER
COOKBOOKS

A CONSOLIDATED GRAPHICS COMPANY

800.548.2537   wimmerco.com

Table of Contents

When You Cook Upon a Star

hen You Cook Upon a Star began as a wish for a handy recipe book of comforting food to share with friends and family. The Auxiliary of St. Luke's Hospital is a close-knit group of people who render service, give financial aid, and promote public awareness of the health and educational initiatives of St. Luke's Hospital for its patients and hospital community. We are also good friends, neighbors, co-workers, family and most importantly-food lovers. Whenever we gather, conversation inevitably turns to the intriguing search for the best-loved recipe. Whether we need a quick cake, an elaborate entree, or crowd-pleasing casserole, someone has a favorite recipe to share.

When You Cook Upon A Star-Shining Recipes from Near and Far is a collection of favorite recipes from Auxilians, volunteers, employees, and friends of St. Luke's Hospital & Health Network. Our St. Luke's community covers a large area, including Bethlehem, Allentown, Easton, Quakertown, and Coaldale. It embraces many cultures and traditions, including the Pennsylvania Dutch, Hungarian, German, Spanish, and Greek. Our recipes reflect the rich ethnic diversity of our communities and the variety of "tastes from home" that we seek in our cooking.

Special thanks to all who shared treasured family recipes and kitchen secrets. We are grateful to all the testers, typists, editors, proofreaders, and researchers. We are indebted to the staff at St. Luke's Hospital & Health Network who generously contributed photography, design and artistic expertise and support.

Please savor this collection of loved food, and share in the warmth, comfort, and enjoyment of our *Shining Recipes from Near and Far.*

Elizabeth Bowyer Malacoff
President, The Auxiliary of St. Luke's Hospital

2006

A special thank you to Lori Diehl and Susan Schantz; their support and guidance throughout this cookbook project was indispensable and greatly appreciated!

Auxiliary Cookbook Committee

Co-Chairmen
Pat Schoenen
Tina Connar

Vice-Chairman
Faith Ann Ryan

Treasurer
Bubsy Kintzer

Historical Facts
Harriet Apfelbaum
Mary Gentry
Judy Waldman

Design Chairperson
Lori Diehl:
Network Director of Graphic Design
St. Luke's Hospital & Health Network

Public Relations Promotions/Marketing
Faith Ann Ryan
Pan Kennedy
Susan Schantz:
Vice President,
Corporate Communications
St. Luke's Hospital & Health Network

Restaurant Contacts
Tina Connar
Lynda Ivarsson
Faith Ann Ryan
Pat Schoenen

Collecting & Distributing Recipes to Testers
Tina Connar
Faith Ann Ryan

Typists and Proofreaders
Harriet Apfelbaum
Tina Connar
Pearl Donaldson
Vilma Harrington
Joy McQuay
Faith Ann Ryan
Jean Schiffert
Pat Schoenen
Jane Stengel
Judy Waldman
Helen Young

Testing Supervisors
Karen Assetto
Joy Cheplick
Lynda Ivarsson
Teresa Kara
Wendy Thomson

Recipe Contributors

Teri Ahmad
Sally Albano
Chris Albeck
Maryjane & Gerald Albeck
Ruth Allen
Elaine Anderson
Helen Anderson
Harriet Apfelbaum
Apollo Grill: Bethlehem, PA
Carla Arbushites
Karen Assetto
Doris Bahner
Rose Ann Bales
Inge Becker
Nancy Becker
Edward Behrens
Lainie Belcastro
Michele Bennett
Sonia Bowyer
Karen Boyer
Joan H. Bray
Brennan's Restaurant:
    New Orleans, LA
Nicole Brewer; Miss Pennsylvania
    2005-2006
Kelly Bruce
Doreen Buchman
Jo-Ann Campbell
Joy Cheplick
Kathy Clark
Anne Clements
Marie Cole
Christina K. Connar
H. Christina Connar
Yvonne & Tom Connar
Sonia Csencsits
Anna Dalesio

Doris W. Davis
Lucinda Dealtrey
Hazel K. Denzel
Sarah Denzel
Susie Deringer
Mary E. Dietz
Chef Brian Donovan
Paula Doto
Lenieve Driver
Terry Edelman
Edge Restaurant: Executive Chef
    Tim Widrick; Bethlehem, PA
Katherine Ely
Anne Elizabeth Evans
Paulette Eyvazzadeh
Carolyn Falasca
Donna Fields
Martha Fisher
Brenda Fox
Katherine Fox
Mary Fox
Pat Fradeneck
Pam Freund
Esther Frisoli
Margaret Fritz
Agnes George
Joan Glancy
Joan P. Glancy
Douglas Godshall
Judy Godshall
Jane Graham
Marianne Gregory
Carole Gressler
Gus's Crossroads Inn:
    Bethlehem, PA
JoAnne Guth
Kathryn Gutshall

Jean D. Hall
Ed Hanna; Chief Meteorologist,
    WFMZ-TV, Channel 69
Eleanor Harbaugh
Lynn Harbold
Diane Harpstar
Nancy Hart
Ethel Harvey
Flo Heacock
Louise Hebert
Kathy & Maury Heller
Mary Jo Hellick
Diane Hess
Donna L. Hoffman
Carol Holbert
Paula K. Horn
Kate Horn
Inez Fungard Horscroft
Gayle Howland
Barbara Hubbard
Jeanne Hunsicker
Inn of the Falcon: Bethlehem, PA
Hallie Iobst
Lynda Ivarsson
Eleanor Johnson
Lois A. Kaercher
Erin Kara
Teresa Kara
Ursula Kennedy
Gloria Kern
Leslie Kingston
Bubsy Kintzer
Maureen Kobasiuk
Susan E. Koch
Judy Kodnovich
Terry Koller
Peg Konold

Recipe Contributors

Gail Korszniak
Eleanor Kravatz
Margie Lehr
Barb Linhart
Steve Link
Cleo Loupos
Janet E. Luther
Elizabeth Malacoff
Mark Malinowski
Belina Mamuzich
Diane Manganiello
Manor House Inn:
    Center Valley, PA
Marblehead Grill and Chowder
    House: Easton, PA
Kay Marstellar
Janet Martin
Susan Master
Joan McEnrue
Sally McFetridge
Carmela McGlade
Lucille McNellis
Katelyn McTague
Chris Mika
Colleen Miller
Sue Mitch
Camie Modjadidi
Jean Montgomery
Mary & Gordon Mowrer
Bob & Joan Murphy
Meg Murphy; Dr. Smilie Pie,
    Caring Clown at St. Luke's
    Hospital, Bethlehem
Helen Najarian
Neiman Marcus
Mary Ann Novatnack
Nutrition Services: St. Luke's
    Hospital & Health Network

Abby Oberbeck
Lesa Oldham
Pat Oravec
Kevin Parker
Lynne Paul
Jocelyn Paulus
Erin Peapos
Ed Petruccelli; Executive Chef, St.
    Luke's Hospital, Bethlehem
Ivy Pychinka
Josephine Quarry
Dawn Ramsden
Cindy Redgate
Kemp Renninger
Barbara Reynolds
Cheryl Reynolds
Cathy Rice
Melissa Riskin
Francie Rodums
Oliver Rodums
Faith Ann Ryan
Jayne Santee
Saucon Valley Country Club:
    Bethlehem, PA
Sheila Saunders
Mary Bridget Sawyer
Nancy Schlegel
Pat Schoenen
Kay Schweyer
Barbara Sciarra
Eva Seibert
Ellen Sheridan
Pat Silfies-Beahm; Dr. Bandaides,
    Caring Clown at St. Luke's
    Hospital, Bethlehem
Susan J. Silvoy
Ashley Smith
Eileen Smith

Lori Smith
Helen K. Snyder
Soho Charcuterie Restaurant:
    Manhatten
Joan Synder
Christina Sotiropoulos
Penny Spugnardi
Leslie Spurlin
Marie Sten
Chrissy Stengel
Jane Stengel
Jean Stoll
Ruth C. Sutherland
Rosemarie Sweeney
Betty Silva
Sandy Szabo
Doris Tatham
Sharon Tennis
Carol Teschke
Terrill E. Theman, MD
Wendy Thomson
Martha Turner
Stephanie Tyrell
Arita Tyson
Rob Vaughn; Anchor, WFMZ-TV,
    Channel 69
Gloria Waas
Judy Waldman
Jim Waters
Cindy Weaver
Marjorie J. Weiss
Linda Wood
Amy Yasso
Elaine Zimmerman
Iona Zimmerman
Mary L. Zimmerman

Recipe Testers

Tara Airoldi
Karen Assetto
Kim Bell
Kelly Bruce
Kathy Calabrese
Rose Marie Chapleski
Joy Cheplick
Anke Christiani
Anne Clements
Christina Connar
Lori Cressman
Gail DeGruccio
Lucinda Dealtrey
Dianne Demko
Pearl Donaldson
Paula Doto
Martha Drust
Dolly Dyer
Quentin Eshleman
Joyce Fosburg
Anna Fritz
Mary Gentry
Ron Gilbert
Joanne Goglia
Elizabeth Greenberg
Licia Grim
Michele Gubich

Stacey Gubich
Eleanor Harbaugh
Lynn Harbold
Diane Harpster
Mary Jo Hellick
Mary Hennigh
Jeanne Hunsicker
Dena Husser
Lynda Ivarsson
Shaku Jain-Cocks
Irene Jordan
Alison Kara
Erin Kara
Myrna Kara
Teresa Kara
Odette Kelly
Pam Kennedy
Helen Kistler
Bernadette Klima
Jana Labelle
Rose Long
Elizabeth Malacoff
Sue Maurer
Mary Rose Mavis
Joan McEnrue
Joy McQuay
Josephine McTague

Katelyn McTague
Anna Miller
Cindy Miller
Camie Modjadidi
Nancy Pittner
Margaret Reczek
Cindy Redgate
Drea Rosko
Faith Ann Ryan
Jayne Santee
Rosemarie Schadle
Nancy Schlegel
Pat Schoenen
Norma Schrey
Judy Siegfried
Jane Stengel
Jean Stoll
Sandy Szabo
Sharon Tennis
Carol Teschke
Wendy Thomson
Maureen Topper
Nikki Vasiliadis
Anne Weeks
Marian Werkheiser

Appetizers & Beverages

When You Cook Upon a Star

A publication of

The Auxiliary of St. Luke's Hospital

The Auxiliary of St. Luke's Hospital

Founded in 1873

The Auxiliary of St. Luke's Hospital enjoys a long and rich history dating back to the year of their founding in 1873, earning the distinction as one of the oldest continuously operating volunteer fund-raising groups in the greater Lehigh Valley.

In the summer of 1873, established and incorporated as the Ladies Aid Society, they successfully launched their first fund-raising project and raised $1,000 toward the cost of furnishings for the "new hospital" originally located within a 20 room renovated home in South Bethlehem.

Today, The Auxiliary of St. Luke's Hospital continues its legacy of fund raising with the same commitment and resolve, helping to improve the quality of health care, as well as supporting medical and nursing education provided by the hospital. Since 1988, when accurate fund-raising records began to be documented, The Auxiliary of St. Luke's Hospital has donated more than $4,500,000 to St. Luke's Hospital & Health Network.

Hot Clam Dip

1 medium onion, chopped

½ bell pepper, chopped

3 tablespoons butter

2 (6½ ounce) cans minced clams, drained

1 cup shredded Cheddar cheese

¼ cup ketchup

1 tablespoon Worcestershire sauce

1 tablespoon Beau Monde seasoning

¼ teaspoon cayenne pepper or to taste

Assorted crackers

- Sauté onions and peppers in butter.
- Add clams, cheese, ketchup, Worcestershire sauce, seasoning, and cayenne.
- Heat until cheese melts.
- Serve with crackers.

Serves 6-8

Note: May be frozen.

Shrimp Dip

1 (8 ounce) package cream cheese, softened

2 tablespoons milk (more or less to soften cream cheese)

Salt and pepper to taste

2 tablespoons chili sauce

3 tablespoons mayonnaise

1 tablespoon lemon juice

1 tablespoon grated onions

1 (4 ounce) can shrimp, chopped

Assorted crackers

- Blend cream cheese, milk, salt, pepper, chili sauce, mayonnaise, lemon juice, and onions with an electric mixer until smooth.
- Blend in shrimp.
- Refrigerate.

Serves 6-8

Note: Crabmeat can be substituted for shrimp. Serve with vegetables or crackers.

Hot Buffalo Dip

2 boneless, skinless chicken breasts, baked and minced

1 (8 ounce) package cream cheese, softened

½ (6 ounce) bottle blue cheese dressing

1 (6 ounce) bottle Tabasco sauce

1 cup shredded Cheddar cheese

Celery sticks or scoop-style corn chips

- Preheat oven to 350 degrees.
- Combine chicken, cream cheese, blue cheese dressing, Tabasco, and Cheddar cheese.
- Divide mixture between two 8 inch pie plates or spoon all into a 13x9x2 inch baking dish.
- Bake for 25 to 30 minutes.
- Serve with celery sticks and corn chips.

Serves 10-12

Hot Crab Dip

1 (8 ounce) package cream cheese, softened

1 tablespoon milk

1 (8 ounce) package fresh back-fin crabmeat

2 tablespoons finely chopped onions

½ teaspoon cream-style horseradish

¼ teaspoon salt

Dash of pepper

⅓ cup toasted sliced almonds

Assorted crackers or Melba toast

- Preheat oven to 375 degrees.
- Blend cream cheese and milk.
- Add crabmeat, onions, horseradish, salt, and pepper.
- Blend well.
- Pour mixture into a 2 quart casserole dish.
- Sprinkle with almonds.
- Bake for 15 minutes.
- Serve with crackers and/or Melba toast.

Serves 6-10

Hot Cheesy Crab Dip

1 cup mayonnaise

1 (6 ounce) can lump crabmeat

½ cup shredded mild Cheddar cheese

½ cup shredded sharp Cheddar cheese

½ cup grated Parmesan cheese

2 tablespoons finely chopped onions

1 garlic clove, minced

½ sweet red pepper, chopped

1 (10 ounce) package bagel chips

- Preheat oven to 350 degrees.
- Blend mayonnaise, crabmeat, all cheeses, onions, garlic, and red pepper.
- Spread mixture into shallow 9 inch dish or pie plate.
- Bake for 20 minutes.
- Serve with bagel chips.

Serves 10-12

Note: May be baked ahead and reheated in microwave.

Baked Holiday Appetizer Dip

1 (8 ounce) package cream cheese, softened

2 tablespoons milk

1 (2½ ounce) jar or package dried beef, chopped

1½ tablespoons instant minced onions

2½ tablespoons chopped bell peppers

1 tablespoon chopped sweet red peppers

¼ teaspoon pepper

½ cup sour cream

¼ cup chopped walnuts or slivered almonds

Assorted crackers

- Preheat oven to 350 degrees.
- Blend cream cheese and milk.
- Stir in dried beef, onions, bell pepper, red peppers, and pepper.
- Mix well and stir in sour cream.
- Spread into a lightly greased shallow baking dish, such as a quiche dish.
- Sprinkle nuts on top.
- Bake for 15 to 20 minutes.

Serves 6

Note: Serve hot with assorted crackers.

3

Artichoke Cheese Dip

1 (14 ounce) can artichoke hearts, well drained and diced

1 (4 ounce) can chopped green chilies

1 cup grated Parmesan cheese

1 cup shredded mozzarella cheese

2 tablespoons grated onions

1 cup mayonnaise

½-1 teaspoon sugar

Tortilla chips

- Preheat oven to 325 degrees.
- Combine artichoke hearts, chilies, Parmesan cheese, mozzarella cheese, onions, mayonnaise, and sugar.
- Spread mixture into a 12 inch pie plate.
- Bake for 20 to 25 minutes.
- Serve warm with tortilla chips.

Serves 10-12

Spinach Artichoke Dip

1 (10 ounce) package fresh spinach, well rinsed and dried

1 (14 ounce) can artichokes, drained and diced

1 cup grated Parmesan cheese

½ cup mayonnaise

½ cup sour cream

1 small onion, chopped

3-4 garlic cloves, diced

Assorted crackers

- Preheat oven to 350 degrees.
- Remove spinach stems.
- Chop in a food processor.
- Add artichokes.
- Stir in Parmesan cheese, mayonnaise, sour cream, onions, and garlic.
- Mix well.
- Pour mixture in an oven safe bowl.
- Bake for 25 to 35 minutes.
- Stir twice while baking.
- Remove from oven.
- Cool for 5 minutes.
- Serve with your favorite crackers.

Serves 10-12

Hot Cheese Dip

2 cups chopped onions

2 cups mayonnaise

1 (8 ounce) package shredded Swiss cheese

- Preheat oven to 325 degrees.
- Combine onions, mayonnaise, and Swiss cheese.
- Spoon mixture into a 1 quart casserole dish.
- Bake for 20 to 25 minutes.

Serves 6-8

Note: Serve with corn chips, tortilla chips, or crackers.

Beer Dip

½ cup blue cheese, crumbled

¾ cup shredded sharp Cheddar cheese

1 teaspoon butter, softened

½ teaspoon dry mustard

⅛ teaspoon Worcestershire sauce

1 teaspoon grated onions

¾ cup beer, room temperature

- Combine blue cheese, Cheddar cheese, butter, mustard, Worcestershire sauce, and onions.
- Add beer and mix well.
- Refrigerate until ready to serve.

Serves 6

Brie Dip

8 ounces Brie cheese, rind removed

2 sticks unsalted butter

1 (8 ounce) package cream cheese, softened

Baguette bread or crackers

- Melt Brie cheese, butter, and cream cheese in the microwave for 1 minute.
- Stir until well blended.
- Microwave an additional 30 seconds.
- Stir again until smooth.
- Serve on baguette bread or favorite crackers.

Serves 8

Evelyn Adam's Taco Dip

1 (8 ounce) package cream cheese, softened

1 (8 ounce) container sour cream

1 (1½ ounce) package taco seasoning mix

1 cup shredded lettuce

1 cup chopped tomatoes

½ cup shredded Cheddar cheese

1 (4 ounce) can sliced black olives

3 green onions, diced

Tortilla chips

- In a blender, mix cream cheese, sour cream, and taco seasoning.
- Spread mixture on the bottom of a 12 inch round dish.
- Top with lettuce, tomatoes, Cheddar cheese, olives, and green onions.
- Refrigerate for 1 hour.
- Serve with tortilla chips.

Serves 6-8

Note: Low fat substitutes may be used.

Amaretto Dip for Fruit

1 (8 ounce) container sour cream

¼ cup powdered sugar

Amaretto liqueur to taste

- Stir sour cream with powdered sugar (enough to make the dip thick enough when amaretto is added).
- Add amaretto by tablespoon to taste.

Serves 6-8

Note: Serve with cold fruit, such as strawberries, pineapple, and cantaloupe.

In February 2002 as a result of a generous gift of about $46,000 from The Auxiliary of St. Luke's Hospital, the St. Luke's Cancer Center began to offer cancer patients free van transportation to their health care appointments.

Vermont Cheddar Spread with Applejack Brandy

1 (10 ounce) package Vermont Cheddar cheese, shredded, room temperature

1 (4 ounce) package cream cheese, softened

2 tablespoons unsalted butter, softened

3 tablespoons applejack brandy

Raw vegetables and crackers

- Combine Cheddar cheese, cream cheese, and butter in a bowl or in a food processor.
- Add brandy.
- Blend thoroughly.
- Pack into a 2 cup container and cover tightly.
- Refrigerate overnight.
- Serve at room temperature with raw veggies or crackers.

Serves 6-8

Note: Store covered and refrigerated for up to one week.

Dilly Smoked Salmon Spread on Cucumber Slices

1 (3 ounce) package reduced-fat cream cheese, softened

1 teaspoon fresh lemon juice

1 tablespoon chopped chives

1 tablespoon chopped dill

3-4 ounces smoked salmon, chopped

25 cucumber slices, about ¼ inch thick

Chopped dill for garnish

- Blend cream cheese, lemon juice, chives, and dill until smooth.
- Stir in salmon.
- Place a spoonful of mixture on each cucumber slice.
- Garnish with dill.

Serves 6-8

The region's first and only permanent and dedicated P.E.T. Scanner was installed at St. Luke's North in July 2001. The scanner offered the newest and most accurate cancer diagnostic technique in the world.

Cream Cheese Tuna Spread

1 (6 ounce) can tuna packed in water, drained and flaked

6 ounces cream cheese, softened

½ teaspoon lemon pepper

1 teaspoon minced onions

¼ teaspoon garlic powder

¼ teaspoon dried dill

¼ teaspoon dried basil

Pinch of salt

¼ teaspoon black pepper

Assorted crackers or bread

- Blend tuna, cream cheese, lemon pepper, onions, garlic powder, dill, basil, salt, and pepper.
- Refrigerate at least 2 hours before serving.
- Spread on crackers or bread.

Makes 1 ½ cups

Note: May be made in advance.

Smoked Salmon Pâté Hors d'oeuvres

¼ pound smoked salmon, diced

2 (8 ounce) packages cream cheese, softened

6 teaspoons minced onions

4 tablespoons chopped fresh dill

3 tablespoons lemon juice

¾ teaspoon Tabasco sauce

Additional chopped dill and dill sprigs for garnish

Assorted crackers or pumpernickel bread

- Combine salmon, cream cheese, onions, dill, lemon juice, and Tabasco.
- Mix thoroughly with a wooden spoon (or your hands) until smooth.
- Transfer to an attractive serving bowl.
- Cover and refrigerate for at least 2 hours.
- Sprinkle with additional chopped dill and garnish with dill sprigs.
- Serve with crackers or pumpernickel bread.

Serves 8-10

Layered Cream Cheese and Smoked Salmon with Dill

6 ounces thinly sliced smoked salmon

2 (8 ounce) packages well chilled cream cheese, halved horizontally

3 tablespoons snipped fresh dill

Assorted breads

- Arrange salmon between cream cheese layers, beginning and ending with cheese.
- Sprinkle layered mixture all over with dill.
- Press in dill to adhere.
- Wrap tightly in plastic wrap.
- Refrigerate up to two days.
- Bring to room temperature.
- Serve with assorted breads.

Serves 8-10

Salmon Roll

1 (8 ounce) can pink salmon

1 (4 ounce) package cream cheese, softened

Salt and pepper to taste

2 teaspoons chopped onions

2 teaspoons lemon juice

¼ cup chopped pecans

2 tablespoons chopped parsley

- Blend salmon, cream cheese, salt, pepper, onions, and lemon juice.
- Shape into a roll. Wrap in plastic wrap and refrigerate.
- Combine pecans and parsley.
- Before serving, roll log in pecan mixture.

Serves 10

Endowed in 1914, the Coxe Ward for Obstetrical Cases was one of the original one-story pavilions built at St. Luke's Hospital. It was funded by the widow and son of coal magnate Eckley B. Coxe. Today, the Coxe Pavilion, as it is now known, is the only original St. Luke's Hospital building that still stands.

Crabmeat Spread

12 ounces cream cheese, softened

1 small onion, minced

2 teaspoons Worcestershire sauce

1 pound crabmeat, drained, no shells

1 cup cocktail sauce
    (see Zippy Cocktail Sauce)

½ cup chopped pecans

3 tablespoons chopped parsley

Assorted crackers

- In food processor or small bowl, blend cream cheese, onions, and Worcestershire sauce.
- Spread mixture on the bottom of a 9 or 10 inch pie plate (or similar serving platter).
- Flake crabmeat and evenly spoon over cream cheese.
- Spoon cocktail sauce over crabmeat.
- Sprinkle with pecans and parsley.
- Refrigerate at least 2 hours or until ready to serve.
- Serve with crackers.

Serves 12

Zippy Cocktail Sauce

½ cup ketchup

1 heaping tablespoon prepared horseradish

3 tablespoons sugar

1 tablespoon steak sauce

1 ½ teaspoons lemon juice

½ teaspoon Worcestershire sauce

8 drops Tabasco sauce

Salt and ground pepper to taste

- Combine ketchup, horseradish, sugar, steak sauce, lemon juice, Worcestershire sauce, Tabasco, salt, and pepper.
- Mix well.
- Cover and refrigerate.

Makes ¾ cup

Note: Best if made a few hours in advance. May be used in the Crabmeat Spread.

In the wake of the terrorist event of September 11, 2001, St. Luke's held various community programs to help adults and children cope with terrorism. In addition, a network-wide Special Bioterrorism Task Force was established to ensure the Network's readiness to respond to potential future bioterrorism attacks.

Salmon Cheese Ball

3 (6 ounce) cans skinless, boneless salmon, drained

1 (8 ounce) package cream cheese, softened

1 tablespoon lemon juice

2 teaspoons grated onions

1 teaspoon horseradish

¼ teaspoon liquid smoke

½ cup chopped pecans

3 tablespoons chopped parsley

Assorted crackers

- Combine salmon, cream cheese, lemon juice, onions, horseradish, and liquid smoke.
- Shape mixture into a ball.
- Refrigerate.
- Remove from refrigerator.
- Press pecans and parsley into ball.
- Press and shape ball into a loaf.
- Serve with crackers.

Serves about 20

Cheese Bombay

1 (8 ounce) package shredded sharp Cheddar cheese, room temperature

1 (8 ounce) package cream cheese, softened

1 tablespoon curry powder

2 tablespoons sherry (scant)

1½ teaspoons fresh garlic, minced

1 (9 ounce) bottle Major Grey's mango chutney

2 tablespoons chopped green onions, white and some green part

Wheat crackers

- Blend Cheddar cheese and cream cheese by hand or in a food processor.
- Add curry, sherry, and garlic.
- Blend well.
- Cover tightly.
- Refrigerate for 24 to 48 hours.
- Bring to room temperature.
- Mound mixture into desired shape on a serving platter.
- Flatten the top.
- Spoon mango chutney on top, chopping any large pieces.
- Sprinkle with green onions.
- Surround with wheat crackers.

Serves 8

Note: Store covered and refrigerated for up to one week.

11

Linda's Special Cheese Ring

1 pound New York sharp Cheddar cheese, shredded, room temperature (or half yellow and half white)

1 cup chopped pecans

½-⅔ cup mayonnaise

2 tablespoons milk (scant)

2 tablespoons finely chopped onions

½ teaspoon Worcestershire sauce

Freshly ground black pepper to taste

Cayenne pepper to taste

Paprika for garnish

Round buttery crackers

- Combine Cheddar cheese, pecans, mayonnaise, milk, onions, Worcestershire sauce, pepper, and cayenne by hand.
- Cover and refrigerate several hours or overnight.
- Bring to room temperature.
- On a dinner-sized plate, mold cheese mixture into a ring around the edges of the plate.
- Garnish with paprika.
- Fill the center of the ring with crackers.

Serves 6

Note: Reduced-fat cheese and mayonnaise can be used. Also, two (4 ounce) jars sliced pimientos may be substituted for the pecans. Pimientos must be drained, patted dry, chopped, and patted dry again.

Brie and Apricot

1 large round or 2 slices Brie cheese

1 (8 ounce) jar apricot preserves

1 sheet frozen puff pastry, thawed

- Preheat oven to 375 degrees.
- Remove rind from cheese and soften in a pie plate.
- Spread cheese evenly in plate.
- Spread preserves over cheese.
- Place pastry over preserves and tuck in the edges.
- Cut several slits in top of pastry.
- Bake about 20 to 25 minutes until lightly browned.
- Serve warm with gourmet crackers.

Serves 8-10

Note: May substitute other preserves to taste.

Blue Cheese Ball

12 ounces cream cheese, softened

4 ounces blue cheese, softened

1 stick butter, softened

5 green onions, chopped, tops only

1 (3½ ounce) can ripe olives, drained and chopped

½ cup slivered almonds, toasted

Cut fresh vegetables or crackers

- Blend cream cheese, blue cheese, and butter.
- Add onions and olives and blend well.
- Refrigerate until firm.
- Shape mixture into a ball.
- Roll cheese ball in almonds.

Serves 6-8

Note: Serve with fresh vegetables or crackers.

Sweet Potato Cheese Ball

1 (8 ounce) package cream cheese, softened

2 cups cold sweet potatoes, cooked and mashed

¼ cup finely chopped onions

2 tablespoons chopped jalapeño peppers (optional)

1 teaspoon seasoned salt

1 teaspoon Worcestershire sauce

1 teaspoon Louisiana hot sauce

¼ cup chopped pecans

Assorted crackers, breadsticks, or raw vegetables

- Beat cream cheese and sweet potatoes until smooth.
- Add onions, peppers, seasoned salt, Worcestershire sauce, hot sauce, and pecans. Mix well.
- Shape mixture into a ball. Cover and refrigerate for 4 hours or more until firm.
- Serve with crackers, breadsticks or vegetables.

Makes about 3 cups

Chocolate Chip Cheese Ball

1 (8 ounce) package cream cheese, softened

1 stick butter, softened

¼ teaspoon vanilla

¾ cup powdered sugar

2 tablespoons packed brown sugar

¾ cup miniature semi-sweet chocolate chips

¾ cup finely chopped pecans

Graham crackers (plain, honey, or chocolate)

- Beat cream cheese, butter, and vanilla until fluffy.
- Gradually beat in powdered sugar and brown sugar just until combined.
- Stir in chocolate chips.
- Cover and refrigerate for 2 hours.
- Place cream cheese mixture on a large piece of plastic wrap and shape into a ball.
- Refrigerate at least 1 hour.
- Just before serving, roll cheese ball in pecans.
- Serve cheese ball with graham crackers.

Serves 6-8

Roasted Red Peppers

6 sweet red peppers, rinsed and halved

2 large garlic cloves, finely chopped

Olive oil

Salt and pepper to taste

Wheat crackers

Parmesan cheese for garnish

- Place peppers on a foil lined broiling pan, cut side down.
- Broil until skin is charred.
- Turn broiler off and cover peppers with foil. Let stand in oven for about 20 minutes.
- Peel off burned skin and lay flat on a plate.
- Sprinkle with garlic, oil, salt, and pepper.
- Serve on wheat crackers and sprinkle with cheese.

Serves 6

Eggplant Appetizer (Caponata-Style)

½ **cup olive oil**

2 **large onions, chopped**

3 **large garlic cloves, minced**

6 **cups diced eggplant (about 1 medium eggplant)**

1 **(14½ ounce) can tomatoes, drained and chopped**

2 **tablespoons fresh lemon juice**

1 ¼ **teaspoons salt**

¾ **teaspoon Tabasco sauce (more to taste)**

¼ **teaspoon pepper**

¼ **cup red wine vinegar**

2 **tablespoons sugar**

Assorted crackers or crisp bread

⅓ **cup pitted black olives, chopped**

- Heat oil in saucepan.
- Add onions and cook for about 3 minutes.
- Add garlic and cook for 3 more minutes.
- Stir in eggplant and cook for at least 15 minutes, stirring often, until eggplant is soft.
- Add tomatoes, lemon juice, salt, Tabasco, and pepper.
- Simmer until mixture is mushy, similar to relish.
- In a separate saucepan, heat vinegar and stir in sugar. Add to eggplant mixture.
- Cook and stir for 2 to 3 minutes.
- May be served warm or cold, with crackers or crisp bread, and garnished with chopped olives.

Serves 6-8

In September 2003, the Board of Trustees unanimously authorized the acquisition of 180 acres in Bethlehem Township, bordered by Route 33 and Interstate 78. The acquisition represented a combined sale and gift agreement with property owner Mrs. Elaine Emrick. For more than 40 years, Elaine and Pete Emrick worked side by side, farming the land. When it came time to make the difficult decision to sell the property, Elaine Emrick wanted to be certain the buyer would use the property for something that would be a source of pride and honor to her family and to Bethlehem Township. She identified St. Like's Hospital & Health Network as an organization that would do just that.

Red Pepper and Corn Relish

1 large sweet red pepper

¼ cup cider vinegar

3 tablespoons pure maple syrup

2½ teaspoons Tabasco sauce

2 teaspoons ground turmeric

1 teaspoon salt

⅓ cup olive oil

3 (10 ounce) packages frozen corn kernels, thawed and drained

½ cup sliced green onions

- Roast pepper over gas grill or under broiler until blackened on all sides.
- Seal in paper bag and let stand 10 minutes.
- Peel, seed, and chop pepper.
- Combine vinegar, syrup, Tabasco, turmeric, and salt in large bowl.
- Gradually whisk in oil.
- Add peppers, corn, and green onions, tossing to coat.
- Cover and refrigerate overnight, stirring occasionally.
- Let stand at room temperature 30 minutes before serving.

Serves 8

Note: May be made 3 days in advance of serving.

Easy Homemade Salsa

4 medium tomatoes, chopped

1 bunch green onions

1 (4 ounce) can black olives, chopped

1 (4½ ounce) can green chiles, chopped

1 tablespoon garlic salt

1 tablespoon vinegar

1 tablespoon olive oil

Assorted chips, crackers, or vegetables

- Combine tomatoes, green onions, olives, chilies, garlic salt, vinegar, and oil.
- Cover and refrigerate for 12 to 24 hours.
- Serve with your favorite chips, crackers, or vegetables.

Serves 8

Note: May add more green onions.

Tex-Mex Salsa

½ **pound tomatoes, seeded and finely chopped**

¼ **pound tomatillos, husked, rinsed, peeled, and finely chopped**

1 **small red onion, finely chopped**

2-4 **fresh serrano, habanera, jalapeño or other hot peppers**

4 **garlic cloves, shredded or finely chopped**

2 **tablespoons lime juice**

2 **tablespoons snipped cilantro**

¼ **teaspoon salt**

- Combine tomatoes, tomatillos, onions, peppers, garlic, lime juice, cilantro, and salt.
- Cover and refrigerate for several hours.
- Cover and store salsa in refrigerator for up to one week.

Serves 10-12

Note: For 4-alarm salsa, leave seeds in peppers before chopping and refrigerate for minimum of 2 to 4 hours. May substitute 1 (13 ounce) can of tomatillos, rinsed, drained and finely chopped for fresh are better.

Bourbon Meatballs

2 **cups ketchup**

2 **cups firmly packed brown sugar**

3 **cups bourbon**

1 **tablespoon dried minced onions or** ¼ **cup finely chopped onions**

½ **teaspoon garlic powder**

1 **(40 ounce) package frozen mild flavored meatballs, thawed**

- Combine ketchup, brown sugar, bourbon, onions, and garlic powder.
- Bring to boil.
- Add meatballs.
- Simmer about 1 hour.
- Refrigerate for 1 to 2 days.
- Remove any excess fat from top.
- Heat and serve warm with toothpicks.

Serves about 20-25

Note: Recipe may be doubled or tripled for large parties, served in a slow cooker set on low.

Sweet-n-Sour Meatballs

1 pound ground beef

½ cup dry bread crumbs

½ cup minced onions

¼ cup milk

1 egg

1 tablespoon dried parsley

1 teaspoon salt

⅛ teaspoon pepper

½ teaspoon Worcestershire sauce

1 (12 ounce) bottle chili sauce

1 (18 ounce) jar grape jelly

- Preheat oven to 350 degrees.
- Combine beef, bread crumbs, onions, milk, egg, parsley, salt, pepper, and Worcestershire sauce.
- Shape mixture into bite-size meatballs. Roll in palm of hand to shape.
- Place meatballs on a baking sheet. Bake about 20 to 25 minutes.
- Heat chili sauce and jelly in a crock pot on low heat. (A regular saucepan on the stove at low heat may be used.)
- Add meatballs and heat, stirring occasionally.

Makes about 30 meatballs.

Note: Triple the ingredients (except onion) for about 80 meatballs. May be made ahead of time and refrigerated.

Pineapple Kielbasa

3 pounds kielbasa, cut into bite-size pieces

1 (20 ounce) can crushed pineapple

1 (12 ounce) bottle chili sauce

½ cup packed brown sugar

- Preheat oven at 350 degrees.
- Mix kielbasa, pineapple, chili sauce, and brown sugar.
- Pour mixture into a 13x9x2 inch baking dish.
- Cover and bake for 1 hour.
- Uncover and bake an additional 30 minutes.

Serves 10-12

Tortilla Wedges

1 (8 ounce) cream cheese, softened

½ cup sour cream

1 (4 ounce) can chopped green chiles

½ cup green onions, sliced

Salt and pepper to taste

10 flour tortillas

Prepared salsa

- Blend cream cheese, sour cream, chiles, green onions, salt, and pepper.
- Spread mixture onto each tortilla.
- Stack tortillas 5 high, making 2 stacks.
- Wrap with plastic wrap and refrigerate.
- When ready to serve, cut each stack into 8 or more wedges each.
- Serve with salsa for dipping.

Serves 8-10

Note: May be made several days in advance.

Tortilla Roll Ups

1 (8 ounce) package cream cheese, softened

½ cup sour cream

1 (4 ounce) can chopped green chilies

1-2 jalapeño peppers, seeded and finely chopped

Chopped black olives to taste

Chopped green onions to taste

2 tablespoons chopped cilantro to taste

6 large flour tortillas

Salsa

- Blend cream cheese and sour cream until smooth.
- Add green chilies, peppers, olives, onions, and cilantro.
- Spread mixture on tortillas.
- Roll up tortillas and cover with plastic wrap.
- Refrigerate.
- Cut into 1 inch pieces and serve with salsa.

Serves 8-10

Bacon Gruyère Rounds

1 (20 ounce) loaf white sandwich bread

1 pound bacon, cooked crisp and crumbled

1 cup grated Gruyère cheese or Swiss cheese

1 cup mayonnaise

1 tablespoon Dijon mustard

1 (4 ounce) can mushroom stems and pieces, drained and chopped

- Using a 1 inch round cutter, cut 3 to 4 circles from each bread slice.
- Combine bacon, Gruyère cheese, mayonnaise, mustard, and mushrooms.
- Mix well.
- Evenly spread mixture onto rounds.
- Freeze rounds in a single layer on baking sheets. Place into freezer bags.
- Preheat oven to 350 degrees.
- Bake frozen rounds for 12 minutes.

Serves 20

French Loaf

1 (12 ounce) package refrigerated crusty French loaf dough

1 (8 ounce) package shredded mozzarella cheese

¼ pound thinly sliced deli ham or salami

1 tablespoon butter, melted

1 tablespoon grated Parmesan cheese

- Preheat oven to 375 degrees.
- On floured board, press loaf into a 14x12 rectangle.
- Sprinkle mozzarella cheese to within ½ inch of the edge.
- Top with ham.
- Roll up from short edge.
- Pinch seams and place seam side down on ungreased baking sheet.
- Brush top with butter and sprinkle with Parmesan cheese.
- Bake for 20-25 minutes or until browned.
- Cool on wire rack for 5 minutes.
- Cut into ½-¾ inch slices with serrated knife.

Serves 8

Stuffed French Loaf

1 (16 ounce) loaf French bread

8 ounces spicy bulk sausage

⅓ cup chopped onions

1 garlic clove, minced

1 egg

1 teaspoon Dijon mustard

2 tablespoons chopped parsley

¾ cup shredded extra sharp Cheddar cheese

½ cup grated Parmesan cheese

¼ cup olive oil

2 teaspoons Dijon mustard

1 teaspoon ground black pepper

- Preheat oven to 350 degrees.
- Slice bread lengthwise and slightly hollow out each half leaving a ½ inch thick layer of bread.
- Place removed bread crumbs in a blender or food processor and process 15 to 20 seconds.
- Cook sausage, onions, and garlic in a heavy skillet over medium heat until meat is browned.
- Drain meat.
- In a large bowl, combine bread crumbs, meat mixture, egg, mustard, and parsley and set aside.
- Combine Cheddar cheese, Parmesan cheese, oil, mustard, and pepper in a food processor.
- Blend about 1 minute into a paste.
- Spread cheese paste evenly over the inside of each bread half.
- Spoon meat mixture into the cavity of each bread half.
- Place bread halves together.
- Wrap in foil.
- Bake for 30 for 35 minutes.
- Cut into 1 inch thick slices and serve immediately.

Serves 12-16

In May 2003, St. Luke's School of Nursing at Moravian College received its first full accreditation from the Commission on Collegiate Nursing Education. Shortly thereafter, the first class of 12 seniors graduated. That same month, St. Luke's Charity Ball raised more than $175,400 to support St. Luke's nursing education programs.

Veggie Wedgies

2 (8 ounce) packages refrigerated crescent rolls

2 (8 ounce) packages cream cheese, softened

1 (1 ounce) package dry ranch dressing mix

1 cup mayonnaise

¾ cup diced tomatoes

¾ cup diced onions

¾ cup diced cauliflower

¾ cup diced broccoli

¾ cup diced mushrooms

1 cup shredded Cheddar cheese

- Press crescent rolls onto a 15x11x2 inch baking sheet, sealing perforations.
- Bake according to package directions.
- Cool.
- Blend cream cheese, dressing mix, and mayonnaise until smooth.
- Spread mixture over cooled crust.
- Add tomatoes, onions cauliflower, broccoli, and mushrooms. Press into cheese lightly.
- Top with Cheddar cheese.
- Place in oven a few minutes to melt cheese.
- Cool.
- Cover with plastic wrap. Refrigerate for 8 to 10 hours.
- Cut into squares.

Serves 12-15

In June 2003, St. Luke's marked the 20th anniversary of the first open-heart surgery performed at the hospital. The program would make St. Luke's the region's most honored heart hospital, earning national recognition for its clinical excellence.

Black Bean Pizza

Pizza shell

1 (15 ounce) can black beans, drained

3 tablespoons vegetable oil

2 tablespoons chopped parsley or cilantro

1 teaspoon ground cumin

1 teaspoon Tabasco sauce

½ teaspoon chopped garlic

1 cup shredded Monterey Jack cheese

1 cup shredded sharp Cheddar cheese

½ cup diced sweet red peppers

¼ cup sliced black olives

¼ cup chopped green onions

Prepared salsa of your choice

- Preheat oven to 425 degrees.
- Place pizza shell on a greased pizza pan.
- Bake for 7 to 10 minutes.
- Blend black beans, oil, parsley, cumin, Tabasco, and garlic in a food processor.
- Spread mixture onto baked pizza shell.
- Top with Monterey Jack cheese, Cheddar cheese, peppers, olives, and green onions.
- Bake for 7 to 12 minutes.
- Serve with salsa.

Serves 8

Note: Can be made as an appetizer or main meal. Use your own set of favorite toppings. To make low fat, substitute low fat cheeses and eliminate olives.

Basil Cream Cheese Bruschetta

12 slices French bread

¾ cup seeded and diced tomatoes

2 tablespoons chopped green onions

1 tablespoon chopped ripe olives

½ teaspoon minced garlic

½ teaspoon salt

¼ teaspoon pepper

4 ounces reduced fat cream cheese, softened

1 tablespoon minced basil

Shredded mozzarella cheese

- Place bread slices on an ungreased baking sheet and broil for 3 to 4 minutes or until golden browned.
- Combine tomatoes, green onions, olives, garlic, salt, and pepper. Set aside.
- Combine cream cheese and basil.
- Spread cream cheese mixture over the untoasted side of bread.
- Spoon tomato mixture over cream cheese.
- Sprinkle mozzarella cheese on top.
- Broil a few minutes until cheese melts.

Serves 4-6

Note: Experiment adding different things to tomato mixture, such as peppers, sweet onions, and various types of tomatoes.   Also, flavored cream cheese, such as chive or vegetable may be used.

St. Luke's Union Station, an outpatient health services center, opened in October 2003. Located in the restored former train station in South Bethlehem, the center provides medical, surgical, pediatric, wound care and dental services. The once magnificent Union Station had been abandoned and was in considerable disrepair when it was purchased by Ashley Development Corporation. St. Luke's worked closely with Lou Pektor of Ashley Development Corporation and Leo Delong of Bucks Development & Contracting Corporation to refurbish the glorious 25,000 square-foot building and transform it into St. Luke's Union Station.

Crostini with California Pistachios

This is an elegant appetizer with a choice of two toppings.

Mediterranean Topping

1 cup roasted red peppers, drained and chopped or diced pimentos

1 cup thinly sliced and crumbled Parmesan cheese

1-2 tablespoons minced garlic

1 tablespoon dried rosemary, crumbled

¼ cup olive oil

Savory Topping

1 (8 ounce) package cream cheese, softened

8 ounces goat cheese

1-2 tablespoons minced garlic

1 teaspoon dried basil

1 teaspoon dried thyme

Crostini

1 (16 ounce) loaf French bread

½ cup pistachios, chopped

1 tablespoon minced parsley

- Combine peppers, Parmesan cheese, garlic, rosemary, and oil.
- Mix well. Set aside.
- Beat cream cheese, goat cheese, garlic, basil, and thyme until smooth. Set aside.
- Preheat oven to 400 degrees.
- Cut bread in half and split lengthwise.
- Spoon topping of choice along length of bread.
- Sprinkle pistachios in diagonal strips across bread.
- Place in a shallow baking pan and loosely cover with foil.
- Bake for 20 minutes or until thoroughly heated.
- Sprinkle with parsley. Cut crosswise into narrow slices.

Makes 5 dozen

Note: To use sourdough baguettes, hollow out some soft bread center, leaving a ½ inch shell.

St. Luke's is designated a major teaching hospital (Solucient) and offers 172 resident/fellowship positions in 17 programs. In 2006, St. Luke's became the only Temple University School of Medicine Clinical Campus in Northeastern Pennsylvania.

Spinach Bars

4 tablespoons butter

3 eggs

1 cup milk

1 cup all-purpose flour

1 teaspoon salt

1 teaspoon baking powder

1 (10 ounce) package frozen spinach, thawed and well drained

1 pound sharp Cheddar cheese, grated

1 small onion, grated

4 garlic cloves, crushed

1 teaspoon freshly squeezed lemon juice

Freshly ground pepper to taste

- Preheat oven to 350 degrees.
- Melt butter in a 13x9x2 inch baking dish in hot oven.
- Blend eggs, milk, flour, salt, baking powder, spinach, Cheddar cheese, onions, garlic, juice, and pepper.
- Add mixture to baking dish.
- Bake for 30 minutes or until golden browned.
- Cool and cut into squares.

Serves 6-8

Crab Appetizer

1 (7½ ounce) can crabmeat

1 (8 ounce) jar sharp processed cheese spread

1 stick butter, softened

2 teaspoons mayonnaise

½ teaspoon garlic powder

8 English muffins

- Combine crabmeat, cheese, butter, mayonnaise, and garlic powder until smooth.
- Separate and quarter English muffins into 64 pieces.
- Spread crabmeat mixture over each muffin piece.
- Place on baking sheet and freeze.
- Store in a zip-top plastic bag in the freezer and use as desired.
- Remove from plastic bag to a baking sheet.
- Place under the broiler for 5 minutes until bubbly and browned.

Serves 10

Cocktail Cheese Rounds

4 tablespoons butter, softened

1 (8 ounce) package shredded sharp
    Cheddar cheese

1 cup all-purpose flour

1 teaspoon salt

Dash of cayenne pepper

50 pecan halves

- Preheat oven to 350 degrees.
- Blend butter, Cheddar cheese, flour, salt, and cayenne.
- Divide mixture into two balls.
- Roll each ball into a long log about 2 inches thick.
- Wrap in wax paper.
- Refrigerate.
- Slice very thin. Place on an ungreased baking sheet.
- Place pecan half on each slice.
- Bake for 10 to 15 minutes.

Makes 50 rounds

Note: Rolls can be made ahead of time and frozen.

St. Luke's continues to work with more than 140 area community, government, educational and social service organizations through the Bethlehem Partnership for a Healthy Community. A national role model for a collaborative approach to improving the health status of the community and reaching those most at risk, the Partnership was established in May 1996 by the Board of Trustees of St. Luke's Hospital & Health Network.

Crab and Brie in Phyllo Dough

2 tablespoons minced shallots

1 tablespoon butter

½ pound crabmeat, well picked over for shells

¼ teaspoon salt

¼ teaspoon pepper

2 teaspoons minced parsley

4 drops Tabasco sauce

½ pound Brie cheese, remove rind and then cut into thin slices

15 sheets of phyllo dough

1 ½ sticks clarified butter

- Preheat oven to 375 degrees.
- Sauté shallots in butter until golden browned.
- Add crabmeat and heat thoroughly.
- Stir in salt, pepper, parsley and Tabasco.
- Spread Brie slices over crabmeat.
- Keep over low heat without stirring until Brie softens enough to be stirred without breaking crabmeat.
- When mixture is fairly homogeneous, set aside and cool.
- Cover 15 phyllo sheets with plastic wrap and top with dish towel. Set aside.
- Reroll remaining phyllo, wrap well in plastic wrap and refrigerate or freeze.
- Lay out 1 phyllo sheet and brush very lightly with butter.
- Fold in half lengthwise and butter again.
- Spoon 1 ½ teaspoons filling at bottom of strip, off to one corner.
- Fold up strip as you would a flag.
- Arrange phyllo packets on a buttered baking sheet and brush lightly with butter.

The Auxiliary of St. Luke's Hospital was named co-recipient of the Most Outstanding Fundraising Group Award presented in November 2003 by the Eastern Pennsylvania Chapter of the Association of Fundraising Professionals. During the 12 years preceding the award, the Auxiliary had raised more then $3.5 million to support St. Luke's Hospital and the St. Luke's School of Nursing.

Crab and Brie in Phyllo Dough, *continued . . .*

- Repeat with remaining sheets, laying out 2 or 3 at a time while keeping rest covered.
- If not serving immediately, cover baking sheet with plastic wrap and refrigerate.
- Bake for 20 to 25 minutes until crisp and golden browned.
- Serve hot.
- To freeze triangles, arrange unbaked packets in single layer on plastic wrap-lined baking sheets.
- Brush packets with butter.

- Wrap each baking sheet tightly with plastic wrap and freeze.
- When frozen, repackage packets more conveniently in layers with wrap between layers.
- Return to freezer.
- To bake, place in preheated oven at 375 degrees.
- Take packets from freezer and place on baking sheet (do not thaw).
- Place directly into the oven and bake until crisp and golden browned.

Serves 12

Note: Freezes well.

Jezabel

1 (12 ounce) jar apple jelly

1 (12 ounce) jar pineapple preserves

½ cup prepared horseradish

1¼ teaspoons dry mustard

Cream cheese, softened

Assorted crackers

- Combine jelly, preserves, horseradish, and mustard.
- Refrigerate overnight.
- Stir until smooth.
- Serve on crackers spread with cream cheese or serve over a block of cream cheese with crackers on the side.

Serves 6-8

The Visiting Nurse Association of St. Luke's opened the region's first freestanding Hospice House in January 2006. Funding for the $2.5 million facility was entirely provided by gifts from the community.

Prosciutto and Gruyère Pinwheels

¾ cup finely grated Gruyère cheese

4 teaspoons chopped fresh sage leaves

1 frozen puff pastry sheet, thawed

1 large egg, slightly beaten

2 ounces thinly sliced prosciutto

- Preheat oven to 400 degrees.
- In a bowl, combine Gruyère cheese and sage.
- On a lightly floured surface, cut pastry sheet in half crosswise.
- Brush the long edge with egg.
- Arrange half of prosciutto evenly on pastry, avoiding egg-brushed edge.
- Top with half of Gruyère cheese mixture.
- Roll pastry up jellyroll fashion into a log, sealing with egg-brushed edge.
- Wrap with wax paper.
- Make another log in the same manner.
- Refrigerate pastry logs, seam side down at least 3 hours until firm or up to 3 days.
- Slice chilled logs crosswise into ⅓ inch thick pinwheels.
- Place slices on a lightly greased baking sheet, cut side down, 1 inch apart.
- Bake for 12 to 16 minutes until golden browned.
- Transfer to a rack and cool slightly.
- Serve warm.

Serves 12-15

In 1999, St. Luke's distributed more than 75,000 Child Emergency Information stickers for car seats to help identify children injured in accidents. The program received the National Health Information Award.

Chicken Broccoli Crescents

1 (3 ounce) package cream cheese, softened

1 (10¾ ounce) can cream of broccoli soup

2 cups cooked cubed chicken

1 (10 ounce) package frozen cut broccoli, cooked

1 tablespoon minced onions

½ teaspoon salt

Dash of pepper

2 (8 ounce) packages refrigerated crescent rolls

½ cup shredded Cheddar cheese

- Preheat oven to 350 degrees.
- Blend cream cheese and soup.
- Stir in chicken, broccoli, onions, salt, and pepper.
- Unroll one package dough into 2 long rectangles.
- Place on an ungreased baking sheet.
- Press to seal perforations.
- Place half mixture on each rectangle to within 1 inch of edge.
- Sprinkle half cheese over each rectangle.
- Unroll second package dough into 2 long rectangles.
- Press perforations to seal.
- Place over chicken mixture.
- Press edges with fork to seal.
- Bake for 22 to 28 minutes.
- Cool 5 minutes.

Serves 8-10

Phase I of the development of the Field of Dreams will include outpatient services such as the region's only freestanding cancer center, two medical office buildings, an ambulatory surgery center and an outpatient testing facility that features a GE Healthcare Global Showsite for radiology and interventional radiology procedures. Phase II will include construction of a new hospital.

Zucchini Appetizers

3 cups thinly sliced, unpeeled zucchini

1 cup biscuit baking mix

½ cup finely chopped onions

½ cup grated Parmesan cheese

2 tablespoons snipped parsley

½ teaspoon salt or to taste

½ teaspoon seasoned salt or to taste

½ teaspoon dried marjoram or oregano leaves

Dash of pepper

1 garlic clove, minced (optional)

½ cup vegetable oil

4 eggs, slightly beaten

- Preheat oven to 350 degrees.
- Combine zucchini, baking mix, onions, Parmesan cheese, parsley, salt, seasoned salt, marjoram, pepper, garlic, oil, and eggs.
- Pour mixture into a greased 13x9x2 inch baking dish.
- Bake about 25 minutes or until golden browned.
- Cut into pieces.

Serves 10-12

Note: May also be baked in a 8 inch pie plate for 45 to 50 minutes. May be prepared with 3 eggs.

The Radiology Department's Picture Archiving Communication Systems (PACS), utilizing computers instead of film to store and display images, became fully operational in February 2004. The PACS system enables several physicians to review an image at the same time from various locations and makes radiographic images available to physicians within minutes of the completion of the examination.

Sausage Stars

1 pound sausage, browned, crumbled and drained

1 (8 ounce) bottle light ranch dressing

½ cup chopped sweet red and/or bell peppers

1½ cups shredded Cheddar cheese

1½ cups shredded Monterey Jack cheese

1 (4 ounce) can sliced black olives

1 package wonton wrappers

Vegetable cooking spray

- Preheat oven to 350 degrees.
- In a bowl, combine sausage, dressing, peppers, Cheddar cheese, Jack cheese, and olives.
- Set aside.
- Carefully press wonton wrappers into greased mini muffin tin to form stars.
- Lightly spray stars with cooking spray.
- Bake wrappers for 5 minutes.
- Remove wrappers from oven and fill each star with sausage mixture.
- Bake for 5 to 10 minutes and serve warm.

Serves 10

Note: May be prepared in advance and heated before serving.

In February 2006, St. Luke's Quakertown Hospital became the first hospital in the region to offer a 64-slice CT Scanner that produces three-dimensional images of the whole, beating heart in just five beats. The technology is ideal for detecting or ruling out coronary artery disease. Subsequently, the technology became available at St. Luke's Miners Memorial Hospital and St. Luke's Hospital-Bethlehem Campus.

Sugar and Spice Pecans

1 egg white

1 tablespoon water

1 pound pecans

1 cup sugar

1 teaspoon cinnamon

- Preheat oven to 200 degrees.
- Beat egg white and water until frothy but not stiff.
- Coat pecans with mixture.
- Combine sugar and cinnamon.
- Mix pecans with sugar mixture.
- Spread pecans on a 13x9x2 inch baking sheet.
- Bake about 45 to 60 minutes, stirring every 15 minutes until pecans appear dry.

Serves 8-10

Candied Pecans

1 stick butter

¼ cup light corn syrup

1 pound pecans

Salt to taste

- Preheat oven to 250 degrees.
- Melt butter and corn syrup.
- Stir in pecans.
- Roast for 1 hour, stirring every 15 minutes to coat pecans.
- Cool on brown paper bag.
- Sprinkle with salt.

Serves 6

In 1999, St. Luke's received its first two awards as one of the nation's 100 Top Cardiovascular Hospitals. The hospital's heart program was honored again in 2001, 2002, and 2003 as one of the nation's 100 Top Cardiovascular Hospitals.

Tid Bits

1 ½ tablespoons butter

1 ½ tablespoons onion salt

1 ½ tablespoons celery salt

1 ½ tablespoons garlic salt

3 tablespoons Worcestershire sauce

3 tablespoons Beau Monde seasoning

1 (15 ounce) box crispy wheat cereal squares

1 (15 ounce) box crispy rice cereal squares

1 (15 ounce) box doughnut-shaped oat cereal

1 (12 ounce) bag pretzel sticks

2 pounds mixed nuts

- Preheat oven to 250 degrees.
- Melt butter in a saucepan.
- Add onion salt, celery salt, garlic salt, Worcestershire sauce, and seasoning.
- In a large bowl, mix all cereals, pretzels, and nuts.
- Spread cereal mixture in a large roasting pan.
- Pour butter mixture over cereal mixture. Stir to coat.
- Bake for 30 minutes.
- Stir ingredients.
- Return to oven and bake an additional 30 minutes.
- Cool completely.

Serves 15-20

Note: May be kept in tin or zip-top plastic bags.

Each year in late fall, managers, physicians and staff participate in the annual Coats for Kids program to provide warm winter clothing, at their personal expense, for about 150 children. Sponsored children are from such organizations as the Fountain Hill Elementary School, South Bethlehem Neighborhood Center, Community Action Committee of the Lehigh Valley and the Visiting Nurse Association of St. Luke's. The 2006 annual shopping trip marked the program's 14th year in which more then 1,200 children have been served.

Fruit Punch

2 cups sugar

1 cup water

3 cups cranberry juice

3 cups orange juice

3 cups pineapple juice

¾ cup reconstituted lemon juice

1 (1 liter) lemon-lime carbonated beverage

- Dissolve sugar in water.
- Add cranberry, orange, and pineapple juices.
- Stir in lemon juice.
- When ready to serve, slowly pour in carbonated beverage.

Serves 15

Champagne Punch

4 (750 ml) bottles champagne

1 (750 ml) bottle apricot brandy

1 (750 ml) bottle vodka

1 (2 liter) ginger ale

Orange slices and cherries for garnish

- Place an ice mold in a large punch bowl.
- Pour in order: the champagne, brandy, vodka, and ginger ale into bowl.
- Make punch just as guests arrive.
- Garnish with orange slices and/or cherries.

Serves 30-40

An outbreak of pertussis (whooping cough) struck the Bethlehem community in October 2003. St. Luke's collaborated with the Centers for Disease Control and Prevention (CDC) and the Pennsylvania Department of Health to manage the outbreak and received commendation from the CDC for its efforts.

Breads & Brunch

St. Luke's Hospital — Bethlehem Campus

Fountain Hill • Lehigh County
Founded in 1872

The Auxiliary of St. Luke's Hospital
has raised more than $3,800,000 to support this campus.

St. Luke's Hospital — Bethlehem Campus

Fountain Hill • Lehigh County
Founded in 1872

St. Luke's Hospital is a non-profit, tertiary-care teaching hospital with campuses in Bethlehem and Allentown. The hospital offers 72 medical specialties and has received more than 25 national awards for clinical excellence and efficient management. St. Luke's has twice been named one of the nation's 100 Top Hospitals.

Apple Bread

3 cups all-purpose flour

1 teaspoon salt

1 teaspoon baking soda

2 teaspoons cinnamon

3 eggs, beaten

⅔ cup vegetable oil

2 cups sugar

2 teaspoons vanilla

2 tablespoons applesauce

3 cups diced apples

1 cup chopped nuts

1 cup raisins

- Preheat oven to 350 degrees.
- Combine flour, salt, baking soda, and cinnamon.
- Add eggs, oil, sugar, vanilla, and applesauce.
- Mix well.
- Stir in apples, nuts, and raisins.
- Pour batter into two greased 9x5 inch loaf pans.
- Bake for 45 minutes until done or tester comes out clean.

Serves 8-10

Simple Banana Bread

3 bananas, previously frozen, thawed

¾ cup sugar

¼ cup vegetable oil

1 egg

2 tablespoons vanilla

1 ½ cups all-purpose flour

1 ½ teaspoons baking powder

½ teaspoon baking soda

½ teaspoon cinnamon

- Preheat oven to 350 degrees.
- Combine bananas, sugar, oil, egg, and vanilla.
- Mix together flour, baking powder, baking soda, and cinnamon.
- Stir banana mixture into flour mixture.
- Using a spatula, spread batter into a buttered 9x5 inch loaf pan.
- Bake about 40 minutes or until bread does not sink when pushed on top.

Serves 6

This recipe is also great with raisins, nuts or chocolate chips.

Lemon Yogurt Bread

2 ¼ cups all-purpose flour

¾ teaspoon baking powder

½ teaspoon baking soda

Pinch of salt

1 stick butter, cut up

1 cup sugar

3 egg whites

Zest of 1 lemon

2 tablespoons fresh lemon juice

1 teaspoon lemon extract

1 (8 ounce) cup nonfat plain yogurt

- Preheat oven to 350 degrees.
- Mix flour, baking powder, and baking soda.
- Add salt.
- In another medium bowl, cream butter and sugar.
- Mix in egg whites. Mixture will look lumpy.
- Add zest, lemon juice, and extract.
- Stir in one-half flour mixture. Add one-half cup yogurt.
- Mix in remaining flour mixture and yogurt.
- Pour batter into greased 9x5 inch loaf pan.
- Bake for 50 minutes or until tester inserted comes out clean.
- Cool in pan about 10 minutes.
- Turn out onto a wire rack to cool completely.

Serves 12

Note: May be frozen for up to 2 weeks.

In September 2006, St. Luke's Hospital-Bethlehem Campus became the first hospital in the region to offer the Trilogy System, the most advanced image-guided intensity modulated radiotherapy and radiosurgery system in the world. This superior treatment is used for treatment of brain tumors, brain abnormalities, and tumors of the lung and spine.

Nut Bread

2½ cups all-purpose flour

4 teaspoons baking powder

1 teaspoon salt

¾ cup sugar

1 egg

2 tablespoons brandy (brandy flavoring)

1 cup milk

1 cup chopped nuts

- Preheat oven to 350 degrees.
- Mix flour, baking powder, and salt and set aside.
- Beat together sugar and egg.
- Add brandy.
- Add milk alternately with dry ingredients to creamed mixture.
- Add nuts.
- Pour batter into a greased and floured 9x5 inch loaf pan.
- Bake approximately 1 hour.

Serves 8-10

Note: English walnuts work well in this recipe.

Pineapple Bread

2 eggs

1 stick butter, melted

1 cup sugar

1 cup crushed pineapple with juice

1 teaspoon vanilla

2½ cups all-purpose flour

3 teaspoons baking powder

½ teaspoon baking soda

¾ teaspoon salt

½ cup chopped walnuts

- Preheat oven to 350 degrees.
- Beat eggs slightly.
- Beat in butter and sugar until smooth.
- Stir in pineapple and vanilla.
- In a separate bowl, combine flour, baking powder, baking soda, salt, and walnuts.
- Stir flour mixture into pineapple mixture until moistened.
- Pour batter into a greased 9x5 inch loaf pan.
- Bake for 50 to 60 minutes.
- Cool in pan for 10 minutes. Remove from pan.
- Cool completely. Wrap in plastic wrap.

Serves 10-12

Pumpkin Bread

2 cups all-purpose flour

2 cups sugar

2 teaspoons baking soda

2 teaspoons cinnamon

1 teaspoon ground cloves

1 teaspoon ground nutmeg

½ teaspoon salt

1 cup vegetable oil

4 eggs, slightly beaten

2 cups pumpkin purée

- Preheat oven to 350 degrees.
- Sift together flour, sugar, baking soda, cinnamon, cloves, nutmeg, and salt.
- Make a well in dry ingredients. Pour oil and eggs into well.
- Beat on low speed until well blended.
- Beat in pumpkin. Pour batter into a greased and floured 10 inch tube pan or two 9x5 inch loaf pans.
- Bake for 1 hour or until top springs back when lightly pressed or tester comes out clean.
- Cool in pan for 15 minutes.
- Turn out onto a wire rack. Cool completely.

Serves 12

Note: Freezes well when wrapped in plastic wrap and foil.

Cortlandt Whitehead, Chaplain, reported that in the first year of operation at St. Luke's Hospital, "those who have been inmates of the Hospital have been connected as follows: Roman Catholics, 20; Lutherans, 10; Episcopalians, 8; Presbyterians, 2; Methodists, 2; Moravian, 1; Baptist, 1. Total 44, The remainder, namely 3 are unrecorded."

Olive Bread

1 cup finely chopped black olives

1 ½ tablespoons finely chopped shallots

1 tablespoon finely chopped garlic

1 tablespoon finely chopped rosemary

1 pound white bread dough, proofed once

1 tablespoon cornmeal

4 tablespoons sun-dried tomato paste

2 (4 ounce) pieces beef tenderloin, cooked, cooled, and sliced

¼ cup feta cheese, crumbled

- Combine olives, shallots, garlic, and rosemary.
- On a floured surface, press out dough to a rectangle, ¾ inch thick.
- Sprinkle olive mixture over dough.
- Fold sides in to hold mixture.
- Beginning with nearest end, roll dough up tightly.
- Transfer carefully to a cornmeal-dusted baking sheet.
- Cover with a towel.
- Set aside in a warm place for 45 minutes to 1 hour or until doubled in size.
- Bake at 400 degrees until bread is deep golden browned and an instant-reading thermometer registers 190 degrees.
- Cool completely on a wire rack before slicing.
- For each sandwich, spread 2 bread slices with sun-dried tomato paste, top with beef slices and sprinkle with feta cheese.
- Serve garnished with some whole olives.

Serves 2

Beer Bread

3 cups self-rising flour

2 tablespoons sugar

1 (12 ounce) bottle beer, room temperature

- Preheat oven to 400 degrees.
- Mix flour, sugar, and beer.
- Pour batter into a greased 9x5 inch loaf pan.
- Bake for 1 hour.

Serves 6-8

Note: To make after Thanksgiving turkey sandwiches, add 1 egg, 1 tablespoon poultry seasoning, and ½ cup finely chopped onions to mixture.

41

Company's Comin' Cornbread

2 (8½ ounce) packages cornbread mix

1 cup cottage cheese

1 (10 ounce) package frozen chopped
  spinach, thawed and drained

2 sticks butter, melted

4 eggs

1 (8 ounce) package shredded Cheddar
  cheese

- Preheat oven to 375 degrees.
- Combine cornbread mix, cottage cheese, spinach, butter, and eggs.
- Add 1 cup Cheddar cheese to mixture and stir well.
- Pour mixture into a greased 13x9x2 inch baking dish.
- Sprinkle remaining cheese on top.
- Bake for 25 to 30 minutes.
- Cool 10 minutes before serving.

Serves 10-12

Note: May use nonfat cottage cheese.

Corn Pone

1 (16 ounce) can cream-style corn,
  undrained

1 (16 ounce) can whole kernel corn,
  undrained

1 (8 ounce) package Jiffy Corn Muffin Mix
  (brand specific)

3 egg yolks

1 stick butter, melted

½-¾ cup finely chopped bell or sweet red
  peppers

¼-⅓ cup finely minced onions

3 egg whites, stiffly beaten

1 cup shredded Cheddar cheese

- Preheat oven to 350 degrees.
- Combine cream-style corn, kernel corn, muffin mix, egg yolks, butter, peppers, and onions.
- Fold in egg whites.
- Pour mixture into 9x9x2 inch baking dish.
- Top with Cheddar cheese.
- Bake for 1 hour.

Serves 8

**Note: The amount of peppers and onions can be varied
according to individual taste. This is a favorite dish to
serve at church or school potluck suppers.**

The Best Coffee Cake Ever

2 sticks butter, softened

2 cups sugar

4 eggs, slightly beaten

1 (16 ounce) container sour cream

2 teaspoons vanilla

3 cups all-purpose flour

2 teaspoons baking soda

½ teaspoon salt

¾ cup sugar

2 teaspoons cinnamon

- Preheat oven to 350 degrees.
- Cream butter and sugar.
- Add eggs, two at a time, mixing well after each addition.
- Blend in sour cream and vanilla.
- Combine flour, baking soda, and salt.
- Add flour mixture and mix well.
- Pour half batter into a greased and floured tube or Bundt pan.
- Combine sugar and cinnamon.
- Sprinkle with half sugar mixture.
- Pour in remaining batter.
- Top with remaining cinnamon mixture.
- Bake for 1 hour.

Serves 10-12

Note: May add apple slices or raisins.

During Fiscal Year 2006, St. Luke's provided more than 100,000 clinic visits to meet the medical needs of children and adults with limited incomes. Clinics are primarily located at the Bethlehem Campus, Allentown Campus, St. Luke's Union Station and the St. Luke's Health Center-Easton.

The Perfect Coffee Cake

1 ½ teaspoons baking powder

1 teaspoon baking soda

¾ teaspoon salt

3 cups all-purpose flour

¾ cup chopped pecans

⅓ cup packed brown sugar

1 ¼ teaspoons cinnamon

1 tablespoon all-purpose flour

1 ½ cups sugar

1 ½ sticks butter, softened

2 teaspoons vanilla

3 large eggs

1 (16 ounce) container sour cream

1 cup powdered sugar

4-6 teaspoons milk

½ teaspoon vanilla

- Preheat oven to 350 degrees.
- Combine baking powder, baking soda, salt, and flour on wax paper.
- Mix pecans, brown sugar, cinnamon, and flour in a bowl. Set aside.
- Beat sugar, butter, and vanilla until creamy. Add eggs, one at a time, beating well after each addition.
- Alternately, blend in flour mixture and sour cream to creamed mixture, beginning and ending with flour mixture.
- Evenly spread 2 cups batter in a greased and floured 12 cup fluted Bundt pan.
- Sprinkle with half nut mixture. Top with 2 cups batter.
- Sprinkle with remaining nut mixture. Top with remaining batter.
- Bake for 55 to 60 minutes or until tester comes out clean.
- Cool in pan on a wire rack for 10 minutes.
- Loosen cake from pan with a small metal spatula. Cool completely.
- Whisk together powdered sugar, milk, and vanilla until smooth. Drizzle over cake.

Serves 16

Note: When adding batter, drop batter by 3 to 4 dollops over nut mixture, gently spreading with a spatula to cover. Be careful not to lift nut mixture out of place. Also, transfer cake to a plate when cool. Decoratively drizzle glaze over cake.

Sour Cream Coffee Cake

2 sticks butter, softened

2 cups sugar

3 eggs

1 (8 ounce) container sour cream

2 cups sifted all-purpose flour

2 teaspoons baking powder

¼ teaspoon salt

1 teaspoon vanilla

¾ cup chopped nuts

2 tablespoons sugar

1 teaspoon cinnamon

- Preheat oven to 350 degrees.
- Cream butter and sugar until light and fluffy.
- Add eggs, one at a time, beating well after each addition.
- Add sour cream and mix well.
- Stir in flour, baking powder, salt, and vanilla.
- Combine nuts, sugar, and cinnamon.
- Pour half of batter into a greased and floured 10 inch fluted tube pan.
- Sprinkle with half nut mixture.
- Repeat with remaining batter and nut mixture.
- Bake for 55 to 60 minutes or until done.
- Cool slightly in pan.
- Remove from pan and cool completely.

Serves 12-16

From 1874 to 1876, the railroad companies, Lehigh Valley, North Penn, and Penna Central, sponsored excursions, free of all expense, for the Ladies' Aid Society. The first was to Onoko Glen which netted $840.65. The second excursion was from Hazelton to the Centennial Buildings at Fairmont Park, raising over $1,600.

Morning Glory Muffins

2 cups all-purpose flour

1½ cups sugar

2 teaspoons baking soda

2 teaspoons cinnamon

½ teaspoon salt

2 cups grated carrots

½ cup raisins

½ cup chopped walnuts or pecans

½ cup shredded coconut

1 apple, peeled and grated or 1 (8 ounce) can crushed pineapple, drained

3 eggs

1 cup vegetable oil

2 teaspoons vanilla

- Preheat oven to 350 degrees.
- Combine flour, sugar, baking soda, cinnamon, salt, carrots, raisins, nuts, coconut, and apples.
- Beat together eggs, oil, and vanilla. Add to dry mixture.
- Do not over-mix.
- Spoon batter into paper-lined muffin cups.
- Bake for 20 minutes.

Makes 14 muffins

Note: May substitute ⅔ cup melted butter for the 1 cup oil. Tastes like carrot cake!

The Ladies' Aid Society resolved at the first meeting, in 1874, that "The Annual meeting shall be held on St. Luke's Day, but if that should fall on Sunday, the said meeting shall be held on the day preceding". St. Luke's Day is celebrated on October 18th.

Baked French Toast

1 (24 inch) loaf French baguette, cut into 20 slices

3 cups milk

6 large eggs

½ teaspoon ground nutmeg

1 teaspoon vanilla

¾ cup packed brown sugar

¼ cup packed brown sugar

Butter

1 cup pecans

1 tablespoon unsalted butter

¼ teaspoon salt

2 cups frozen or fresh berries (optional)

- Preheat oven to 350 degrees.
- Arrange bread slices in bottom of a buttered 13x9x2 inch baking dish.
- Whisk together milk, eggs, nutmeg, vanilla, and ¾ cup brown sugar.
- Pour over bread.
- Cover and refrigerate overnight, turning bread once.
- Sprinkle with ¼ cup brown sugar and dot with butter.
- Bake 20 to 40 minutes or until firm.
- Toast pecans on baking sheet for 8 minutes.
- Toss pecans in butter and salt.
- Sprinkle pecans and berries on baked French toast.

Serves 8

Norwegian Waffles

1 cup all-purpose flour

½ cup sugar

4 eggs

1 (8 ounce) container sour cream

1 stick butter, melted

- Blend flour, sugar, eggs, sour cream, and butter until smooth.
- Pour batter into hot waffle iron.
- Cook until done.

Serves 4-6

The foundation of the Bach Choir was in the Bethlehem Choral Union organized in 1882 by Dr. Wolle, the young organist in the Moravian school and the church. Dr. Wolle's passion for Bach resulted in the Choral Union singers mastering the difficulties of Bach's St. John Passion and St. Matthew Passion.

Blueberry French Toast

French Toast

12 slices day old white bread, crusts removed and cubed

2 (8 ounce) packages cream cheese, cut into 1 inch cubes

1 cup fresh or frozen blueberries, thawed

12 eggs

2 cups milk

⅓ cup maple syrup or honey

- Arrange half bread cubes in greased 13x9x2 inch baking dish.
- Scatter cream cheese cubes over bread.
- Top with blueberries and remaining bread.
- In large bowl, beat eggs.
- Add milk and syrup and mix well.
- Pour egg mixture over top of bread. Cover and refrigerate 8 hours or overnight.
- Remove from refrigerator 30 minutes before baking.
- Cover and bake at 350 degrees for 30 minutes.
- Uncover and bake an additional 25 to 30 minutes or until golden browned and center is set.
- Pour warm blueberry sauce over toast.

Note: For a lighter recipe, use one regular and one reduced fat cream cheese.

Blueberry Sauce

¾-1 cup sugar, as desired

2 tablespoons cornstarch

1 cup water

1 cup fresh or frozen blueberries, thawed

1 tablespoon butter

- Combine sugar and cornstarch in a saucepan.
- Add water and bring to boil over medium heat.
- Boil for 3 minutes, stirring constantly.
- Stir in blueberries and reduce heat.
- Simmer for 8 to 10 minutes or until berries burst.
- Stir in butter until melted.
- Keep sauce warm until ready to serve.

Serves 8-10

As a demonstration of its corporate citizenship, St. Luke's employees volunteer at more than 100 area organizations, exclusive of their volunteer involvement with various religious organizations.

Almond-Anise Biscotti

½ **cup packed brown sugar**

½ **cup sugar**

4 **tablespoons butter, softened**

1 **tablespoon anise seeds**

3 **eggs**

1 **teaspoon almond extract**

1 **teaspoon vanilla**

2½-3 **cups all-purpose flour**

1 **tablespoon baking powder**

¾ **cup blanched almonds**

- Preheat oven to 350 degrees.
- Beat brown sugar, sugar and butter until smooth.
- Add anise seeds and eggs. Mix well.
- Stir in almond extract and vanilla.
- Add flour and baking powder and mix well.
- Stir in almonds.
- Shape dough into rectangle approximately 6-8 inches wide, 1-1 ½ inches thick and 12 inches long.
- Bake about 25 to 35 minutes until golden browned. Test with toothpick to make sure middle is done.
- Remove from oven and cool completely.
- Cut into ½ inch thick slices.
- Arrange slices on their side on a baking sheet.
- Bake for 6 to 10 minutes or until golden browned.
- Remove from oven and turn slices over.
- Bake an additional 3 to 5 minutes until crisp.
- Let cool. Slices become crisper as they cool.
- Store in airtight container.

Serves 12-15

Note: Store for a month in air tight container but anise flavor may get stronger over time.

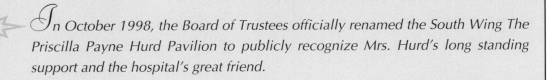

In October 1998, the Board of Trustees officially renamed the South Wing The Priscilla Payne Hurd Pavilion to publicly recognize Mrs. Hurd's long standing support and the hospital's great friend.

Chocolate Chip Scones

2 cups biscuit baking mix

½ cup semi-sweet chocolate chips

⅓ cup whipping cream

3 tablespoons sugar

1 egg

1 teaspoon vanilla

Whipping cream and sugar

- Preheat oven to 425 degrees.
- In large mixing bowl, combine baking mix, chocolate chips, whipping cream, sugar, egg, and vanilla.
- Shape dough into an 8 inch round.
- Place on a greased baking sheet.
- Brush with extra cream and sprinkle with sugar.
- Cut into 8 wedges, do not separate.
- Bake for 12 minutes or until golden browned.
- Serve warm.

Serves 8

Note: If desired, cut 12 smaller scones or drop dough in mounds and bake at 400 degrees until golden browned. To make Raisin Scones, omit chocolate chips and vanilla and add 1 cup raisins. Drizzle top of scones with mixture of one-half cup powdered sugar and one tablespoon whipping cream.

Pineapple Casserole

1 cup sugar

4 eggs

3 tablespoons all-purpose flour

1 (20 ounce) can crushed pineapple

5 slices bread, crust removed and cubed

1 stick butter, melted

- Preheat oven to 350 degrees.
- Beat together sugar, eggs, and flour.
- Add pineapple.
- Pour mixture into buttered 1 ½ quart casserole dish.
- Stir bread cubes into butter.
- Sprinkle on top.
- Bake, uncovered, for 1 hour.

Serves 8

Eggs, Sausage and Cheese Breakfast Casserole

1 pound lightly seasoned bulk sausage

9 eggs

3 cups milk

1 ½ teaspoons seasoned salt

Pepper to taste

10 slices white sandwich bread, crusts removed and cubed

1 (8 ounce) package shredded sharp Cheddar cheese

- Brown and drain sausage. Let cool.
- Beat eggs with milk, salt, and pepper.
- Add cubed bread and cheese.
- Pour mixture into a 13x9x2 inch baking dish.
- Crumble cooled sausage on top.
- Cover and refrigerate overnight.
- Preheat oven to 350 degrees.
- Remove from refrigerator 15 minutes before baking.
- Bake for 45 minutes.
- Let stand 10 minutes before cutting.

Serves 8-10

Note: A Christmas morning breakfast tradition.

In 1922, The Bethlehem Community Chest was established consisting of 12 agencies: The Blind Association, Boy Scouts, Children's Aid Society, Children's Home, Community Center, Day Nursery, Family Welfare Association, Girls Scouts, St. Luke's Hospital, Salvation Army, Visiting Nurse Association, and YMCA.

Easy Cheese Strata

16 slices white sandwich bread

16 slices of Old English Cheese (sharp process cheese spread)

8 eggs, beaten

3 cups milk

2 teaspoons dry mustard

½ teaspoon onion salt

- Arrange 8 slices of bread on bottom of a greased 13x9x2 inch baking dish.
- Top each slice with a cheese slice.
- Repeat with a second layer of bread and cheese.
- Blend eggs, milk, mustard, and onion salt.
- Pour egg mixture over bread and cheese.
- Cover and refrigerate overnight.
- Bake, uncovered, at 400 degrees for 45 to 50 minutes.

Serves 8

Note: This also tastes good with ham, bacon or sausage layers.

Breakfast Casserole

7 slices white sandwich bread, crusts removed and cubed

1 (8 ounce) package shredded Cheddar cheese

6 eggs

3 cups milk

1 teaspoon ground mustard

½ teaspoon salt

¼ teaspoon pepper

6 slices bacon, cooked and crumbled

- Arrange bread cubes in a greased 11x7x2 inch baking dish and top with cheese.
- In a bowl, whisk together eggs, milk, mustard, salt, and pepper.
- Pour egg mixture over bread and cheese.
- Top with bacon.
- Cover and refrigerate overnight.
- Bake, uncovered, at 350 degrees for 50 to 55 minutes or until knife inserted in center comes out clean.

Serves 6-8

Note: To double recipe, use a 13x8x2-inch baking dish and bake at 325 degrees until done.

Sherry Crab Quiche

1 tablespoon butter, softened

1 (9 inch) deep dish pie crust, unbaked

2 cups heavy cream

4 eggs

¾ teaspoon salt

1 cup shredded Swiss cheese

3 tablespoons butter

2 tablespoons chopped onions

2 (6 ounce) cans crabmeat, drained

2 tablespoons sherry

⅛ teaspoon cayenne pepper

- Preheat oven to 425 degrees.
- Spread butter over pie crust.
- Whisk together cream, eggs, and salt.
- Stir in cheese and set aside.
- Melt butter in a saucepan. Add onions and cook until tender.
- Stir in cream mixture.
- Add crabmeat, sherry, and cayenne.
- Pour filling into pie crust.
- Bake for 15 minutes.
- Reduce heat to 325 degrees. Bake an additional 35 minutes until knife inserted in center comes out clean.

Serves 12

Veggie Quiche Cups

1 (10 ounce) package frozen chopped spinach, thawed and well drained

¾ cup egg substitute or 3 large eggs or ¾ cup egg whites

¾ cup shredded reduced fat Cheddar cheese

¼ cup diced bell or sweet red peppers or mixture

¼ cup diced onions

Tabasco sauce and salt to taste

- Preheat oven to 350 degrees.
- Line a 12 cup muffin pan with foil baking cups.
- Spray baking cups with cooking spray.
- Combine spinach, eggs, cheese, peppers, onions, Tabasco, and salt. Divide mixture evenly between 12 cups.
- Bake for 20 minutes or until tester comes out clean.
- Remove from cups to serve.

Serves 8

Company Crêpes

1 pound mild sausage

1 onion, minced

1 (8 ounce) package of cream cheese, softened

1 (7 ounce) can mushroom pieces and stems, drained

1 (8 ounce) can chopped water chestnuts, drained

¼ teaspoon dried thyme

¼ teaspoon garlic salt

12 store-bought crêpes

½ cup sour cream

1 stick butter, softened

½ cup shredded Cheddar cheese

- Brown sausage and onions in a skillet. Drain well.
- Add cream cheese, mushrooms, water chestnuts, thyme, and garlic salt.
- Fill each crêpe with 2 tablespoons sausage filling.
- Roll gently and place crêpes seam side down in a 13x9x2 inch glass baking dish.
- Blend sour cream and butter and pour over crêpes.
- Top with Cheddar cheese.
- Heat in a microwave or oven until warm.

Serves 4-6

Muhlenberg College, in Allentown, PA, was founded in 1848. The name Muhlenberg College was adopted in honor of the patriarch of the Lutheran Church in America, Henry Melchior Muhlenberg. It is an independent, undergraduate, coeducational institution.

Soups & Salads

St. Luke's Hospital — Allentown Campus

Lehigh County
Joined Network in 1997

The Auxiliary of St. Luke's Hospital
has raised more than $67,000 to support this campus.

St. Luke's Hospital — Allentown Campus

Lehigh County
Joined Network in 1997

St. Luke's Hospital – Allentown Campus is undergoing a revitalization resulting from a major facility investment projected to be in excess of $108 million over a five-year period. Since becoming part of the St. Luke's Hospital & Health Network, admissions in all clinical areas have experienced consecutive years of double digit growth. In addition, clinical services and technology have been greatly enhanced.

Butternut Squash Soup

2 tablespoons unsalted butter

1 shallot, chopped or 1 onion

1 butternut squash, peeled and cut into
    1-2 inch pieces

6 cups chicken or vegetable broth

Salt, pepper, and ground nutmeg to taste

- Melt butter in a large stockpot.
- Sauté shallots about 7 minutes or until translucent.
- Add squash and broth.
- Bring to simmer and cook until squash is tender.
- Purée soup with an immersion blender or transfer to a blender.
- Return to pot. Add salt, pepper, and nutmeg. Reheat slowly.

Serves 4-6

Butternut Squash and Pear Soup

3 tablespoons extra virgin olive oil

3 green onions, finely chopped

3 large shallots, finely chopped

1 medium onion, finely chopped

1 ¼ pound butternut squash, peeled and
    cut in 1 inch pieces

½ pound Yukon gold potatoes, peeled and
    cut in 1 inch pieces

4 cups chicken or vegetable broth or
    2 cups broth and 2 cups water

1 tablespoon sugar

2 teaspoons ground coriander seeds

2 teaspoons fine sea salt

Fresh ground black peppercorns

1-2 ripe Bartlett pears (2 if small)

2 tablespoons unsalted butter

Chopped cilantro and chives for garnish

- Heat oil in 4-5 quart heavy stockpot over moderate heat.
- Heat until hot but not smoking.
- Cook and stir green onions, shallots, and onions until soft but not browned.
- Add squash, potatoes, broth, sugar, coriander seeds, salt, and peppercorns.
- Cover and simmer about 15 to 20 minutes until squash is tender.
- Core pears and cut into 1 inch pieces.
- Add pears to soup.
- Remove from heat and cool 10 minutes.
- Purée in blender in batches.
- Return to stockpot to reheat.
- Add butter and stir.
- Garnish with cilantro and chives.

Serves 10-12

Cauliflower Soup

½ cup chopped onions

1 cup chopped celery

½ cup chopped carrots

1 head cauliflower, cut into florets

1 tablespoon chopped parsley

6 cups chicken broth

1 stick butter

¾ cup all-purpose flour

2 cups milk

1 cup light cream

- Simmer onions, celery, carrots, cauliflower, and parsley in broth until tender.
- In a separate saucepan, melt butter and whisk in flour.
- Gradually add milk and cook until creamy.
- Remove from heat and stir in light cream.
- Purée vegetable and broth mixture.
- Add puréed vegetables to thickened cream sauce.
- Gently reheat and serve.

Serves 6

Note: Lighten up by reducing butter amount and using reduced fat milk for milk and nonfat light cream.

Doug's Gazpacho Soup

1 (15 ounce) can Italian or Mexican stewed tomatoes

2 cups vegetable juice cocktail

½ tablespoon Worcestershire sauce

½ tablespoon wine vinegar

1 tablespoon olive oil

¼ cup finely chopped bell peppers

1 tablespoon finely chopped green onion tops

2 shallots, finely chopped

3 tablespoons mild salsa, green chile

½ cup peeled, seeded and chopped cucumber

1 stalk celery, chopped including leaves

- Purée stewed tomatoes with immersion blender.
- Add juice cocktail, Worcestershire sauce, vinegar, oil, peppers, onions, shallots, salsa, cucumbers, and celery.
- Blend mixture.
- Refrigerate at least 4 hours or recommended 8 to 12 hours.

Serves 4

Italian Soup-Maness

5 slices bacon, diced

3 garlic cloves, crushed

1 (16 ounce) can crushed tomatoes

2 (10 ounce) packages frozen chopped spinach

1 cup water (more or less)

2 (15 ounce) cans cannellini beans, undrained

Salt to taste

Grated Parmesan or Romano cheese for garnish

- Cook bacon in a large skillet until lightly browned.
- Add garlic and cook until bacon is crispy.
- Stir in tomatoes and simmer about 10 minutes.
- Add frozen spinach and water. Cook until spinach is completely thawed.
- Add beans and salt and simmer an additional 15 minutes.
- Sprinkle cheese on top before serving.

Serves 6

Note: Enjoy with a good loaf of Italian bread.

Jewish Chicken Soup

("Jewish Penicillin")

4-5 pound chicken, quartered

3 carrots, sliced

3 stalks celery, sliced

1 onion, chopped

1 parsnip, peeled and diced

Salt and pepper to taste

3 sprigs dill, chopped

2 tablespoons kosher instant chicken soup mix

1 sweet potato, peeled, cooked and puréed

- Place chicken in a 6 quart stockpot. Cover with water and bring to boil.
- Skim and discard top of soup when boiling.
- Add carrots, celery, onions, parsnips, salt, and pepper.
- Simmer for 1 hour to 1 hour, 30 minutes.
- Remove chicken pieces.
- Add dill, soup mix, and sweet potatoes.
- Remove chicken meat from bones and return meat to soup.

Serves 6-8

Note: May add orzo, rice, noodles, or matzo balls to soup. Soup may be frozen and reheated.

Mulligatawny Soup

2 cups diced onions

1 cup diced carrots

1 cup diced celery

2 tablespoons butter

2 apples, peeled and diced

2 bananas, diced

2⅓ quarts chicken broth

2 tablespoons curry powder

3 pinches of ground allspice

3 pinches of cayenne pepper

½ cup mango chutney

¼ cup packed dark brown sugar

6 tablespoons butter

6 tablespoons all-purpose flour

1⅓ cups heavy cream

½ pound boneless, skinless chicken breast halves, grilled and diced into ¼ inch pieces

1 cup cooked rice

- Sauté onions, carrots, and celery in butter.
- Add apples and sauté until tender.
- Add bananas and sauté.
- Add broth, curry, allspice, cayenne, chutney, and brown sugar.
- Simmer for 1 hour.
- Melt butter and whisk in flour to make roux. Set aside.
- Strain vegetables and fruit from broth and purée in blender or food processor.
- Return to broth.
- Bring to boil.
- Whisk in roux and stir until thickened.
- Add cream and chicken.
- Simmer for 3 more minutes.
- Add rice and serve.

Serves 10-12

Note: Canned low-sodium chicken broth, reduced by half, may be used instead of chicken broth. This recipe makes a slightly sweet, savory curried cream of chicken soup. Recipe may be halved.

 In 1754, Hans Christiansen, a Dane, erected the first water works in Bethlehem. This first water works, a small frame structure, forced water by pump through wooden pipes to a central water tower.

Mushroom Soup

½ **ounce dried porcini mushrooms**

½ **cup hot water**

2 **tablespoons butter**

1 **small onion, chopped**

4½ **cups diced mushrooms**

3½ **cups vegetable broth**

Salt and pepper to taste

⅔ **cup light cream**

- Soak mushrooms in hot water for 20 minutes.
- Melt butter in a stockpot. Add onions and sauté for 5 minutes.
- Add mushrooms and cook for 5 minutes.
- Add dried mushrooms and the liquid.
- Cook gently for 15 minutes.
- Stir in broth, salt, and pepper.
- Bring to boil. Reduce heat and simmer for 15 minutes.
- Remove from heat. Purée with an immersion blender or transfer to blender and purée in batches.
- Return to pot and stir in light cream.

Serves 4

In 1929, the Ward Packard Laboratory of Electrical and Mechanical Engineering was built, a gift of $1,200,000 from James Ward Packard. James Ward Packard, a benefactor of Lehigh University, was the originator of the Packard automobile and founder of the Packard Electric Company.

Portuguese Soup

5 pounds ground beef chuck

6 large hot or sweet Italian sausages, sliced

7 large yellow onions, minced

1 (1 ounce) envelope dry onion soup mix

1 (1 ounce) package Knorr's Oxtail soup mix

3 (28 ounce) cans whole tomatoes

1 liter hearty burgundy wine

½ cup chopped parsley

1 tablespoon dried basil

1 tablespoon ground marjoram

2 bay leaves

1 tablespoon garlic powder

2 tablespoons sugar

1 (15 ounce) can red kidney beans, drained

1 (58 ounce) can B&M baked beans

- Brown beef and drain fat.
- Brown sausage with onions. Drain well.
- Add to beef.
- Stir in onion soup and oxtail soup mix.
- Add tomatoes, wine, parsley, basil, marjoram, bay leaves, garlic powder, and sugar.
- Cover and simmer for 4 hours, stirring every 30 minutes to prevent scorching.
- Add kidney beans and baked beans.
- Simmer an additional hour, stirring several times.
- Refrigerate overnight. Remove fat from top before serving.

Serves 16

Note: Soup is very thick, almost like chili. Can be made 2 days ahead and the flavor improves. Freezes beautifully and improves in flavor. May substitute Knorr's Tomato with Oxtail or Lipton's Beef Onion Soup for Knorr's Oxtail.

The first fire engine in America was brought to Bethlehem by Captain Jacobsen in 1763. It was so efficient, it sent a water stream 75 feet high and flowed at 78 gallons per minute.

Potato Cheese Soup

1 cup chopped onions

1 garlic clove, minced

3 tablespoons butter

4 cups chicken broth (may use 1 box of chicken broth organic and 99% fat free)

1 (10¾ ounce) can cream of chicken soup

4 pounds russet potatoes, cubed

1 tablespoon chopped parsley

Salt and pepper to taste

1 (8 ounce) package shredded Cheddar cheese

- Sauté onions and garlic in butter for 5 minutes in stockpot.
- Add broth and soup.
- Add potatoes, parsley, salt, and pepper.
- Cover and simmer for 20 to 30 minutes.
- When potatoes become soft, mash them in the pot with a potato masher.
- Add cheese.
- Simmer until cheese melts.

Serves 6-8

Note: This is an easy porridge like soup.

Stilton Cheese Soup

1¾ cups milk

1 small onion, sliced

12 whole black peppercorns

1 bay leaf

2 tablespoons butter

2 tablespoons all-purpose flour

1½ cups chicken broth

1 cup Stilton or blue cheese, crumbled

Assorted crackers

- In medium saucepan, bring milk, onions, peppercorns, and bay leaf to boil.
- Reduce heat and simmer for 15 minutes.
- Strain, reserving milk. Discard onions, peppercorns, and bay leaf.
- In same saucepan, melt butter and remove from heat.
- Whisk in flour until smooth.
- Gradually return milk and add broth. Bring to boil, stirring constantly.
- Reduce heat. Simmer for 1 minute.
- Stir in cheese until melted.
- Serve hot with crackers.

Serves 4

Taco Bean Soup

1 pound bulk pork sausage

1 pound ground beef

1 (1½ ounce) envelope taco seasoning mix

4 cups water

2 (16 ounce) cans kidney beans, rinsed and drained

2 (15 ounce) cans pinto beans, rinsed and drained

2 (15 ounce) cans garbanzo beans, rinsed and drained

2 (14½ ounce) cans stewed tomatoes

2 (14½ ounce) cans Mexican diced tomatoes, drained

1 (16 ounce) jar chunky salsa

Sour cream, shredded Cheddar cheese, and sliced ripe olives for garnish

- In a stockpot, cook sausage and beef over medium heat until no longer pink.
- Drain meat mixture.
- Add taco seasoning and mix well.
- Stir in water, kidney beans, pinto beans, garbanzo beans, stewed tomatoes, diced tomatoes, and salsa.
- Bring to boil.
- Reduce heat.
- Simmer, uncovered, for 30 minutes, stirring occasionally.
- Garnish with sour cream, Cheddar cheese, and olives.

Serves 18-20

Note: In place of Mexican diced tomatoes, use diced tomatoes with jalapeños.

Use 2 pounds of ground beef and omit the sausage.

Brown the meat and put in crock pot. Add all other ingredients except for sour cream, cheese and olives and cook on high for 3 hours.

The first pharmacy in America, at 420 Main Street, was founded by Dr. John Frederic Otto in 1745, and later known as the Simon Rau Drug Store.

White Bean Soup

2 cups dry cannelloni beans or Great
Northern beans

3 tablespoons butter

½ cup finely diced Canadian bacon or
smoked ham

2 tablespoons chopped garlic

1 medium sweet onion, chopped

4 medium carrots, sliced

2 medium turnips, peeled and diced

1-2 parsnips, peeled and diced

3-4 stalks celery, diced

2 leeks, white part sliced

7 cups water

2 beef bouillon cubes

4 bay leaves

1 teaspoon white pepper

1 teaspoon marjoram leaves

- Cover beans with water in a large bowl. Soak overnight.
- Melt butter over medium heat in a large stockpot.
- Add bacon and garlic and cook 3 minutes.
- Add onions, carrots, turnips, parsnips, celery, and leeks.
- Cook for 6 to 7 minutes until soft.
- Add water, bouillon cubes, drained beans, bay leaves, pepper and marjoram.
- Cover and bring to boil.
- Reduce heat and simmer about 1 hour, 30 minutes until beans are soft.
- Remove bay leaves before serving.

Serves 8

**Note: Substitute 2 cups dry white wine for 2 of the
7 cups of water.**

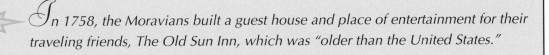

*In 1758, the Moravians built a guest house and place of entertainment for their
traveling friends, The Old Sun Inn, which was "older than the United States."*

Pasta and Bean Soup

2 tablespoons extra virgin olive oil

2 carrots, diced

2 stalks celery, diced

1 garlic clove, minced

¼ teaspoon crushed red pepper

3 cups vegetable or chicken broth

½ cup small whole wheat pasta (elbows, gemelli, or small shells)

1 (14½ ounce) can seasoned diced tomatoes, undrained

1 (16 ounce) can red kidney beans, rinsed and drained

1 (16 ounce) can black beans, rinsed and drained

¼ cup fresh basil, chopped

¼ cup grated Romano or Asiago cheese for garnish

- Heat oil in a stockpot.
- Sauté carrots and celery for 5 minutes.
- Add garlic and red pepper and cook 1 minute.
- Add broth and pasta.
- Bring to boil. Reduce heat and simmer for 10 minutes.
- Stir in tomatoes, and beans. Simmer an additional 15 minutes.
- Serve in bowls and top with basil and cheese.

Serves 4-6

Tortellini Soup

2 garlic cloves, minced

1 tablespoon olive oil

3 (14 ounce) cans chicken broth

1 (16 ounce) package refrigerated cheese tortellini

1 (10 ounce) package frozen chopped spinach, thawed and squeezed dry

1 (16 ounce) can stewed tomatoes

1 cup Parmesan cheese

- Sauté garlic in oil for 2 minutes.
- Add broth and bring to boil.
- Add tortellini. Reduce heat and simmer for 10 minutes.
- Stir in spinach and tomatoes. Simmer an additional 5 minutes.
- Sprinkle with cheese and serve immediately.

Serves 6

Vegetable Bean Soup

3 tablespoons olive oil

1 large onion, chopped

2 garlic cloves, minced

4 cups water

2 (30 ounce) cans garbanzo beans, undrained

½ cup diced celery

½ cup diced carrots

1 large bay leaf

1 teaspoon salt or to taste

1 (28 ounce) can tomatoes, undrained

1 teaspoon dried basil

½ teaspoon freshly ground black pepper

2 cups chopped spinach or kale

- Heat oil in medium stockpot.
- Sauté onions and garlic for 3 to 4 minutes.
- Add water, beans, celery, carrots, bay leaf, and salt.
- Cover and bring to boil. Reduce heat and simmer for 10 to 15 minute or until vegetables are tender.
- Add tomatoes and liquid, basil, and pepper.
- Cover and simmer an additional 15 minutes. Add spinach during last 5 minutes.
- Remove bay leaf.

Serves 6-8

Moravian Academy, in Bethlehem, PA, descends from the first school for girls founded in the American colonies in 1742. It is the ninth oldest independent school in the United States. Moravian Academy was incorporated in 1971 with the merger of Moravian Seminary for Girls and Moravian Preparatory School.

Vegetable Beef Soup

1 pound beef chuck, diced

1 tablespoon vegetable oil

2 cups beef broth

1 teaspoon salt

½ teaspoon dried basil

½ teaspoon dried thyme

⅛ teaspoon pepper

1 bay leaf

3 cups water

1 cup canned or frozen corn

3 medium carrots, sliced

2 stalks celery, sliced

1 medium onion, chopped

1 (16 ounce) can whole tomatoes,
   undrained

- Brown beef in oil.
- Add broth, salt, basil, thyme, pepper, bay leaf, and water.
- Cover and simmer for 1 hour to 1 hour, 30 minutes until beef is tender.
- Stir in corn, carrots, celery, onions, and tomatoes.
- Cover and simmer an additional 35 minutes until carrots are tender.

Serves 8

The first uniform for the St. Luke's School of Nursing was of durable blue cotton with a white stripe. It consisted of a blouse with a stiff white bishop collar, and long full sleeve with a wide stiff detachable white cuff. The skirt was full, nearly floor length, with a self-belt. Over the skirt was a long, full white apron that tied in the back. High-laced black shoes were barley visible. The cap was made of delicate organdy with a little frill at the edge and was shaped like a large tea strainer.

Italian Fish Soup

1-2 tablespoons olive oil

½ pound hot sausage, remove skin and cut into ½ inch slices

½ sweet red pepper, chopped

1 small onion, diced

1 (16 ounce) can Italian tomatoes

4 garlic cloves, chopped

½ pound chopped clams

½ pound shrimp, peeled and cleaned

2 small lobster tails

½ pound fresh clams, with shells

½ pound fresh or frozen mussels, with shells

½ pound fresh or frozen fish (salmon, cod, or haddock), cut into 1 inch squares

Salt, pepper, and cayenne pepper to taste

Chopped fresh basil, thyme, and parsley to taste

- Heat oil in large stockpot until hot.
- Brown sausage. Remove from pan and drain.
- Sauté peppers and onions until slightly tender.
- Return sausage and add tomatoes.
- Fill tomato can with water and add to pot. Add garlic and bring to boil.
- Boil gently for 10 minutes.
- Add chopped clams, shrimp, and lobster tails.
- Simmer over low heat for 5 minutes.
- Remove lobster tails. Cool and remove lobster meat from tails.
- Dice lobster meat and return to soup.
- Add clams, mussels, and fish to soup.
- Stir in salt, pepper, cayenne, basil, thyme, and parsley.
- Heat thoroughly until clams and mussels open.

Serves 10

Note: Crabmeat can also be added just before serving. Also, a cup of red or white wine can be added to the broth.

The only team of fellowship-trained surgical oncologists in the region is at the St. Luke's Cancer Center.

Creamy Scallop Soup

4 tablespoons butter

1 onion, finely chopped

1 pound potatoes, diced

Salt and pepper to taste

2½ cups hot fish stock

12 ounces scallops (and corals, if available)

1¼ cups milk

2 egg yolks

¾ cup heavy cream

1 tablespoon fresh chopped parsley for garnish

- Melt butter in large saucepan.
- Add onions and cook gently for 10 minutes until softened but not browned.
- Add potatoes, salt, and pepper.
- Cover and cook over low heat for 10 minutes.
- Pour in hot fish stock and bring to boil.
- Reduce heat and simmer for 10 to 15 minutes until potatoes are tender.
- Coarsely chop scallops and combine with milk in a second saucepan. If corals are available, chop and set aside.
- Simmer scallops gently for 6 to 8 minutes until tender.
- Transfer potatoes and cooking liquid to a food processor or blender. Blend to a purée. (Alternately, press through a sieve.)
- Add puréed mixture to scallops and milk. Add corals if available. Do not heat.
- Whisk together egg yolks and cream and add to scallops.
- Return soup to low heat, stirring constantly, until slightly thickened. (Do not boil because soup will curdle.)
- Serve hot and sprinkle with fresh parsley.

Serves 4

---

*C*edar Crest College, a liberal arts college in Allentown, PA, was founded in 1867.

Aidens Favorite Cream of Crab Soup

6 tablespoons butter

9 tablespoons all-purpose flour

1 (14 ounce) can chicken broth

4 cups light cream

1 tablespoon chopped parsley

1 tablespoon chopped chives

1 (1 pound) can crabmeat

½ cup cooking sherry

1 tablespoon Old Bay seasoning

- Melt butter in stockpot.
- Blend in flour.
- Stir in chicken broth.
- Cook and stir constantly until smooth.
- Add light cream, parsley, chives, crabmeat, sherry, and seasoning.
- Mix well.
- Heat until ready to serve.

Serves 6

Note: Old Bay seasoning is the secret. May add more to taste.

Seafood Bisque

1 pound mushrooms, chopped

1 whole bunch celery, chopped

2 large Bermuda onions, chopped

2 sticks butter

4 tablespoons all-purpose flour

1 quart light cream

1 quart nonfat light cream

2 pounds crabmeat

2 pounds small shrimp, cleaned

½ cup white wine

2 tablespoons Old Bay seasoning

1 tablespoon paprika

1 quart whole milk

Chopped parsley for garnish

- Sauté mushrooms, celery, and onions in butter until tender in a large stockpot.
- Stir in flour and brown lightly.
- Slowly stir in light cream and nonfat light cream.
- Add crabmeat, shrimp, and wine.
- Stir in seasoning and paprika.
- Simmer but do not boil.
- Thin with milk to desired consistency.
- Heat thoroughly.
- Garnish with parsley.

Serves 12

Crab Bisque

4 tablespoons butter

¼ cup cooking sherry

6 cups heavy cream or light cream

1 (29 ounce) can tomato sauce

1½ tablespoons Old Bay seasoning

1 tablespoon finely chopped parsley

½ teaspoon Tabasco sauce (optional)

3 (7½ ounce) cans crabmeat, drained or
   1 container fresh crabmeat

- In a large stockpot, heat butter and sherry until butter melts.
- Add cream, tomato sauce, seasoning, parsley, and Tabasco.
- Blend until smooth.
- Add crabmeat and serve immediately.

Serves 8 small portions

Broccoli Chowder

2 (10 ounce) packages frozen chopped
   broccoli, thawed

3 cups chicken broth

3 tablespoons chicken bouillon powder

3 cups hot water

4 tablespoons butter

1 cup milk

1 cup light cream or skim milk

1 (8 ounce) package shredded Swiss cheese

1 teaspoon salt

1 teaspoon pepper

- Cook broccoli with chicken broth according to package directions. Do not drain.
- Dissolve bouillon powder in water.
- Add bouillon, butter, milk, light cream, cheese, salt, and pepper to broccoli.
- Stir and simmer until thoroughly heated.

Serves 6

"St. Luke's has been such an important part of my life for forty-seven years. It's hard to imagine the day when I hang up my uniform and am no longer able to offer my somewhat limited services to help others!" Victoria "Lala" Leach

Fresh Corn Chowder

2 cups chopped onions

4 tablespoons butter

1 cup minced celery

2 sweet red bell peppers, chopped

8 cups fresh sweet corn (about 8-10 cobs)

1 teaspoon salt

Pepper to taste

½ teaspoon ground thyme

1 teaspoon dried basil

2 cups vegetable broth

2 cups light cream

- Sauté onions in butter for 3 to 5 minutes over medium-low heat, stirring constantly.
- Add celery and cook 5 minutes.
- Stir in peppers, corn, salt, pepper, thyme, and basil.
- Stir well and cover.
- Reduce heat and cook for 5 minutes.
- Add broth.
- Cover and simmer about 10 minutes.
- Using a blender or food processor, purée about half the solids in the soup liquid.
- About 10 minutes before serving, add light cream.
- Slowly reheat soup but do not boil.

Serves 6

Ideal Corn Chowder

1 pound bacon

1 small onion, diced

2 cups water

4 large potatoes, cubed

1 (15 ounce) can Mexican corn or whole kernel corn

2 (15 ounce) cans cream-style corn

2 tablespoons butter

½ cup heavy cream

2 cups light cream

Salt and pepper to taste

- Cook bacon until crisp in a deep stockpot.
- Add onions and sauté.
- Pour off drippings.
- Add water and potatoes.
- Cook until tender.
- Add Mexican corn, cream-style corn, and butter.
- Bring to boil.
- Reduce heat.
- Stir in cream and light cream.
- Add salt and pepper.
- Remove from heat.

Serves 10-12

Chili Con Carne

1 onion, chopped

2 garlic cloves, crushed

3 tablespoons olive oil

1 ½ pounds ground beef

3 cups water

1 ⅓ cups tomatoes

1 bell pepper, chopped

2 tablespoons chili powder

1 ½ teaspoons salt

1 teaspoon cumin seed, crushed

½ teaspoon celery seed

¼ teaspoon cayenne pepper

⅛ teaspoon dried basil

1 small bay leaf

1 (6 ounce) can tomato paste

- Sauté onions and garlic in oil.
- Add ground beef.
- Cook until browned.
- Transfer mixture to a saucepan.
- Add water, tomatoes, peppers, chili powder, salt, cumin seed, celery seed, cayenne, basil, bay leaf, and tomato paste.
- Simmer, uncovered, for 3 hours.
- Remove bay leaf before serving.

Serves 4

Note: May add 1 (16 ounce) can kidney beans (drained and rinsed) just before serving. You may add less water for a thicker chili.

Moravian College in Bethlehem was founded in 1742 and is the sixth oldest college in America.

Spicy Turkey Chili

1 small finely chopped onion

3 tablespoons olive oil

1 (4 ounce) can diced jalapeño peppers

3 tablespoons all-purpose flour

3 teaspoons ground cumin

2 (16 ounce) cans Great Northern beans

1 (8 ounce or 14 ounce) can turkey broth

1 pound finely chopped seasoned cooked turkey

Salt and pepper to taste

Shredded Cheddar cheese

- In large skillet, sauté onions in oil for 4 minutes.
- Add jalapeños, flour, and cumin.
- Cook and stir for 2 minutes.
- Add beans and broth.
- Bring to boil.
- Reduce heat.
- Simmer for 10 minutes or until thickened.
- Add turkey, salt, and pepper.
- Cook until hot.
- Garnish with cheese.

Serves 5-6

Note: To reduce spiciness, use 2 ounces of jalapeños and 2 teaspoons of cumin.

In 1954 the men's and women's institution of Moravian College merged making it the first coed institution in the Lehigh Valley.

Southwest White Chili

1 teaspoon garlic powder

1 teaspoon ground cumin

½ teaspoon dried oregano

½ teaspoon dried cilantro leaves (optional)

¼ teaspoon cayenne pepper

1 tablespoon olive oil

1 pound boneless, skinless chicken breast halves, cubed

¼ cup chopped onions

1 cup chicken broth

1 (4 ounce) can chopped green chilies

1 (19 ounce) can white kidney beans, undrained (cannelloni)

Shredded Monterey Jack cheese and chopped onions for garnish

- Combine garlic powder, cumin, oregano, cilantro, and cayenne in a small bowl. Set aside.
- Heat oil in 2 to 3 quart saucepan over medium-high heat.
- Add chicken and cook 4 to 5 minutes, stirring often.
- Remove chicken with slotted spoon. Cover and keep warm.
- Add onions to saucepan and cook 2 minutes.
- Stir in broth, chilies, and spice blend.
- Simmer for 30 minutes.
- Return chicken and add beans.
- Simmer an additional 10 minutes.
- Garnish with Monterey Jack cheese and onions.

Serves 4

Note: Cheddar cheese and sour cream are also good garnishes.

St. Luke's Cancer Center is the only cancer center in Pennsylvania to be recognized with the 2004 Cancer's (CoC) Outstanding Achievement Award.

Vegetarian Chili

1 sweet red pepper, cut into 1 inch pieces

1 yellow pepper, cut into 1 inch pieces

1 medium onion, chopped

2 garlic cloves, minced

1 (1 inch) piece fresh ginger, chopped

2 teaspoons vegetable oil

1 (15 ounce) can black beans, drained

1 (15 ounce) can chili beans in sauce

1 (4 ounce) can chopped green chilies, drained

1 (15 ounce) can tomato sauce

1 (14½ ounce) can diced tomatoes, undrained

1 (12 ounce) package frozen meatless ground burger

1 tablespoon chili powder

½ teaspoon ground cumin

- Cook peppers, onions, garlic, and ginger in oil for 3 minutes.
- Add black beans, chili beans, green chilies, tomato sauce, tomatoes, burger, chili powder, and cumin.
- Bring to boil.
- Reduce heat and simmer for 30 minutes, stirring occasionally.

Serves 6-8

Note: Use organic beans when available. Top with sour cream or shredded Cheddar cheese.

DeSales University, in Center Valley, PA was founded in 1964. It is a private, four-year Catholic university for men and woman administered by the Oblates of St. Francis de Sales.

Cajun Okra Stew

1-2 teaspoons olive oil

1 onion, chopped

2-3 garlic cloves, chopped

6-7 fresh large tomatoes, chopped

1 (15 ounce) can lima beans

1 (15 ounce) can black-eyed peas

1 tablespoon Cajun seasoning

1 cup chopped okra

Salt and pepper to taste

Cooked brown rice

- Heat olive oil in a large stew pot.
- Add onions and garlic.
- Sauté for 2 to 3 minutes.
- Add tomatoes, lima beans, black-eyed peas, and Cajun seasoning.
- Bring to boil.
- Stir well.
- Reduce heat and simmer on low for 30 minutes, stirring occasionally.
- If the stew gets too thick, add water as needed.
- Add okra, salt, and pepper.
- Stir well.
- Simmer an additional 15 minutes.
- Serve over brown rice.

Serves 6-8

 The annual subscription request of the members of the Ladies' Aid Society was begun in 1906. Monies collected in the late 19th and early 20th centuries were used to repair, paint, and furnish the nurses' residence, the wards and the doctor's offices.

Cachupinha

1 large onion, chopped

1 pound linguica, Portuguese smoked
    sausage, can substitute sliced chorizo

2 peppercorns

2 tablespoons olive oil

1 pound bag dried samp or 5 ears fresh
    corn, cut kernels off cob

1 (16 ounce) package dry lima beans

1 yellow or zucchini squash, sliced

2 ripe tomatoes, chopped or 1 (6 ounce)
    can tomato paste

Salt and ground pepper to taste

Fresh cilantro for garnish

- Gently sauté onions, linguica and peppercorns in olive oil in a large stockpot.
- Add corn.
- Stir in beans, squash, tomatoes and sauté mixture.
- Add water to cover.
- Bring to boil, reduce heat and simmer 1 hour, 30 minutes to 2 hours or until beans are soft.
- Add water as needed to maintain stew consistency.
- Sprinkle with salt and pepper. Garnish with cilantro.

Serves 4-6

Note: Hearty stew from Cape Verde Islands off the coast of Africa. Tastes even better the second day.

Apricot Gelatin Salad

1 (6 ounce) box apricot flavored gelatin

2 cups boiling water

1 (20 ounce) can crushed pineapple,
    undrained

2 (11 ounce) cans Mandarin oranges,
    undrained

1 cup whipped topping, thawed

- Dissolve gelatin in boiling water in a large bowl.
- Add pineapple and oranges and the juices. Refrigerate until slightly firm.
- Stir in whipped topping.
- Pour mixture into an oiled mold.
- Refrigerate overnight.

Serves 12

Note: May substitute orange gelatin, use fruit in light syrup or own juice, use light whipped topping, or omit mold and chill in bowl.

Cranberry Fruit Salad

1 (8 ounce) can crushed pineapple

½ cup cranberry juice

2 tablespoons lemon juice

1 (3 ounce) package raspberry flavored gelatin

1 (16 ounce) whole berry cranberry sauce

½ cup chopped walnuts

½ (11 ounce) can Mandarin oranges, drained (optional)

- Drain pineapple, reserving juice. Set pineapple aside.
- Combine pineapple juice, cranberry juice, and lemon juice in a medium saucepan.
- Bring to boil and remove from heat.
- Stir in gelatin until completely dissolved.
- Break up cranberry sauce with a fork.
- Stir into gelatin mixture.
- Refrigerate until mixture begins to set.
- Stir in pineapple, walnuts, and oranges.
- Pour mixture into a 4 cup mold.
- Refrigerate until firm.

Serves 8

Cranberry Mold

1 (3 ounce) package cherry flavored gelatin

1 (3 ounce) package raspberry flavored gelatin

3 cups boiling water

1 (16 ounce) can whole cranberry sauce

1 cup sour cream, room temperature

1 (11 ounce) can Mandarin oranges, drained

1 cup chopped walnuts or pecans

- Dissolve cherry and raspberry flavored gelatin in boiling water.
- Stir in cranberry sauce.
- Refrigerate until gelatin begins to thicken.
- Blend in sour cream.
- Add oranges and nuts and mix well.
- Pour mixture into 11x7x2 inch baking dish or gelatin mold.
- Refrigerate several hours until set.

Serves 8-10

Pretzel Salad

2 cups thin pretzels, crushed

3 tablespoons sugar

1 ½ sticks butter

1 (8 ounce) package cream cheese, softened

1 cup sugar

1 (12 ounce) container frozen whipped topping, thawed

1 (6 ounce) package strawberry flavored gelatin

2 cups hot water

1 pint frozen strawberries

- Preheat oven to 400 degrees.
- Combine crushed pretzels, sugar and butter.
- Press mixture into a 13x9x2 inch baking dish.
- Bake for 8 minutes. Cool completely.
- Beat cream cheese and sugar until smooth.
- Stir in whipped topping.
- Spread mixture over crust.
- Blend gelatin, water, and strawberries.
- Allow to set until slightly firm.
- Spread strawberry mixture over whipped topping.

Serves 10-12

Note: May add extra strawberries over whipped topping mixture before adding gelatin mixture. Do not pour bag of pretzels into food processor for crushing. Crust will be too salty if salt in bottom of bag is mixed in.

Cucumber Mousse

1 (3 ounce) package lime flavored gelatin

1 cup boiling water

1 tablespoon vinegar

1 tablespoon horseradish

1 tablespoon grated onions

½ cup mayonnaise

½ cup sour cream

2 cups grated well-drained cucumbers

- Combine gelatin, water, vinegar, horseradish, onions, mayonnaise, sour cream, and cucumbers.
- Blend well.
- Refrigerate until set.

Serves 6-8

Jellied Vegetable Salad

1 (3 ounce) package lemon flavored gelatin

2 vegetable bouillon cubes

¼ teaspoon salt

1 cup boiling water

2 tablespoons tarragon vinegar

Dash of pepper

1 cup sour cream

½ cup diced celery

⅓ cup diced carrots

⅓ cup thinly sliced radishes

⅓ cup diced cucumbers

2 tablespoons diced bell peppers

3 tablespoons thinly sliced green onions

Curly lettuce for garnish

- Dissolve gelatin, bouillon cubes, and salt in boiling water.
- Add vinegar and pepper.
- Refrigerate until slightly thickened.
- Blend in sour cream, celery, carrots, radishes, cucumbers, peppers, and onions.
- Pour mixture into a 3 cup mold.
- Refrigerate about 4 hours or until firm.
- Unmold and garnish with curly lettuce.

Serves 5-6

Note: Serve with French dressing or mayonnaise, if desired.

The first diplomas from St. Luke's School of Nursing were awarded to Mary Augusta Camp of Brooklyn, NY, Minnie Agnes Ernst of Bethlehem, PA, and Minerva Anne Jordan of Riegelsville, PA on October 18, 1886.

Hidden Treasures

2 cups mayonnaise

½ cup horseradish, well drained

2 teaspoons dry mustard

½ teaspoon salt

2 teaspoons lemon juice

2 pounds shrimp, shelled, cleaned, and
    cooked

1 basket cherry tomatoes

2 (6 ounce) cans pitted black olives,
    drained

1 (8 ounce) can whole water chestnuts,
    drained

2 (6 ounce) cans whole button mushrooms,
    drained

½ small head cauliflower, cut into bite size
    pieces

- Blend mayonnaise, horseradish, mustard, salt, and lemon juice.
- Add shrimp, tomatoes, olives, water chestnuts, and mushrooms.
- Stir gently.
- Add cauliflower just before serving.

Serves 12-15

Note: Best made early in the day or the night before.

Fruited Spinach Salad with Currant Vinaigrette

¼ cup currant jelly

3 tablespoons red wine vinegar

8 cups spinach leaves, cleaned

1 cup strawberries, halved

1 (11 ounce) can Mandarin oranges,
    drained

¼ cup sliced green onions

- Combine jelly and vinegar in saucepan.
- Cook and stir over medium heat until smooth.
- Place in freezer for about 10 minutes.
- Combine spinach, strawberries, oranges, and green onions in large bowl.
- Drizzle vinaigrette over spinach mixture.
- Toss to mix.
- Serve immediately.

Serves 6

Arugula, Endive, and Apple Salad with Gorgonzola

Dressing

1 cup Chianti wine

2 tablespoons red wine vinegar

1 tablespoon chopped fresh chives

1 teaspoon chopped fresh rosemary

1 teaspoon sugar

1 garlic clove, minced

½ cup olive oil

Salad

4 ounces baby arugula

4 heads Belgian endive, sliced thin
    diagonally

1 tart apple, julienne cut

⅓ cup Gorgonzola cheese, crumbled

¼ cup chopped fresh chives

½ cup chopped walnuts for garnish

- Whisk together wine, vinegar, chives, rosemary, sugar, garlic, and oil and set aside.
- In large salad bowl, mix arugula, endive, apples, Gorgonzola cheese, and chives.
- Pour one-third cup dressing over greens and toss to coat.
- Divide salad onto six plates.
- Garnish with walnuts.

Serves 6

Note: Pass the remaining dressing, if desired.

*I*n 1919, the Executive Committee of the Board of St. Luke's Hospital asked the Ladies' Aid Society to form committees to assist on the wards. They were also asked to visit the wards regularly and report back to the hospital's directors on what was needed. These Visiting Committee members took the responsibility very seriously and documented all problems they saw inside the hospital.

Melissa Riskin's Strawberry-Chicken Salad

Raspberry Vinaigrette

¾ **cup pear nectar**

⅓ **cup vegetable oil**

⅓ **cup raspberry vinegar**

3 **tablespoons fresh chopped basil**

1 **tablespoon Dijon mustard**

1 **tablespoon sesame oil**

½ **teaspoon freshly ground pepper**

¼ **teaspoon salt**

Salad

4 **boneless, skinless chicken breast halves**

8 **cups mixed salad greens**

1 **quart strawberries, sliced**

2 **pears, sliced**

2 **avocados, peeled and sliced**

½ **small sweet onion, diced**

½ **cup pecan halves, toasted**

- Combine nectar, oil, vinegar, basil, mustard, sesame oil, pepper, and salt in a tightly covered jar and shake until blended.
- Store up to 2 weeks in refrigerator.
- Combine chicken and one-half cup raspberry vinaigrette in large zip-top bag.
- Seal and refrigerate for 1 hour.
- Remove chicken from marinade. Grill, covered, 4 minutes per side over medium high heat.
- Let stand 10 minutes, then slice.
- Place salad greens, strawberries, pears, avocados, onions, and pecans in a large bowl and gently toss.
- Add sliced chicken.
- Serve with remaining vinaigrette.

Serves 8

*D*r. William L. Estes came to St. Luke's Hospital from New York City on November 21, 1881. He wanted to start a school of nursing based on Bellevue Hospital's training school, which was started in 1873 on the Nightingale Plan.

Taco Salad

1 pound ground beef

1 (1½ ounce) envelope taco seasoning mix

¾ cup water

1 medium head lettuce, shredded

½ cup pitted sliced olives

1 cup shredded sharp Cheddar cheese

1 (15½ ounce) can pinto or kidney beans, drained

1 large tomato, diced

1 small onion, sliced into rings

1 avocado, peeled and sliced

Tortilla chips or hard taco shells, crushed

- Brown ground beef and drain.
- Add seasoning mix and water.
- Simmer, uncovered, for 15 to 20 minutes.
- In salad bowl, toss lettuce, olives, and Cheddar cheese.
- Spread beef mixture on top of salad.
- Layer with beans, tomatoes, onions, and avocados.
- Top with crushed tortilla chips or shells.

Serves 4

Note: Serve with taco sauce or sour cream.

Meatless Taco Salad

1 (12 ounce) container sour cream

2 (8 ounce) packages cream cheese, softened

1 (1½ ounce) package taco seasoning mix

1 (12 ounce) jar taco sauce or salsa

1 head lettuce, shredded

2 tomatoes, diced

1 red onion, diced

Sliced black olives

Shredded Mexican blend cheese

Tortilla chips

- Blend sour cream, cream cheese, and seasoning mix.
- Spread mixture in a 13x9x2 inch foil baking pan.
- Pour taco sauce on top and spread evenly.
- Top with lettuce, tomatoes, red onions, olives, and cheese.
- Serve with tortilla chips.

Serves 8-10

Note: May use reduced fat sour cream and cream cheese.

Couscous Salad

Dressing

¾ cup olive oil

Juice of 2 lemons

3 garlic cloves, minced

1 teaspoon Dijon mustard

1 teaspoon ground coriander

1 teaspoon salt

Pepper to taste

Salad

2 cups cooked couscous

3 plum tomatoes, chopped

1 cucumber, peeled, seeded, and chopped

½ cup chopped green onions

½ medium red onion, chopped

1 (8 ounce) can garbanzo beans, drained

½ cup chopped parsley

½ cup chopped cilantro

Chopped fresh mint to taste

- Whisk together oil, lemon juice, garlic, mustard, coriander, salt, and pepper. Refrigerate until ready to use.
- Prepare couscous according to package directions, fluff with a fork, and refrigerate.
- Remove couscous from refrigerator and add tomatoes, cucumbers, green onions, red onions, beans, parsley, cilantro, and mint.
- Pour dressing over couscous mixture just before serving.

Serves 6

Note: For a twist, add one or more of the following: dried cranberries or raisins, chopped celery, radishes, or pineapple chunks.

Linens, mattresses, beds, rugs, wheel chairs, clothing, electric fans, a gas stove, refrigerators, kitchen, bathroom, and laundry fixtures were bought with money raised by the Ladies' Aid Society in the early 1900's.

Linguine Vegetable Salad

1 pound linguine, cooked

1 onion, chopped

1 cucumber, peeled and chopped

1 tomato, chopped

1 bell pepper, chopped

1 (8 ounce) bottle Italian salad dressing

¾ jar Salad Supreme dry spice

- Cook and drain linguine.
- Add onions, cucumbers, tomatoes, and peppers.
- While still warm, pour dressing over linguine and vegetables.
- Add Salad Supreme.
- Toss and mix well.
- Refrigerate and serve cold.

Serves 8

Note: Make 1 day in advance.

Broccoli Salad

3 cups broccoli florets

1 cup chopped red onions

½ cup grated Cheddar cheese, more or less to taste

6 slices bacon, cooked and crumbled or 1 (2 ounce) jar bacon bits

1 cup mayonnaise

⅓ cup sugar

4 tablespoons vinegar

- Combine broccoli, onions, Cheddar cheese, and bacon.
- Blend mayonnaise, sugar, and vinegar until smooth.
- Pour dressing over salad and mix well.

Serves 6-8

Note: May substitute 1 (10 ounce) package frozen broccoli, thawed for fresh broccoli. May add 1 finely chopped hard-cooked egg white.

 St. Luke's was named one of the Best Places to Work in PA in 2003, an award it would also receive in subsequent years.

Savory Winter Salad

2 teaspoons tarragon vinegar

½ teaspoon minced shallots

½ garlic clove

2 sprigs thyme

½ teaspoon coarse salt

⅛ teaspoon ground pepper

⅓ cup extra virgin olive oil

1 head Belgian endive, separated into
   leaves

1 small head radicchio, torn

½ cup mixed greens

1 cup blue cheese, crumbled

2 pears, sliced lengthwise

⅓ cup coarsely chopped walnuts

- Whisk together vinegar, shallots, garlic, thyme, salt, and pepper.
- Slowly whisk in oil.
- Cover and let stand overnight at room temperature.
- Strain dressing.
- Combine endive, radicchio, greens, blue cheese, pears, and walnuts in a large bowl.
- Pour on dressing and toss to coat.

Serves 6

Note: Dressing may be made several hours before serving and strained, but yields best flavor if left overnight.

Elizabeth's Spinach Salad

2 tablespoons sesame seeds, toasted

½ cup vegetable oil

¼ cup fresh lemon juice

2 tablespoons soy sauce

1 (8 ounce) package sliced mushrooms

⅛ teaspoon salt

⅛ teaspoon Tabasco sauce

1 (8 ounce) can sliced water chestnuts

1 (10 ounce) package fresh spinach,
   chopped

- Combine sesame seeds, oil, lemon juice, soy sauce, mushrooms, salt, Tabasco, and water chestnuts.
- Marinate overnight.
- Immediately before serving, toss with the spinach.

Serves 8-10

Spinach Salad

Dressing

⅔ cup olive oil

2 teaspoons vinegar

1 teaspoon prepared mustard

2 teaspoons seasoned salt

1 tablespoon sugar

1 garlic clove, crushed

3 tablespoons lemon juice

1 tablespoon mayonnaise

Salad

1 pound baby spinach

8-10 slices bacon, cooked and crumbled

Red onion slices to taste

Radishes, thinly sliced

1 ½ cups shredded sharp Cheddar cheese

- Whisk together oil, vinegar, mustard, salt, sugar, garlic, lemon juice, and mayonnaise until smooth.
- Combine spinach, bacon, red onions, radishes, and cheese in a salad bowl.
- Just prior to serving, pour dressing over salad and toss to coat.

Serves 6-8

In one year, 1920-1921, members of the Auxiliary sewed 36 towels, 18 covers, 7 pair girls drawers, 6 petticoats, 5 heavy wrappers, 3 doctors' gowns, 19 infant slips, 30 operating boots, 6 bed curtains, 18 pillow-slips, 12 nightingales, 10 doctors' operating shirts, 52 napkins, and 6 flannels skirts for infants.

Spinach Salad with Pomegranate Dressing

2 tablespoons Enova oil

⅓ cup fresh orange juice

4 tablespoons pomegranate juice

1 tablespoon toasted sesame seeds

½ teaspoon salt

⅛ teaspoon pepper

6 ounces baby spinach, torn

¾ cup sliced red onions

2 (11 ounce) cans Mandarin oranges, drained

4 tablespoons pomegranate seeds

½ cup baked wontons

- Whisk together oil, orange juice, pomegranate juice, half sesame seeds, salt, and pepper.
- In a large bowl, combine spinach, onions, oranges, and pomegranate seeds.
- Pour dressing over salad.
- Toss well.
- Sprinkle with remaining sesame seeds and baked wontons.

Serves about 8

Note: Wontons can be baked at 350 degrees for about 12 minutes until golden browned and dry in order to crumble.

Napa Cabbage Oriental Salad

1 head Napa cabbage, chopped

1 bunch green onions, chopped

1 bell or sweet red pepper, chopped

1 cup slivered almonds, toasted

½ (1 ounce) jar sesame seeds, toasted

½ cup vegetable oil

6 tablespoons rice wine vinegar

¼ cup sugar

½ teaspoon white pepper

1 (3 ounce) package chicken flavored Ramen noodles

- Combine cabbage, green onions, peppers, almonds, and sesame seeds.
- Blend oil, vinegar, sugar, pepper, and seasoning packet.
- Pour over salad and toss to coat.
- Crumble noodles and spread on top.

Serves 8-10

Joy's Layered Salad

1 head iceberg lettuce, sliced into 6 pieces

1 bunch green onions, chopped

2 stalks celery, chopped

½ bell pepper, chopped

1 (8 ounce) can sliced water chestnuts, drained

1 (10 ounce) package frozen peas, do not thaw

2 cups mayonnaise

2 teaspoons sugar

½ cup Parmesan cheese

1 teaspoon salt

¼ teaspoon garlic powder

15 slices bacon, cooked and crumbled

3 hard-cooked eggs, sliced

2 tomatoes, sliced

- Layer lettuce in a deep salad bowl.
- Layer in order the green onions, celery, peppers, water chestnuts, and peas.
- Blend mayonnaise, sugar, Parmesan cheese, salt, and garlic powder.
- Spread over peas.
- Top in order with bacon, eggs, and tomatoes.
- Refrigerate at least 4 hours.

Serves 8-10

Note: May be assembled up to 24 hours in advance.

The Ladies' Aid Society solicited donations of clothing, fruit and vegetables in the late 1800's. Some early donations included: Mrs. E.P. Wilbur, 15 jars preserved fruit and jelly; Mrs. T. Jeter, 6 quarts cherries, 3 barrels apples, 3 pounds grapes; Mrs. Cortlandt Whitehead, 4 cans corn, 5 jars fruit, basket apples, jelly cake, glass jelly, 2 chickens; Church of the Nativity Sewing School, 3 bed quilts, 5 sheets, 27 pillow cases; Mrs. Henry Coppée, 2 wrappers, 2 pair pantaloons, 2 vests, coat, cap, 4 dresses, 21 pieces underclothing.

Orange Vinaigrette Dressing

1 cup orange juice

1 cup wine vinegar

¾ cup sugar

1 ½ teaspoons salt

¼ teaspoon pepper

- Blend together juice, vinegar, sugar, salt, and pepper.
- Pour over salad.

Makes 2 ¾ cups

Bacon Dressing

6 slices bacon, cut into 1 inch pieces

½ cup sugar

½ teaspoon salt

1 tablespoon cornstarch

1 egg

¼ cup vinegar

1 cup water

- Fry bacon. Set aside.
- In a medium bowl, combine sugar, salt, and cornstarch.
- Add egg and vinegar.
- Mix well.
- Stir in water.
- Pour mixture into pan with hot bacon and drippings.
- Bring to boil until thickened.

Serves 4

Note: The dressing is good hot on lettuce, dandelion, endive, spinach, or other greens.

In 2005, The Auxiliary, through the St. Luke's Ball Committee, partnered with Hospice of the Visiting Nurse Association to raise both funds and awareness for hospice services. Artist Deborah Todd agreed to donate her talent to create a beautiful mosaic of the Tree of Life, which was installed in the new inpatient Hospice House in Lower Saucon Township. The public was offered a unique opportunity to purchase one of the 650 tiles in the memorial mosaic to honor a loved one of show support for the extraordinary work of the hospice team.

Poppy Seed Dressing

⅓ cup sugar

½ teaspoon salt

½ teaspoon dry mustard

3 tablespoons vinegar

1 teaspoon finely chopped onions

½ cup olive oil

2 teaspoons poppy seed

- Combine sugar, salt, mustard, vinegar, and onions in a blender.
- Blend until combined.
- Add oil in a slow, steady stream with machine running.
- Blend until thickened and smooth.
- Add poppy seeds.
- Blend a few seconds.
- Refrigerate.

Serves 4

Note: Good on spinach salad with toasted almonds, sliced peaches, and blue cheese.

Bacon Dressing

3-4 slices bacon

1 egg, beaten

6 tablespoons sugar

1 tablespoon cornstarch

½ teaspoon dry mustard

6 tablespoons white vinegar

Water

Onion salt to taste (optional)

- Cook bacon until crisp.
- Remove from pan and crumble. Reserve drippings.
- Combine egg, sugar, cornstarch, mustard, and vinegar.
- Add enough water to make 2 cups liquid.
- Pour mixture into bacon drippings. Cook over low heat and stir constantly until thickened.
- Add bacon.

Serves 4

Note: Great on endive, lettuce, or warm potatoes as German potato salad.

Pasta, Rice & Grains

St. Luke's "Field of Dreams"

**Outpatient Center
Coming to Bethlehem Township**

The Auxiliary of St. Luke's Hospital designated the more than $300,000 proceeds from the 2006 Charity Ball to support the development of the new St. Luke's Cancer Center to be located in the Outpatient Center.

St. Luke's Field of Dreams"

Outpatient Center
Coming to Bethlehem Township

The rendering on the front of this page illustrates an Outpatient Center to be constructed during the Phase I development of a 200+ acre site owned by St. Luke's near the intersection of Route 33 and I-78. Phase II will include construction of a new hospital.

In addition to the St. Luke's Cancer Center, Phase I will include a pavilion to house a GE Healthcare Global Showsite, one of only five in the world, and other outpatient testing services; an ambulatory surgery center; and medical office buildings.

Cajun Fettuccine

1 stick butter

1 tablespoon chopped garlic

½ cup diced andouille sausage

¼ cup chopped green onions

¼ cup mushrooms, sliced

½ cup tomatoes, diced

2 tablespoons dry white wine

1 tablespoon lemon juice

1 cup heavy cream

¼ cup sweet red pepper, diced

1 tablespoon chopped parsley

Salt and cracked black pepper to taste

3 cups spinach fettuccine, cooked al dente

- In a 2 quart heavy saucepan, melt butter over medium-high heat.
- Add garlic, andouille sausage, green onions, mushrooms, and tomatoes.
- Sauté 3 to 5 minutes or until all vegetables are crisp-tender.
- Deglaze pan with wine and lemon juice. Cook until liquid is reduced by half.
- Add heavy cream, stirring constantly.
- Cook and stir about 5 minutes until thickened and reduced.
- Add peppers.
- Remove from heat.
- Add parsley, salt, and pepper.
- Gently fold in fettuccine and serve immediately.

Serves 6

The Ladies' Aid Society of St. Luke's Hospital was organized and had its first meeting on August 6, 1874. Mrs. Robert H. Sayre, the first President of the Ladies' Aid Society, was the wife of the Chief Engineer of the Lehigh Valley Railroad. Mrs. Tinsley Jeter was Secretary and Mrs. B.C. Webster served as Treasurer. The proposed annual subscription was set at $2.00. At the end of its first year, the Ladies' Aid Society was able to present $1,221.49 to the Hospital.

Fettuccine with White Clam Sauce

2 dozen littleneck clams or
    2 (6 ounce) cans minced clams

1 tablespoon chopped yellow onions

½ cup olive oil

2 teaspoons chopped garlic

2 tablespoons chopped Italian parsley

½ teaspoon crushed red pepper

¼ cup dry white wine

1 tablespoon butter (optional)

2 tablespoons freshly grated Parmesan
    cheese (optional)

Salt and pepper to taste

1 pound fettuccine, cooked al dente

- Wash and scrub clams.
- Cook in covered saucepan over medium high heat until clams open.
- Reserve liquid.
- Shuck clams, chop and place in a bowl.
- If using canned clams, drain and reserve liquid.
- Sauté onions in oil over medium high heat until translucent.
- Add garlic and sauté until lightly browned.
- Add parsley and red pepper.
- Add wine and reduce by half.
- Add about ⅔ cup clam liquid.
- Reduce by half.
- Add clams, butter, and Parmesan cheese.
- Stir in salt and pepper.
- Add sauce to pasta and toss to coat and serve immediately.

Serves 4-6

The Fowler Family Community Health Endowment Fund was generously established by Linny and Beall Fowler to support the many St. Luke's Community Health Programs for the benefit of children from low-income families. Children in need of vision and dental care, treatment for asthma, as well as other medical concerns, are helped through the generosity of the Fowler Family.

Linguine with Clam Sauce

3 garlic cloves, minced

½ cup olive oil or canola oil

1 (7½ ounce) can minced clams

3 teaspoons dried sweet basil

½ teaspoon dried oregano

¼ teaspoon salt

¼ teaspoon pepper

½ cup white wine

½ pound linguine, cooked al dente

¾ cup grated Parmesan cheese

- Sauté garlic in oil.
- Drain juice from clams and add water to equal one cup.
- Stir in clams, liquid, basil, oregano, salt, and pepper.
- Simmer for 10 minutes.
- Add white wine.
- Serve sauce over linguine and top with Parmesan cheese.

Serves 2-3

Note: May double recipe for 6 or more.

Pasta with Peas and Onions

4 medium onions, thinly sliced

1 tablespoon olive oil

4 cups fresh or frozen tiny green peas (about 1 pound)

Salt and fresh ground pepper to taste

2 tablespoons hot water

1 pound orecchiette pasta or other small shell pasta, cooked al dente

1 cup freshly grated pecorino or Parmesan cheese

- In a large pot, heat water to boiling for pasta.
- Heat olive oil in a saucepan over medium high heat.
- Sauté onions until browned.
- Add peas, salt, and pepper and heat through.
- Add hot water to saucepan.
- Cover and simmer.
- Drain pasta and toss with some cheese.
- Pour peas and onions mixture over pasta.
- Serve immediately with remaining cheese on the side.

Serves 4-6

Pasta with Crab, Tomatoes, Cream and Tarragon

Cream Sauce

3 tablespoons minced shallots (optional)

¼ cup Madeira wine

½ cup dry white wine

¾ teaspoon dried tarragon

½ teaspoon pepper

1⅔ cups heavy cream

¼ teaspoon lemon zest

1 teaspoon salt

1 cup peeled, seeded, and chopped tomatoes

1 tablespoon lemon juice

Crabmeat

4 tablespoons butter

3 tablespoons minced green onions

¼ teaspoon dried tarragon

½ cup peeled, seeded, and chopped tomatoes

½ teaspoon salt

⅛ teaspoon pepper

2 tablespoons lemon juice

½ pound lump or backfin crabmeat

½ pound fresh cappellini pasta or ⅓ pound dried, cooked al dente

1 tablespoon minced parsley

- In a wide saucepan, combine shallots, Madeira wine, white wine, tarragon, and pepper.
- Bring to boil and reduce to one-fourth cup.
- Toward the end of reduction, tilt pan back and forth so mixture does not burn around the edges.
- Add cream, lemon zest, and salt.
- Bring to hard boil for 5 minutes, stirring occasionally.
- Stir in tomatoes and lemon juice.
- Set aside.
- In a sauté pan, heat butter and add green onions, tarragon, tomatoes, salt, pepper, and lemon juice.
- Heat until very hot.
- Add crabmeat and shake pan gently to heat the crab without breaking up the lumps.
- Cover and keep hot.
- Combine hot pasta and cream sauce, bringing it just to a boil.
- Divide pasta among individual plates and top each with crabmeat mixture.
- Sprinkle with parsley.

Serves 4

Spicy Pepper Pasta

¾ **cup extra virgin olive oil**

¾ **cup finely chopped parsley**

1 **bell pepper, chopped**

1 **sweet red bell pepper, chopped**

1 **small bunch green onions, chopped**
   (including some green)

3 **large garlic cloves, finely minced**

1 **(35 ounce) can Italian plum tomatoes,**
   coarsely chopped

2 **teaspoons dried basil**

1 **teaspoon dried mint**

¼ **teaspoon red cayenne pepper or more**
   to taste

Salt to taste

3 **tablespoons butter**

2 **tablespoons cognac**

1 **(16 ounce) package pasta, cooked**
   al dente

- Heat oil in heavy saucepan over medium high heat.
- Add parsley, peppers, green onions, and garlic.
- Stir in tomatoes.
- Add basil, mint, cayenne, and salt.
- Simmer for 5 minutes.
- Add butter and cognac to sauce and serve over pasta immediately.

Serves 4-6

Note: Great with shrimp or chicken added. Add fresh grated Parmesan cheese when serving.

The mission of St. Luke's Hospital & Health network is "to provide compassionate, excellent quality and cost-effective health care to residents of the communities we serve regardless of their ability to pay". Rick Anderson, President's Dinner, October, 2006.

Spinach Lasagna

1 (16 ounce) container ricotta cheese

1 cup shredded mozzarella cheese

1 egg, slightly beaten

1 (10 ounce) package frozen chopped spinach, thawed and well drained

½ teaspoon salt

⅛ teaspoon pepper

¾ teaspoon Italian seasoning

1 (32 ounce) jar spaghetti sauce or equal amount homemade sauce

1 (8 ounce) package lasagna noodles, uncooked

1 cup shredded mozzarella cheese

1 cup water

- Preheat oven to 350 degrees.
- Combine ricotta cheese, mozzarella cheese, egg, spinach, salt, pepper, and Italian seasoning in a large bowl.
- Stir well.
- Spread one-half cup spaghetti sauce in the bottom of a greased 13x9x2 inch baking dish.
- Arrange one-third noodles over sauce.
- Spread with half of cheese mixture.
- Layer with one-third spaghetti sauce, one-third noodles and remaining half cheese mixture.
- Top with remaining noodles, remaining spaghetti sauce and mozzarella cheese.
- Pour water around edges.
- Cover securely with foil.
- Bake for 1 hour, 15 minutes.
- Remove foil.
- Bake an additional 15 minutes until lightly browned.

Serves 6-8

Note: Freezes well. Add the water after defrosted and ready to bake. May also be made with meat based sauce (ground turkey, beef, or sweet Italian sausage).

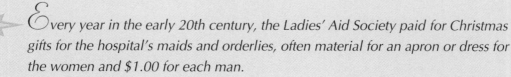

Every year in the early 20th century, the Ladies' Aid Society paid for Christmas gifts for the hospital's maids and orderlies, often material for an apron or dress for the women and $1.00 for each man.

Spaghetti Casserole

2 tablespoons butter

1 teaspoon sugar

1 teaspoon salt

Pinch of pepper

1 garlic clove, minced

1 ½ pounds ground beef

2 (8 ounce) cans tomato sauce

1 (3 ounce) package cream cheese, softened

1 ½ cups sour cream

6 green onions, chopped

1 (8 ounce) package spaghetti, cooked al dente

1 (8 ounce) package shredded Cheddar cheese

- Preheat oven to 350 degrees.
- Place butter in cold skillet.
- Add sugar, salt, and pepper.
- Mix well.
- Cook until butter is melted.
- Brown garlic and ground beef.
- Add tomato sauce.
- Simmer, uncovered, for 20 minutes.
- Combine cream cheese, sour cream, and green onions.
- Spread spaghetti in greased 13x9x2 inch baking dish.
- Top with cream cheese mixture.
- Spread meat mixture on top.
- Sprinkle with Cheddar cheese.
- Bake, uncovered, for 30 minutes.

Serves 6-8

In the late 19th century and early 20th centuries, each year the Ladies' Aid Society purchased material so that the Mother's Meeting of the Church of the Nativity could sew garments for the hospital's patients.

Spaghetti Pie

1 pound ground beef round

2 garlic cloves, crushed

¼ teaspoon black pepper

2 teaspoons Italian Seasoning

2 (8 ounce) cans tomato sauce

1½ cups reduced fat or nonfat sour cream

¼ cup reduced fat or nonfat cream cheese, softened

1 (8 ounce) package spaghetti, cooked al dente

1⅓ cups shredded reduced fat extra-sharp Cheddar cheese

- Cook ground beef and garlic in a large nonstick skillet over medium heat until browned.
- Stir while cooking to crumble meat.
- Drain well and return meat to pan.
- Stir in pepper, Italian seasoning, and tomato sauce.
- Bring to boil.
- Reduce heat and simmer for 20 minutes.
- Preheat oven to 350 degrees.
- Combine sour cream and cream cheese in a small bowl.
- Set aside.
- Place spaghetti a greased 2 quart in casserole dish.
- Spread sour cream mixture over spaghetti.
- Top with meat mixture.
- Sprinkle with Cheddar cheese.
- Cover and bake for 25 minutes.
- Uncover and bake an additional 5 minutes or until cheese is bubbly.

Serves 6

At their annual meeting, on October 18, 1916, the Ladies' Aid Society decided to have their first Charity Ball to raise money for their hospital projects. A great success, the event brought in $4,617.14.

Sausage and Bow-Tie Pasta

1 (16 ounce) package bow-tie pasta,
  cooked al dente

½ sweet red pepper, chopped

½ bell pepper, chopped

3 garlic cloves, minced

1 pound savory sausage, cooked and
  crumbled

½ cup Parmesan cheese (optional)

1 bunch green onions, chopped (optional)

Chopped parsley to taste

½ cup olive or canola oil

1 cup white wine (table or cooking wine)

Chopped parsley for garnish

- Preheat oven to 350 degrees.
- Arrange pasta in a 13x9x2 inch baking dish.
- Add peppers and garlic.
- Top with sausage.
- Sprinkle with Parmesan cheese, green onions, and parsley.
- Pour oil and wine over all.
- Bake about 30 minutes.
- Sprinkle with parsley before serving.

Serves 6

Angel Hair and Fresh Tomato Sauce

3 large tomatoes

½ cup olive oil

2 bunches green onions (white part only),
  sliced

3 garlic cloves, minced

1 cup fresh basil, finely chopped

Dash of dried oregano

Salt to taste

1 (12 ounce) package angel hair pasta,
  cooked al dente

- Blanch tomatoes in boiling water. Peel, seed, and chop tomatoes.
- Heat olive oil in pan on stove.
- Sauté green onions and garlic in oil for 3 minutes, do not brown.
- Add tomatoes, basil, oregano, and salt.
- Bring to boil.
- Reduce heat to low.
- Simmer for 3 minutes.
- Pour over cooked pasta.

Serves 4-6

Note: Angel hair pasta cooks quickly.

Special Tortellini

1 (10 ounce) package frozen chopped spinach, thawed

1 (16 ounce) package frozen tortellini, thawed

2 (14½ ounce) cans diced tomatoes

1 pint half-and-half

- Cook spinach according to package directions and drain.
- Cook tortellini according to package directions and drain.
- Place tortellini and spinach in a large stockpot.
- Mix in tomatoes.
- Heat until bubbly.
- Stir in half-and-half and heat thoroughly.
- Serve promptly.

Serves 4-5

Note: Experiment with the flavored canned diced tomatoes that are available now, such as garlic and onion or garlic and basil.

If a sweeter sauce is desired, add sugar according to taste. Try adding pieces of cooked chicken or cooked, sliced Italian sausage, and heat through before serving. Serve with a salad and fresh garlic bread.

In 1920, committees of the Ladies' Aid Society were formed to come to the hospital weekly to help make bandages, surgical dressings, and to sew and mend clothing and linens.

Chickpea Cassoulet with Tomatoes and Chard

1 onion, diced

3 garlic cloves, minced

2 pinches crushed red pepper

½ teaspoon ground thyme

½ teaspoon paprika

Pinch of saffron threads (optional)

1 (15 ounce) can chickpeas, reserve liquid

2 cups chopped tomatoes

1 bunch chard, leaves only

Salt to taste (optional)

Ground pepper to taste

1 (12 ounce) package spaghetti, cooked al dente

½ cup soy cheese, grated

Grated Parmesan cheese (optional)

- Preheat oven to 350 degrees.
- Sauté onions, garlic, red pepper, thyme, paprika, and saffron.
- Cook over medium-high heat for 8 minutes, stirring frequently, until onions are soft.
- Add chickpeas, one-half cup of reserved liquid, and tomatoes.
- Add pepper, lower heat and simmer for 15 minutes.
- If pan becomes dry, add a little water to keep it moist.
- Steam chard until bright green and tender. Remove and drain.
- Coarsely chop chard. Sprinkle with salt and pepper.
- Place pasta in a casserole dish. Add chickpea-tomato mixture, chard, and cheese.
- Toss until well mixed.
- Cover with foil and bake about 20 minutes or until thoroughly warmed.
- Serve with additional cheese.

Serves 4-6

Note: Firm, crumbled tofu may be used instead of soy cheese.

In 1920, the Ladies' Aid Society started donating baby clothes to mothers who had none for their babies when they left the hospital.

Pasta with Pink Vodka Sauce

5 tablespoons unsalted butter

¾ cup vodka

¼ teaspoon crushed red pepper

1 (16 ounce) can plum tomatoes, seeded and puréed

¾ cup heavy cream

½ teaspoon salt

1 (16 ounce) package penne pasta, cooked al dente

¾ cup freshly grated Parmesan cheese

- In saucepan, melt butter over moderate heat.
- Add vodka and red pepper and simmer for 2 minutes.
- Add tomatoes and cream and simmer an additional 5 minutes.
- Stir in salt.
- Add pasta.
- Reduce heat to low.
- Add Parmesan cheese and mix thoroughly.
- Pour into heated serving bowl and serve immediately.

Serves 4-6

Note: Easy and elegant.

Easy Brown Rice Almandine

1 ½ cups instant brown rice

1 ¼ cups chicken broth

1 medium onion, chopped

1 tablespoon lemon juice

1 tablespoon butter

1 cup fresh or frozen green beans, thawed if frozen

2 tablespoons sliced toasted almonds

Lemon slices for garnish

- Combine rice, broth, onions, lemon juice, and butter in microwave dish.
- Cover.
- Microwave on high for 5 minutes.
- Stir in string beans.
- Cover.
- Microwave on high for 5 minutes.
- Stir in almonds.
- Garnish with lemon slices.

Serves 4

Spiced Couscous

3 tablespoons olive oil

1 cup sliced almonds

3 garlic cloves, finely chopped

1 teaspoon paprika

1 teaspoon ground cumin

¾ teaspoon ground coriander

½ teaspoon cayenne pepper

2½ cups vegetable broth

2 cups cooked chickpeas, drained and rinsed

1 cup chopped dates

1¼ cups couscous

Salt and freshly ground black pepper to taste

½ cup chopped green onions, including green tops

- Heat oil in a large skillet.
- Sauté almonds about 2 minutes over medium heat, stirring frequently, until fragrant and lightly toasted.
- Add garlic. Cook and stir for 1 minute.
- Stir in paprika, cumin, coriander, and cayenne.
- Add broth, chickpeas, and dates.
- Bring to boil.
- Add couscous.
- Stir once to combine.
- Cover pan and remove from heat.
- Let stand for 5 minutes until couscous absorbs liquid.
- Fluff couscous mixture with a fork.
- Sprinkle with salt and pepper.
- Top with green onions before serving.

Serves 4

 The Industrial Revolution brought steel mills and other heavy production to the Lehigh Valley. Industrial accidents occurred and the injured were taken, by wagon, to Philadelphia for treatment. Many died during the long trip.

Dirty Rice with Andouille

3 garlic cloves, minced

1 teaspoon olive oil

1 teaspoon olive oil

¼ cup chopped onion

½ cup chopped celery

¼ cup chopped bell pepper

1 cup diced andouille sausage

1 cup cooked and diced chicken breast

1 cup uncooked long-grain rice

2½ cups chicken broth

1 teaspoon thyme leaves

1 teaspoon salt

½ teaspoon ground pepper

Pinch of cayenne pepper

- In a large skillet, sauté garlic in oil for 1 minute until lightly browned.
- Add oil.
- Sauté onions, celery, and peppers for 5 minutes over low heat until softened.
- Add sausage, chicken, and rice. Sauté 2 minutes more, stirring constantly.
- Add broth and thyme and bring to boil.
- Cover and simmer for 20 minutes until rice is just about cooked.
- Stir in salt, pepper, and cayenne. Cook for 5 minutes or until rice is dry and tender, but firm to the bite.

Serves 6

Broccoli Green Rice

2 (10 ounce) packages frozen chopped
   broccoli, thawed

1 stick butter

¾ cup chopped celery

¾ cup chopped onions

½ cup chopped bell pepper

1 (8 ounce) jar processed cheese sauce

2 (10¾ ounce) cans cream of mushroom
   soup

2 cups cooked rice

- Preheat oven to 350 degrees.
- Cook broccoli according to package directions and drain.
- Melt butter in skillet.
- Sauté celery, onions, and peppers in butter until tender.
- Add broccoli to sautéed vegetables.
- Stir in three-fourths cheese sauce and all mushroom soup.
- Add rice and mix well.
- Pour mixture into a lightly greased 2 quart casserole dish.
- Spread remaining cheese sauce on top.
- Bake for 30 minutes.

Serves 8-10

The women's group of the Church of the Nativity incorporated themselves as the Ladies' Aid Society of St. Luke's Hospital which today operates as St. Luke's Hospital Auxiliary.

Barley-Pine Nut Casserole

⅓ cup pine nuts

2 tablespoons butter

1 cup uncooked barley

1 onion, chopped

4 tablespoons butter

½ cup minced parsley

¼ cup minced chives

Salt and pepper to taste

3 ½ cups beef or chicken broth

- Preheat oven to 375 degrees.
- Cook pine nuts in butter until lightly toasted.
- Remove nuts from pan.
- Sauté barley and onions in butter until tender.
- Remove pan from heat.
- Stir in nuts, parsley, chives, salt, and pepper.
- Spoon mixture into a greased 1 ½ quart casserole dish.
- Bring broth to boil. Pour over barley mixture.
- Bake for 1 hour until liquid is absorbed.

Serves 6

In 1872, Tinsley Jeter suggested the Water Cure property as ideal location for St. Luke's and purchased the property with his own funds to keep it from being developed. Mr. Jeter envisioned the Fountain Hill property as the medical campus of a state-of-the-art hospital.

Barley Risotto

4 cups chicken or vegetable broth

2½ cups water

2 tablespoons extra-virgin olive oil

1 medium leek, chopped, both white and green parts or chopped onion

1 garlic clove, minced

¾ cup medium pearl barley

½ teaspoon dried tarragon

¼ teaspoon pepper

½ cup frozen peas

¼ cup Parmesan cheese

1 tablespoon fresh chives

- Combine broth and water in a medium saucepan.
- Bring to boil.
- Reduce heat, cover and simmer.
- In a large saucepan, heat oil over medium heat.
- Sauté leek and garlic for 4 minutes, stirring constantly.
- Add barley, tarragon, and pepper. Stir until barley is coated.
- Add one-half cup hot broth mixture at a time, stirring frequently after each addition until liquid is nearly evaporated.
- Continue adding one-half cup broth at a time until used up and barley is very tender and creamy, about 55 minutes.
- Stir in peas, Parmesan cheese, and chives.
- Cook for 5 minutes or until heated through.

Serves 6-8

In late 1875, Tinsley Jeter's Water Cure property in Fountain Hill was purchased for $25,000, with $10,000 of the cost donated by Asa Packer and sons. This along with the acquisition of an adjacent land parcel gave the hospital more than 40 acres.

Pierogies in a Casserole

5 or 6 red potatoes

4 medium onions, diced

1 stick butter

¾ (16 ounce) package large wide egg noodles, cooked al dente

1 pound American cheese

Butter

- Preheat oven to 350 degrees.
- Boil potatoes until tender and mash.
- Sauté onions in butter until soft.
- Spread half the noodles and half the potatoes in a buttered 13x9x2 inch baking dish.
- Spoon onions on top.
- Top with five cheese slices.
- Layer with remaining noodles and potatoes.
- Top with remaining cheese.
- Dot with margarine.
- Cover with foil.
- Bake for 30 minutes.

Serves 8-10

Asa Packer died in 1879 willing $300,000 in Lehigh Valley Railroad stock to St. Luke's Hospital directing the income to pay for the treatment of railroad employees, injured, wounded, sick, or disabled by age or other cause.

Gloria's Best Ever Noodle Kugel

1 (13½ ounce) package graham cracker crumb crust mix

1 (16 ounce) package noodles, cooked al dente

2 sticks unsalted butter, softened

1½ cups sugar

1 cup golden raisins

2 (8 ounce) containers cottage cheese

Pinch of salt

1 pint sour cream

6 eggs, beaten

1½ cups graham cracker crumbs

- Preheat oven to 350 degrees.
- Make graham cracker crust according to package directions and press on the bottom of a 13x9x2 inch baking dish.
- Bake for 5 minutes.
- Combine noodles, butter, sugar, raisins, cottage cheese, salt, and sour cream.
- Add eggs.
- Spoon mixture onto crust.
- Dot with butter.
- Sprinkle with graham cracker crumbs.
- Cover with foil and bake for 1 hour, 15 minutes, removing foil for the last 5 minutes.
- Cut into squares and serve in place of rice or potato.

Serves 8-10

Note: This recipe can be baked and frozen, then reheated.

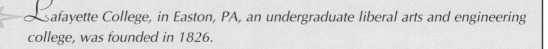

Lafayette College, in Easton, PA, an undergraduate liberal arts and engineering college, was founded in 1826.

Wild Rice with Mushrooms

3 cups chicken broth

¾ cup wild rice

1 stick butter

1½ pounds sliced mushrooms

½ teaspoon dried rosemary

¼ teaspoon dried sage

Pinch of cayenne pepper

6 tablespoons dry sherry

- Combine broth and rice in a heavy saucepan.
- Cover and simmer about 1 hour until tender and liquid is absorbed.
- Remove from heat.
- Melt butter in a heavy skillet. Sauté mushrooms, rosemary, sage, and cayenne about 12 minutes until golden browned.
- Add sherry. Cook and stir about 2 minutes until mushrooms are dry.
- Stir in rice. Heat thoroughly.

Serves 4

Bulgur Pilaf

3 tablespoons olive oil

4 green onions, chopped

1 large sweet red pepper, chopped

2 large fresh or 1 (16 ounce) can diced tomatoes

1 cup basil leaves, chopped

2 cups medium or coarse bulgur

5 cups hot chicken broth or water

1 teaspoon salt

Basil leaves for garnish

- Heat oil in a large saucepan over medium high heat.
- Sauté green onions and peppers for 2 minutes until soft.
- Add tomatoes and basil.
- Cook for an additional 2 minutes.
- Stir in bulgur.
- Pour in hot broth or water.
- Add salt and mix well.
- Bring to boil.
- Reduce heat to low.
- Cook, uncovered, about 15 minutes until liquid is absorbed, stirring occasionally to prevent bulgur from sticking to pan.
- Add salt to taste.
- Serve hot on a platter garnished with basil leaves.

Serves 8

St. Luke's Quakertown Hospital

Bucks County
Joined Network in 1995

The Auxiliary of St. Luke's Hospital
has raised more than $35,000 to support this campus.

St. Luke's Quakertown Hospital

Bucks County
Joined Network in 1995

St. Luke's Quakertown Hospital has undergone a transformation with the addition of a new and expanded Emergency Department, as well as a new entrance and adjacent medical office building. The hospital has also added a number of leading-edge technologies, such as a 64-slice CT scanner. Recently, St. Luke's Quakertown Hospital was ranked first in Pennsylvania for overall patient satisfaction.

Brussels Sprouts with Hazelnuts

8 ounces hazelnuts

2 pounds Brussels sprouts, trimmed and halved

6 tablespoons butter

6 shallots, chopped

2 teaspoons fresh lemon juice

1 teaspoon grated lemon zest

Salt and pepper to taste

- Preheat oven to 350 degrees.
- Toast hazelnuts about 10 minutes or until lightly browned.
- Cool slightly then rub skins off.
- Halve hazelnuts and set aside.
- In a large saucepan, boil water.
- Cook sprouts in boiling water for 3 to 4 minutes until crisp-tender.
- Drain in a colander.
- Melt butter over medium heat in a large skillet.
- Add shallots and cook 1 to 2 minutes, stirring frequently.
- Add sprouts.
- Sprinkle with lemon juice, lemon zest, salt, and pepper.

Serves 4-6

The Emrick Family's extraordinary gift of 25 acres creates an unprecedented opportunity to brink nationally recognized health care services to their neighbors and friends. On this site where Elaine Emrick and her husband, Pete, worked side by side for more than 40 years farming land, we will create a health care campus that will bring honor to both the Emrick Family and to St. Luke's Hospital & Health Network, and that will serve the health care needs of our region for generations to come." Richard Anderson, President & CEO, St. Luke's Hospital & Healthcare Network.

Cabbage Casserole

1 medium head cabbage, cut up

4 tablespoons butter

1 small garlic clove, crushed (optional)

¼ cup all-purpose flour

½ teaspoon salt

¼ teaspoon pepper

2 cups milk

1 (8 ounce) package processed cheese loaf, sliced

Bread crumbs for topping (optional)

- Preheat oven to 350 degrees.
- Cook cabbage in salted water for 10 to 15 minutes until tender, do not overcook.
- Drain well.
- In a small saucepan, melt butter and add garlic.
- Slowly stir in flour, salt, and pepper, to make a smooth paste.
- Gradually add milk, stirring constantly until smooth.
- Stir constantly until thickened.
- In a 2-quart casserole dish, layer cabbage and cheese slices.
- Pour in white sauce until dish is full.
- Sprinkle bread crumbs over top.
- Bake for 30 to 40 minutes.

Serves 4-6

The first class of St. Luke's School of Nursing started on December 1, 1884.

Carrot Apple Side Dish

1 ½ cups diced carrots (about 6)

2 cups water

1 tablespoon butter

¼ cup packed brown sugar

1 tablespoon lemon juice

⅛ teaspoon ground cinnamon

1 cup peeled and diced apples

1 tablespoon cornstarch

2 tablespoons cold water

- Cook carrots in water until crisp-tender.
- Drain carrots.
- Return carrots to stockpot and add butter, brown sugar, lemon juice, and cinnamon.
- Mix well.
- Stir in apples.
- Cover and simmer for 10 minutes, stirring occasionally.
- Whisk together cornstarch and cold water.
- Stir into carrot mixture.
- Bring to boil.
- Cook and stir about 1 minute until thickened.
- Simmer for 2 minutes, stirring occasionally.

Serves 4

Gold pins were given at the first graduation in 1886. On the pins was the winged ox, the evangelistic symbol of St. Luke the Physician.

Marinated Carrots

2 pounds carrots, sliced

1 (10¾ ounce) can tomato soup, undiluted

1 teaspoon salt

1 teaspoon pepper

¾ cup sugar

¼ cup vinegar

1 teaspoon Worcestershire sauce

½ teaspoon prepared mustard

3 small onions, sliced into rings

½ bell pepper, diced

½ cup vegetable oil

- Cook carrots in lightly salted water until crisp-tender.
- Set carrots aside to cool.
- Blend soup, salt, pepper, sugar, vinegar, Worcestershire sauce, mustard, onions, peppers, and oil.
- Add cooled carrots.
- Refrigerate for several days or at least overnight.

Serves 6-8

Note: May store for several weeks.

Corn Pudding

6 ears corn, cooked with kernels removed

3 egg yolks, beaten

1 tablespoon cornstarch

1 teaspoon salt

4 tablespoons butter, melted

1 cup milk

3 egg whites

- Preheat oven to 350 degrees.
- Combine egg yolks, cornstarch, salt, butter, and milk.
- Beat egg whites until stiff. Fold into egg yolk mixture.
- Spoon mixture in a greased casserole dish.
- Bake for 35 to 40 minutes.

Serves 4-6

Note: May substitute 1 (15 ounce) can whole kernel corn for fresh corn.

Fountain Hill and St. Luke's Hospital intertwine: the original property was owned by a Frenchman, Auguste Fiote, who named the property Fountainbleau.

Ham and Corn Bake

4 eggs

1½ cups milk

1½ cups shredded Cheddar cheese

¼ teaspoon salt

¼ teaspoon pepper

¼ teaspoon ground thyme

½ teaspoon dry mustard

2 green onions, minced

2 cups frozen corn, thawed or canned corn, drained

1½ cups coarsely chopped ham

1 bell pepper, finely chopped

1 tablespoon butter

- Preheat oven to 350 degrees.
- Beat eggs in mixing bowl.
- Add milk, cheese, salt, pepper, thyme, mustard, green onions, corn, and ham. Mix well.
- Sauté peppers in butter until slightly softened. Add to mixture.
- Pour mixture into a buttered 11x7x2 inch baking dish.
- Bake for 40 to 45 minutes or until set and knife comes out clean.

Serves 6

Barbeque Green Beans

4 slices bacon, diced

¼ cup chopped onions

½ cup ketchup

⅓-½ cup packed brown sugar

2 (16 ounce) cans French style green beans, drained or 1 pound fresh

Salt and pepper to taste (optional)

- Preheat oven to 350 degrees.
- Fry bacon with onions until browned.
- Drain bacon and onions.
- Add ketchup and brown sugar and heat a few minutes.
- Pour beans into 1½ quart casserole dish.
- Sprinkle with salt and pepper.
- Pour sauce over beans and mix.
- Bake, uncovered, for 45 minutes.

Serves 4-6

Aloo Gobi

(Punjabi-Style Cauliflower and Potatoes with Ginger)

Peanut or canola oil

1 pound baking potatoes, peeled and cut into 2x1x1 inch thick fries

1 head cauliflower (1¾ pounds), cut into delicate florets

1 tablespoon finely chopped ginger

½ teaspoon ground turmeric

¾-1 teaspoon salt

¼ teaspoon cayenne pepper

1 teaspoon ground cumin

1 teaspoon ground coriander

3 tablespoons water

2 tomatoes, chopped

½ teaspoon garam masala

2-3 tablespoons coarsely chopped cilantro leaves

- Heat oil in a large frying pan over medium heat. When hot, fry potatoes about 10 minutes until golden browned and almost tender.
- Remove potatoes with a slotted spoon to drain on paper towels.
- Turn heat to medium-high.
- Add cauliflower florets and fry for 3 to 4 minutes or until golden browned.
- Remove cauliflower with a slotted spoon to drain on paper towels.
- Turn heat off.
- Remove all except 2 tablespoons oil from pan, (extra oil can be drained and reused).
- Heat to medium-high and add ginger.
- Stir for 10 seconds.
- Return potatoes and cauliflower to pan.
- Reduce heat to medium.
- Add turmeric, salt, cayenne, cumin, and coriander.
- Stir gently to coat vegetables with spices.
- Add water, tomatoes, and masala.
- Stir once and cover the pan.
- Reduce heat to low and cook very gently for 4 minutes.
- Add cilantro and toss gently.

Serves 4

Note: This everyday cauliflower and potato dish is generally eaten with flatbreads (rotis or parathas) as well as a yogurt relish and some pickles. You may serve it as part of any meal along with greens, beans, and rice or bread.

Sautéed Green Beans with Tomatoes and Basil

1 ½ **pounds green beans, trimmed**

2 **tablespoons butter**

2 **tablespoons olive oil**

3 **large shallots, thinly sliced**

2 **garlic cloves, minced**

1 **(14½ ounce) can diced tomatoes**

¼ **cup dry white wine**

2 **tablespoons thinly sliced basil**

Salt and ground pepper to taste

- Cook green beans in boiling water about 3 minutes until crisp-tender.
- Drain and immerse in cold water.
- Drain well.
- Melt butter and oil in a heavy skillet.
- Sauté shallots and garlic 3 for minutes until tender.
- Add tomatoes and cook for 3 minutes.
- Add beans and cook until juices evaporate and beans are tender.
- Stir in wine and basil and simmer for 2 minutes.
- Add salt and pepper.

Serves 6-8

Note: Wonderful side dish with meat, fish, or pasta dinner.

Baked Beans

2 **(16 ounce) cans baked beans**

½ **cup packed dark brown sugar**

1 **small onion, diced**

Dash of ground nutmeg

Dash of cinnamon

¾ **cup ketchup**

2 **slices bacon, diced**

1 **cup cornflakes cereal**

- Preheat oven to 350 degrees.
- Combine beans, brown sugar, onions, nutmeg, cinnamon, and ketchup.
- Pour mixture into greased bean pot or baking dish.
- Top with bacon.
- Cover with cereal.
- Bake for 1 hour or until slightly moistened.
- Serve warm.

Serves 4-6

Note: For variety, add 1 package of miniature frankfurters.

New Orleans Spinach

2 (10 ounce) packages frozen chopped spinach, thawed

1 (8 ounce) package cream cheese, softened

1 stick butter, cut up

Zest of 1 lemon

Juice of ½ lemon

Pinch of nutmeg or mace

Salt to taste

Crushed red pepper or cayenne pepper to taste

1 cup herb flavored stuffing mix

- Preheat oven to 350 degrees.
- Cook spinach and drain well.
- While still hot, add cream cheese and butter.
- Mix well.
- Add lemon zest, lemon juice, nutmeg, salt, and red pepper.
- Spoon mixture in greased casserole dish.
- Sprinkle with stuffing mix.
- Bake about 30 minutes or until thoroughly heated.

Serves 8

Italian Potato Pancakes

6 potatoes, cooked and mashed

¾ cup grated Romano cheese

1 large garlic clove, minced

1 tablespoon minced parsley

2 eggs

Salt to taste

All-purpose flour

Olive oil

- Combine potatoes, Romano cheese, garlic, parsley, eggs, and salt.
- Add water if necessary to soften mixture.
- Shape mixture into patties. Dredge in flour.
- Fry in hot oil until lightly browned.
- Serve hot.

Serves 6

Oven Fried Potatoes

3 medium potatoes, sliced into ⅛ inch pieces, do not peel

¼ cup olive oil

1 tablespoon grated Parmesan cheese

½ teaspoon garlic powder or 1 garlic clove, minced

½ teaspoon paprika

Dash of cayenne pepper

- Preheat oven to 450 degrees.
- Arrange potato slices in an overlapping fashion in a lightly greased 13x9x2 inch baking dish.
- Blend oil, Parmesan cheese, garlic powder, paprika, and cayenne.
- Brush mixture over potatoes.
- Bake for 45 minutes.
- Potatoes will be fork tender and crisp around the edges and golden browned.

Serves 4

Note: Red new potatoes work well.

Donations received by St. Luke's Hospital in 1874 included 4 shirts, magazines, 4 jars of fruit, 2 bottles of raspberry vinegar, a box of mustard, a jar of pickles, 2 pounds of sugar, and a jar of butter.

Tourte aux Pommes de Terre (Potato Torte)

2 sheets puff pastry, each cut into a
    9½ inch circle

2 large potatoes, peeled and very thinly
    sliced, almost transparent

4 tablespoons butter

1 large shallot, finely minced

½ garlic clove, finely minced

3 tablespoons finely minced parsley

1 egg yolk, beaten

2 tablespoons cold water

- Preheat oven to 475 degrees.
- Arrange an even, thin layer potatoes over one puff pastry circle, leaving one inch pastry edge.
- Dot generously with butter.
- Combine shallots, garlic, and parsley.
- Spread evenly over potatoes.
- Cover with other puff pastry circle and pinch edges together.
- Beat egg yolk with water.
- Brush top of torte with egg wash.
- Pierce a hole in the center for steam to escape. Otherwise your torte may fall when removed from the oven.
- Bake for 15 minutes or until torte has visibly risen.
- Reduce temperature to 375 degrees.
- Bake for an additional 30 minutes.

Serves 8-10

Note: For a creative look, use some of the leftover puff pastry and decorate the top of the torte before brushing with egg.

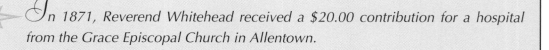

In 1871, Reverend Whitehead received a $20.00 contribution for a hospital from the Grace Episcopal Church in Allentown.

Grammy Borath's Cheese Stuffed Baked Potatoes

8 large baking potatoes, cleaned and patted dry

½ cup milk

4 tablespoons butter

½ cup sour cream

1 cup diced Swiss cheese

1 ½ teaspoons salt

¼ teaspoon pepper

¼ cup shredded Swiss cheese

- Preheat oven to 425 degrees.
- Pierce potatoes with a fork.
- Place in a shallow pan and bake for 55 minutes.
- Cut a thin lengthwise slice from top of each potato.
- Scoop out the pulp leaving a ¼ inch shell.
- Place pulp in bowl and cover.
- Return shells to baking pan.
- Combine milk and butter in small saucepan. Heat slowly until butter melts.
- Add milk to potato pulp and beat with electric mixer until fluffy.
- Stir in sour cream, Swiss cheese, salt and pepper.
- Spoon potato mixture back into shells.
- Bake for 25 minutes.
- Top with shredded Swiss cheese and bake an additional 5 minutes until cheese is browned.

Serves 8

Sweet Potato Casserole

4 tablespoons butter, melted

¼ cup milk

2 cups sweet potatoes, mashed

1 teaspoon vanilla

1 medium ripe banana, mashed

¼ cup undiluted frozen orange juice, thawed

¼ cup sugar

- Preheat oven to 350 degrees.
- Combine butter, milk, potatoes, vanilla, bananas, juice, and sugar.
- Pour mixture into a 3 quart casserole dish.
- Bake for 30 minutes.

Serves 4

Whipped Sweet Potatoes with Cornflake Topping

Sweet Potatoes

3 large sweet potatoes, peeled and cut into 1 inch pieces

6 tablespoons butter, softened

1 large egg

6 tablespoons sugar

1 teaspoon pumpkin pie spice

Pinch of salt

Cornflake Topping

1 ½ cups crushed cornflakes

½ cup packed brown sugar

½ cup chopped pecans

6 tablespoons butter, melted

- Cook sweet potatoes in large pot of boiling water about 15 minutes or until tender.
- Drain and transfer potatoes to large bowl.
- Add butter and beat until smooth.
- Blend in egg, sugar, spice, and salt.
- Pour mixture into a 9x9x2 inch baking dish.
- Cover and refrigerate.
- Bring to room temperature.
- Bake at 400 degrees about 25 minutes or until edges are browned and slightly puffed.
- Combine cornflake crumbs, brown sugar, pecans, and butter.
- Spoon topping evenly over potatoes.
- Bake an additional 10 minutes or until golden browned and crispy.

Serves 6

Reverend Whitehead and Tinsley Jeter, a church member and businessman, asked the state legislature for a state charter to establish a hospital, circa 1872.

Portobello Mushroom Parmesan

4-6 Portobello mushrooms, stemmed

3 tablespoons extra virgin olive oil

½ teaspoon salt

¼ teaspoon pepper

2 tablespoons extra virgin olive oil

1½ cups marinara or tomato sauce

**4-6 slices mozzarella cheese or ¾ cup
    shredded**

¼ cup grated Parmesan cheese

1 tablespoon butter, cut into pieces

- Preheat oven to 400 degrees.
- Preheat grill pan on stove.
- Drizzle oil over both sides of mushrooms.
- Sprinkle both sides of mushrooms with salt and pepper.
- Drizzle oil on grill pan.
- Grill mushrooms on both sides about 6 minutes per side until tender.
- Spread one-half cup sauce on bottom of a 13x9x2 inch baking dish.
- Place mushrooms in dish, gill side up.
- Top with mozzarella cheese and remaining sauce.
- Sprinkle with Parmesan cheese and dot with butter.
- Bake about 15 minutes until cheese melts and is golden browned.

Serves 4-6

On March 29, 1872 Governor Geary signed the state approved charter establishing a church hospital.

Squash Casserole

2 pounds small yellow squash, sliced

1 tablespoon chopped onions

2 eggs, beaten

1 cup shredded sharp Cheddar cheese

½ cup crushed round buttery crackers

4 tablespoons butter

Paprika and black pepper to taste

- Preheat oven to 350 degrees.
- Cook squash and onions in salted water until tender.
- Drain and cool.
- Add eggs and mix well.
- Pour mixture into a lightly greased casserole dish.
- Sprinkle with cheese.
- Scatter cracker crumbs on top.
- Dot with butter. Sprinkle with paprika and black pepper.
- Bake about 20 minutes or until browned.

Serves 6

Zucchini Pie

4 eggs

½ cup vegetable oil

1 cup biscuit baking mix

¼ teaspoon salt

Pepper to taste

4 cups grated zucchini

1 small onion, chopped

1 (8 ounce) package shredded extra sharp Cheddar cheese

½ cup shredded Parmesan cheese

½ teaspoon dried parsley

Ground nutmeg to taste

- Preheat oven to 350 degrees.
- Whisk together eggs and oil.
- Add baking mix, salt, and pepper.
- Stir in zucchini, onions, Cheddar cheese, and Parmesan cheese.
- Add parsley.
- Pour mixture into a lightly greased 9 inch pie plate.
- Sprinkle with nutmeg.
- Bake for 45 to 60 minutes, or until browned, and knife comes out clean.

Serves 6

Summer Zucchini Casserole

3 medium zucchini, sliced into ¼ inch slices

1 large Vidalia onion, sliced

2 small sweet red peppers, sliced

1-2 medium tomatoes, sliced

2 tablespoons all-purpose flour

3 tablespoons butter

½ cup shredded mozzarella cheese

- Preheat oven to 350 degrees.
- Layer half zucchini in a greased 2 quart casserole dish.
- Continue layering with half onions, peppers and tomatoes.
- Sprinkle with 1 tablespoon flour.
- Dot with 1 tablespoon butter.
- Top with ¼ cup cheese.
- Repeat vegetable layers. Repeat layers of flour, butter, and cheese.
- Top with butter.
- Cover and bake for 45 minutes.
- Uncover and bake for 10 minutes or until golden browned.

Serves 4-6

Amazing Pineapple Stuffing

1 stick butter, softened

1 cup sugar

6 eggs, beaten

1 (20 ounce) can crushed pineapple, undrained

15-18 slices white sandwich bread, crust removed and cubed

- Preheat oven to 350 degrees.
- Cream butter and sugar.
- Add eggs.
- Stir in pineapple with juice.
- Add bread cubes and mix well.
- Pour mixture into a greased 2 quart casserole dish.
- Bake for 1 hour.

Serves 6-8

Note: Very good served with ham.

127

Yorkshire Pudding

1 ½ cups all-purpose flour

¾ teaspoon salt

¾ cup milk, room temperature

3 eggs, room temperature

¾ cup water

½ cup beef drippings

- Mix together flour and salt.
- Make a well in the flour. Add milk and mix well.
- Beat eggs into batter.
- Add water and beat again until mixture is light and frothy.
- Set aside for an hour, or if making ahead, cover and refrigerate overnight.
- If batter has been refrigerated, bring to room temperature and stir before continuing.
- Preheat oven to 400 degrees.
- Pour beef drippings into a lightly greased 13x9x2 inch baking dish.
- Place dish in the oven and heat until the drippings sizzle.
- Pour batter over drippings.
- Return to oven and bake for 30 minutes or until the sides have risen and are golden browned.
- Cut into eight portions and serve immediately.

Serves 8

Note: This is a delicious addition to a roasted prime rib dinner. As indicated above, it can be partially prepared the night before.

 In late 1872, the charter was modified stating that St. Luke's Hospital should be non-denominational, as it remains today.

St. Luke's Hospice House

A service of The Visiting Nurse Association of St. Luke's
Joined Network in 1993

The Auxiliary of St. Luke's Hospital
has raised more than $235,000 to support the Maternal Child Program
and the new Hospice House.

St. Luke's Hospice House

A service of The Visiting Nurse Association of St. Luke's
Joined Network in 1993

The Visiting Nurse Association of St. Luke's provides a wide range of home care services, as well as inpatient and outpatient hospice programs. Home care services, for adults and children, include: mother/baby care; home health care; physical, occupational and speech therapy and private duty services.

Honey-Mustard Marinade for Chicken or Pork

1 tablespoon curry powder

2 tablespoons soy sauce

½ cup Dijon mustard

½ cup honey

- Combine curry, soy sauce, mustard, and honey in a large zip-top plastic bag.
- Add chicken or pork and seal the bag.
- Marinate for 2 to 4 hours.

Makes 1 cup marinade

Note: Excellent for thick pork chops or boneless, skinless chicken breast halves prior to grilling. Can also be used to spread over boneless pork tenderloin or a small chicken prior to baking in the oven.

Mango Avocado Salsa

1 large mango, peeled, pitted and diced

3 tablespoons minced onion

3 tablespoons diced bell pepper

3 tablespoons diced sweet red pepper

1½ tablespoons white wine vinegar

1 tablespoon fresh chopped cilantro

1 tablespoon olive oil

1 tablespoon chopped chives

½ large avocado, pitted and diced

Salt and pepper to taste

- Combine mango, onions, bell peppers, red peppers, vinegar, cilantro, oil, and chives until well blended.
- Cover and refrigerate up to 3 hours.
- Just before serving, stir in avocado.
- Add salt and pepper.

Serves 4

Note: Delicious with chicken or fish.

The first fund raising campaign raised $9000 in one month in 1873.

Basil Cheese Sauce for Pasta

2 tablespoons butter

4 garlic cloves, minced

2 tablespoons all-purpose flour

1 ½ cups milk

½ cup half-and-half

½ cup ricotta cheese

¼ cup grated Parmesan cheese

1 cup grated mozzarella cheese

¼ cup finely chopped fresh basil

½ teaspoon salt

¼ teaspoon pepper

- Melt butter in 2 quart saucepan over medium-low heat.
- Sauté garlic for 1 minute. Do not brown.
- Stir in flour to coat garlic.
- Add milk, half-and-half, ricotta cheese, Parmesan cheese, and mozzarella cheese.
- Cook and stir over medium-low heat until cheese melt.
- Add basil, salt, and pepper.
- Cook over low heat for 15 minutes, stirring once in a while to prevent sticking.
- Serve over your favorite pasta.
- Sprinkle with additional Parmesan cheese.

Serves 4-6

In 1846, Dr. Francis Henry Oppelt applied to the Moravian Church for permission to build a hydropathy institute at the source of a spring of chemically pure water.

Raisin Sauce for Ham

1 cup raisins

1 cup water

1 cup orange juice

½ cup orange marmalade

¼ cup sugar

2 tablespoons cornstarch

¼ teaspoon salt

¼ teaspoon ground cloves

- Bring raisins, water, orange juice, and marmalade to boil.
- Add sugar, cornstarch, salt, and cloves.
- Stir until dissolved.
- Pour sauce over cooked ham.

Serves 4

Barbecue Sauce

1 ½ cups molasses

1 cup prepared mustard

⅓ cup Worcestershire sauce

½ cup vinegar

2 teaspoons Tabasco sauce

¼ teaspoon ground marjoram

¼ teaspoon dried oregano

- Pour molasses into large mixing bowl.
- Gradually blend in mustard.
- Add Worcestershire sauce, vinegar, Tabasco, marjoram, and oregano.
- Mix well.
- Store in tightly covered jar in refrigerator.

Makes about 1 quart

Note: Great basting sauce for chicken and ribs.

In 1874, the hospital's operating budget was $11,742.

Carpaccio Sauce

2 cups mayonnaise

4 anchovy filets

2 teaspoons capers

1 ½ cups coarsely chopped parsley, without stems

4 teaspoons red wine vinegar

¼ teaspoon salt

¼ teaspoon pepper

- Combine mayonnaise, anchovies, capers, parsley, vinegar, salt, and pepper in a blender.
- Blend until very smooth.
- Cover and store in refrigerator.

Serves 6-8

Note: Great served with any meat, especially roast beef.

Cocktail Hot Dogs

(For Slow Cooker)

2 (16 ounce) packages hot dogs

2 (8 ounce) jars brown mustard

2 (12 ounce) jars currant jelly

- Slice hot dogs into bite size pieces.
- Mix together mustard and jelly in a slow cooker.
- Add hot dog pieces and stir well.
- Cook on high for 20 minutes or on low for 1 hour.
- Check and stir occasionally.

Serves 10-12

There were 47 beds in the first year at St. Luke's Hospital and 400 in the 100th year.

Slow Cooker French Dip

4 pound boneless sirloin tip roast

2 (0.7 ounce) envelopes dry Italian dressing mix

2 cups water

1 (16 ounces) jar mild pepper rings, undrained

Hoagie rolls

- Place roast in slow cooker.
- Combine dressing mix and water. Pour over roast.
- Cook on low about 9 hours.
- Remove meat and shred.
- Return meat to slow cooker. Add pepper rings and liquid to slow cooker.
- Stir and heat thoroughly.
- Serve on hoagie rolls.

Serves 6-8

Note: Add Swiss or mozzarella cheese to sandwiches. May substitute thick sliced specialty breads for hoagie rolls.

Sausage Sandwiches

(For Slow Cooker)

2 pounds favorite sausage

1 large onion, sliced

4-6 garlic cloves, minced

1 bell pepper, red, yellow or orange, chopped

1 tablespoon dried parsley

1 tablespoon dried basil

1-2 tablespoons dried oregano

1 (28 ounce) can tomato purée

1 jalapeño pepper, chopped (optional)

Sandwich rolls

- Boil sausages 5 minutes to remove fat.
- Place sausages, onions, garlic, peppers, parsley, basil, oregano, tomato purée, and jalapeños into slow cooker.
- Cook 4 hours on high or 8 hours on low.
- Serve sausages on rolls with tomato sauce on top.

Serves 6

Slow Cooker Meatball Stew

1 (10¾ ounce) can condensed cream of
   mushroom soup with roasted garlic

½ cup beef broth

4 large red potatoes, cut in 1 inch cubes

1½ cups baby carrots

1 cup chopped celery

1 pound lean ground beef

½ cup grated Parmesan cheese

⅓ cup seasoned dry bread crumbs

1 large egg

2 tablespoons chopped parsley

½ teaspoon salt

½ teaspoon pepper

Chopped parsley for garnish

- Blend soup and broth in a slow cooker.
- Stir in potatoes, carrots, and celery.
- Mix beef, Parmesan cheese, bread crumbs, egg, parsley, salt, and pepper in a bowl by hand or with a spoon until blended.
- Shape meat mixture into 1 ½ inch balls, and place on top of vegetable mixture.
- Cover and cook on low for 7 to 9 hours or until meatballs are cooked through and vegetables are tender.
- Transfer meatballs and vegetables to a platter with a slotted spoon.
- Whisk sauce until smooth and pour over meatballs and vegetables.
- Sprinkle with parsley before serving.

Serves 4

Note: To cut down on preparation time, premade meatballs may be used.

By 1875, there was an obvious need for a larger hospital campus.

Hamburger Soup

(For Slow Cooker)

1 pound ground beef

1 (14½ ounce) can stewed or diced tomatoes

1 (8 ounce) can tomato sauce

2 cups water

1 (16 ounce) package frozen mixed vegetables

1 (1 ounce) envelope dry onion soup mix

1 teaspoon sugar

1 (16 ounce) loaf French bread, sliced

- Brown ground beef and drain.
- Combine beef, tomatoes, tomato sauce, water, vegetables, soup mix, and sugar in slow cooker and mix well.
- Cook on low for 4 to 5 hours, stirring occasionally.
- Serve with a loaf of fresh bread.

Serves 4-6

May 24, 1876, when St. Luke's Hospital moved into the old water cure building, the era of modern medicine in the Lehigh Valley had begun.

Flemish Carbonades

(For Slow Cooker)

2-3 pounds boneless beef chuck, cubed

½ cup all-purpose flour

4 tablespoons butter, melted

1 onion, sliced

1 ¼ teaspoons salt

¼ teaspoon pepper

1 garlic clove, chopped

2 cups beer

¼ cup all-purpose flour

- Coat beef with flour.
- Brown meat in butter in a large skillet.
- Drain off excess fat.
- Combine beef, onions, salt, pepper, garlic, and beer in a slow cooker.
- Cover and cook on low for about 5 hours or until meat is tender.
- Increase heat to high.
- Dissolve flour in small amount of water. Stir into meat mixture.
- Cook on high for about 30 minutes.

Serves 6

Note: Dark beer gives stronger flavor.

In 1885 The Women's Pavilion and the Boiler House were completed at St. Luke's. An Isolation Pavilion was erected in 1893, to treat any infectious diseases which might develop in the institution.

Dilled Pot Roast

(For Slow Cooker)

3 pounds beef pot roast

1 teaspoon salt

¼ teaspoon pepper

1 teaspoon dried dill

⅓ cup water

1 ½ tablespoons vinegar

¼ cup all-purpose flour

1 teaspoon dried dill

1 cup sour cream

- Rub all sides of meat with salt, pepper, and dill.
- Place in slow cooker.
- Add water and vinegar.
- Cover and cook on low about 8 hours or until tender.
- Remove meat from cooker and keep warm.
- Increase heat to high.
- Dissolve flour in small amount of cold water. Stir into meat drippings.
- Add dill.
- Cook on high about 20 minutes or until slightly thickened.
- Stir in sour cream and heat thoroughly.
- Serve sauce with sliced meat.

Serves 5-6

In 1878, a telephone was installed at St. Luke's Hospital, the cutting edge of communication technology.

Crock Pot Lasagna

(For Slow Cooker)

1 pound ground beef

¾ **teaspoon garlic powder**

½ **teaspoon onion powder**

¼ **teaspoon salt**

1 (26 ounce) jar marinara sauce

1 (20 ounce) jar Alfredo sauce

¾ **(12 ounce) package lasagna noodles, uncooked and broken in thirds**

1 (12 ounce) package shredded mozzarella cheese

Parmesan cheese

- Brown hamburger with garlic powder, onion powder, and salt.
- Coat inside of slow cooker with cooking spray.
- Spread a layer marinara sauce, Alfredo sauce, noodles, beef mixture, and mozzarella cheese in cooker.
- Repeat layers two to three times.
- End with a layer of mozzarella cheese.
- Sprinkle with Parmesan cheese.
- Cook on low 4 to 5 hours.

Serves 4-6

On November 1, 1881, the first buildings of the present pavilion establishment were completed and opened for the treatment of patients at St. Luke's Hospital.

Mission-Style Chicken

(For Slow Cooker)

2 (2½ pound) whole chickens or
    1 large chicken, cut into pieces

4 tablespoons butter

¼ teaspoon ground cinnamon

¼ teaspoon ground cloves

1 teaspoon salt

1 teaspoon seasoned salt

1 (6 ounce) can frozen orange juice
    concentrate, thawed

½ cup water

2-3 drops Tabasco sauce

1 cup halved seedless grapes

½ cup slivered toasted almonds (optional)

- In a large skillet, brown chicken in butter.
- Place chicken in slow cooker.
- Combine cinnamon, cloves, salt, seasoned salt, juice concentrate, water, and Tabasco. Pour over chicken.
- Cover and cook on low for 4 to 5 hours or until chicken is done.
- Stir in grapes.
- To serve, place chicken on a platter. Drizzle with some sauce and sprinkle with almonds. Pass remaining sauce separately. If desired, thicken sauce with flour dissolved in a small amount of water.

Serves 6-8

The first three pavilions at St. Luke's were the Men's Pavilion, an Operation Pavilion and a Kitchen and Laundry Pavilion.

White Chicken Chili

(For Slow Cooker)

1 pound Great Northern beans, soaked overnight

2 pounds boneless, skinless chicken breast halves, cut into one inch cubes

1 medium onion, chopped

3 garlic cloves, minced

2 (4 ounce) cans green chilies, chopped

2 teaspoons ground cumin

1 teaspoon dried oregano

1½ teaspoons cayenne pepper

1 (14½ ounce) can reduced sodium chicken broth

1 cup water

- Place beans in medium pot and cover with water.
- Bring to boil, reduce heat, and simmer for 20 minutes.
- Drain beans and discard water.
- Brown chicken.
- Place beans, chicken, onions, garlic, chilies, cumin, oregano, cayenne, broth, and water into slow cooker.
- Cover and cook on low for 10 hours or high for 6 hours.

Serves 6

Eckley B. Coxe, Jr., of Philadelphia donated the Coxe Pavilion, which opened July 1, 1914. The Coxe Pavilion is the only original St. Luke's Hospital building that still stands.

Coq Au Vin

4-6 slices bacon

3-4 tablespoons butter

1 (3-3½ pound) whole chicken, cut up

1 pound small white onions, peeled, parboiled, and drained

4 garlic cloves, finely minced

½ pound (or more) small button mushroom caps, stems removed and cleaned

¼ cup warm cognac or brandy

1 bouquet garni (fresh parsley, thyme, and bay leaf bundled together to be simmered in broth and removed)

½ teaspoon pepper

½-1 teaspoon salt

1½-2 cups dry red wine

Beurre Manié

3 tablespoons butter, softened

2 tablespoons all-purpose flour

Salt and pepper to taste

- Brown bacon in large, heavy stockpot over moderate heat.
- Remove bacon with slotted spoon. Crumble and reserve.
- Add 3 tablespoons butter to bacon fat in pot. Brown chicken a few pieces at a time. Remove and reserve.
- Add onions and brown about 10 minutes, adding more butter if necessary. Push onions to side of pot.
- Add garlic and mushrooms and cook 3 to 5 minutes until lightly browned.
- Return chicken pieces.
- Scatter bacon over top of chicken.
- Pour cognac or brandy over chicken and ignite.
- When flames die, add garni, pepper, salt, and wine.
- Cover and simmer about 45 minutes until chicken is tender. Remove garni.
- Transfer chicken and vegetables to a large platter or casserole dish.
- Cover and keep warm.
- To make beurre manié, blend butter and flour until smooth.
- Pinch off 3 tablespoons beurre manié into pot juices. Heat, whisking constantly, until thickened and smooth.
- Add salt and pepper.
- Strain gravy over chicken and serve.

Serves 4-6

Note: Good with mixed long grain and wild brown rice. Makes about 3 tablespoons beurre manié, enough to thicken 1½ cups liquid.

141

Chicken Marsala

4 boneless, skinless chicken breasts or 2 pounds chicken tenderloins

¼ **cup all-purpose flour**

½ **teaspoon salt**

¼ **teaspoon pepper**

½ **teaspoon dried oregano**

¼ **cup olive oil**

4 tablespoons butter

1 (8 ounce) can sliced mushrooms

½ **cup Marsala wine**

¼ **cup cream sherry**

- Pound chicken until flat.
- Combine flour, salt, pepper, and oregano.
- Dredge chicken in flour mixture.
- Heat oil and butter in a skillet until melted.
- Brown chicken on both sides.
- Top with mushrooms, wine, and sherry.
- Cover and simmer for 10 minutes, turning a few times.

Serves 4

In 1881, 25 year old Dr. William L. Estes was appointed the first superintendent and surgeon-in-chief marking the transformation of St. Luke's from emergency treatment center to a general hospital.

Chicken Sauté with Mango Sauce

Chicken

4 boneless, skinless chicken breast halves (1-1¼ pounds), trimmed

¼ cup all-purpose flour

½ teaspoon salt or to taste

Pepper to taste

1 tablespoon olive oil or canola oil

Sauce

1 jalapeño pepper, seeded and minced

2 garlic cloves, minced

2 teaspoons minced fresh ginger

½ cup reduced-sodium chicken broth

½ cup orange juice

1 tablespoon packed brown sugar

¾ teaspoon cornstarch

1 mango, cut into ½ inch dice, about 1 cup

2 tablespoons lime juice

2 tablespoons chopped fresh cilantro or mint

- Remove chicken tenders (long thin flaps) from breast. Reserve for another use (great in a stir-fry).
- Place trimmed chicken breasts between 2 pieces of plastic wrap.
- Flatten chicken breast with a rolling pin, meat mallet, or heavy skillet until an even thickness, about ½ inch.
- Combine flour, salt, and pepper in a shallow glass dish.
- Dredge chicken in seasoned flour, shaking off excess. Discard any leftover flour.
- Heat oil in a large nonstick skillet over medium-high heat.
- Cook chicken for 4 to 5 minutes per side until well browned and no longer pink in the center.
- Transfer to a plate, cover, and keep warm.
- Add jalapeños, garlic, and ginger to skillet. Cook and stir over medium heat about 1 to 2 minutes until softened.
- Add broth and deglaze pan for 1 minute, scraping up any browned bits.
- In a small bowl, blend orange juice, brown sugar, and cornstarch.
- Add to pan and bring sauce to simmer.
- Cook about 4 minutes, stirring often, until thickened and slightly reduced.
- Stir in mango and cook about 1 minute until heated thoroughly.
- Remove from heat and stir in lime juice.
- Spoon sauce over chicken and sprinkle with cilantro.

Serves 4

Lori's Glazed Chicken

½ cup steak sauce

2 tablespoons honey

2 tablespoons orange juice

1 tablespoon lemon juice

2 tablespoons olive oil

10 (6 ounce) boneless, skinless chicken breasts

- Blend steak sauce, honey, orange juice, lemon juice, and oil.
- Place chicken breasts in marinade. Refrigerate overnight.
- Cook marinated chicken over grill until meat registers 165 degrees.

Serves 8-10

Amaretto Chicken

1 (6¼ ounce) can frozen orange juice concentrate, thawed

3 tablespoons all-purpose flour

1½ teaspoons salt

¾ teaspoon pepper

2 teaspoons paprika

½ teaspoon garlic powder

5 boneless, skinless chicken breasts, cut in half

1 tablespoon vegetable oil

3 tablespoons butter

1½ tablespoons Dijon mustard

1¼ cups amaretto

- Preheat oven to 350 degrees.
- Combine juice concentrate with a half of can of water.
- Combine flour, salt, pepper, paprika, and garlic powder. Dredge chicken in mixture.
- Heat oil and butter in skillet. Sauté chicken until browned.
- Transfer chicken to a lightly greased 13x9x2 inch baking dish.
- Add juice mixture, mustard, and amaretto to skillet.
- Increase heat and bring to boil, stirring until slightly thickened.
- Pour sauce over chicken. Bake, uncovered, for 45 minutes.

Serves 8-10

Note: Very good when served with couscous.

Marinated Chicken Breasts

2 cups sour cream

¼ cup lemon juice

4 teaspoons Worcestershire sauce

2 teaspoons paprika

½ teaspoon garlic powder

¾ tablespoon salt

1 teaspoon pepper

8 boneless, skinless chicken breasts

1½ cups crushed round buttery crackers

1½ cups crushed saltine crackers

2 sticks butter, melted

- Preheat oven to 300 degrees.
- Combine sour cream, lemon juice, Worcestershire sauce, paprika, garlic powder, salt, and pepper.
- Add chicken and toss to coat.
- Refrigerate overnight in marinade.
- Remove chicken from sauce.
- Combine cracker crumbs. Dredge chicken in crumbs.
- Place in lightly greased 13x9x2 inch baking dish.
- Spoon half butter over chicken.
- Bake for 1 hour.
- Spoon remaining butter over chicken.
- Bake for an additional 45 minutes.

Serves 8

The St. Luke's School of Nursing remains the nation's oldest hospital-based, diploma nursing school in continuous operation.

Chicken Olivia

3 cups cooked and diced chicken

2 cups chopped celery

1 cup cooked rice

¾ cup mayonnaise

2 tablespoons chopped onions (more to taste)

1 teaspoon lemon juice

1 (10¾ ounce) can cream of chicken soup

1 (8 ounce) can water chestnuts

3 hard-cooked eggs, chopped

1 stick butter, melted

1 cup crushed corn flakes cereal or round buttery crackers

½ cup sliced almonds

- Preheat oven to 350 degrees.
- Combine chicken, celery, rice, mayonnaise, onions, juice, soup, water chestnuts, and eggs.
- Pour mixture into a 13x9x2 inch baking dish.
- Mix butter, cereal crumbs, and almonds. Spread topping over chicken mixture.
- Bake for 30 minutes or until hot and bubbly.

Serves 8-10

"What's in This Chicken?" Chicken

½ cup warm ketchup

1 cup cola-flavored carbonated beverage

1 pound cut-up chicken

- Preheat oven to 350 degrees.
- Mix ketchup and carbonated beverage.
- Place chicken in a roasting pan. Pour sauce over chicken.
- Bake, uncovered, for 30 minutes.
- Turn chicken over and bake for an additional 30 minutes.

Serves 4

Note: The sauce tastes very similar to a BBQ sauce. Great with rice or mashed potatoes.

146

Baked Chicken Supreme

½ cup all-purpose flour

1 teaspoon salt

¼ teaspoon pepper

8 boneless, skinless chicken breasts

5 tablespoons butter

¼ cup minced green onions

¼ cup chicken broth

¾ cup dry white wine

½ pound mushrooms, sliced

3 tablespoons butter

2 cups seedless grapes

- Preheat oven to 350 degrees.
- Combine flour, salt, and pepper.
- Dredge chicken in seasoned flour.
- Brown chicken in butter.
- Transfer chicken to a 13x9x2 inch baking dish.
- Add onions to pan drippings and cook until tender.
- Add broth and wine.
- Bring to boil and pour over chicken.
- Cover and bake for 45 minutes to 1 hour or until tender.
- Cook mushrooms in butter.
- Add mushrooms and grapes to chicken.
- Cover and bake an additional 5 to 10 minutes.

Serves 8

A children's ward was added to St. Luke's in 1887, bringing total beds to 60.

Creamy Baked Chicken Breasts

4 boneless, skinless chicken breast halves, split

½ cup water

8 (4x4 inch) slices Swiss cheese

1 (10¾ ounce) can cream of chicken soup, undiluted

½ cup dry white wine

1 cup seasoned stuffing, crushed

4 tablespoons butter, melted

- Preheat oven to 325 degrees.
- Arrange chicken in a lightly greased 13x9x2 inch baking dish.
- Add water and cover with foil.
- Bake for 25 minutes.
- Remove from oven. Drain water.
- Increase oven to 350 degrees.
- Top each breast with cheese.
- Blend soup and wine. Spoon sauce over chicken.
- Sprinkle with stuffing crumbs and drizzle with butter.
- Bake, uncovered, for 1 hour.

Serves 8

Baked Chicken with Sauce

1 (8 ounce) jar apricot preserves

4 heaping tablespoons orange marmalade

1 (16 ounce) bottle Russian dressing

½ (1 ounce) package dry onion soup mix

4 boneless, skinless chicken breasts

Hot cooked rice

- Preheat oven to 350 degrees.
- Blend together apricot preserves, orange marmalade, dressing, and onion soup.
- Dip chicken in mixture and coat well.
- Place chicken in baking dish.
- Bake for 1 hour to 1 hour, 30 minutes.
- May need to add some water while baking.
- Serve over fluffy rice.

Serves 4

Hot and Sticky Apricot-Glazed Chicken

⅔ cup apricot preserves

¼ cup white wine vinegar

2 tablespoons hot mustard

2 large garlic cloves, finely chopped

8 chicken thighs with skin, excess fat trimmed

Salt and pepper to taste

- Prepare barbecue for medium-high heat.
- Combine apricot preserves, vinegar, mustard, and garlic in a small saucepan.
- Whisk over medium heat until preserves melt.
- Set glaze aside.
- Sprinkle chicken generously on all sides with salt and pepper.
- Place chicken, skin side down, on outer edges of grill rack.
- Cover grill and cook about 15 minutes until golden browned, turning occasionally.
- Brush glaze over chicken.
- Grill an additional 10 minutes, turning occasionally, until blackened in spots and juices run clear when pierced with a fork.

Serves 4

The Ladies' Aid Society held the first St. Luke's Charity Ball on February, 6 1890, historical sources believe.

Easy Chicken

1 whole chicken, cut up

1 (8 ounce) can tomato sauce

¼ cup honey

¼ cup prepared mustard

- Preheat oven to 400 degrees.
- Arrange chicken, skin side down in a greased 13x9x2 inch baking dish.
- Blend tomato sauce, honey, and mustard. Pour over chicken.
- Bake, uncovered, for about 30 minutes.
- Turn chicken and spoon sauce and drippings on top.
- Bake an additional 20 to 30 minutes until tender.

Serves 4

St. Luke's was the first hospital to have one individual responsible for both medical and administrative functions, a system studied and copied by other hospitals.

Capital Chicken

4 tablespoons butter

1 tablespoon vegetable oil

3 pounds boneless, skinless chicken breasts, cut in half or thirds

½ pound (or more) fresh mushrooms, sliced

1 tablespoon all-purpose flour

1 (10¾ ounce) can cream of chicken soup

1 cup dry white wine

½ cup heavy cream

¼ teaspoon dried tarragon

Salt and pepper to taste

1 (15 ounce) can artichoke hearts, drained

6 green onions, chopped

Chopped parsley

- Preheat oven to 350 degrees.
- Heat butter and oil in a large skillet.
- Brown chicken on all sides for about 10 minutes.
- Transfer chicken to a 13x9x2 inch baking dish.
- Sauté mushrooms in same skillet for about 5 minutes.
- Stir in flour.
- Add soup and wine. Simmer until thickened.
- Add cream, tarragon, salt, and pepper.
- More cream or wine may be added for taste or thickness of sauce.
- Pour sauce over chicken. Bake, uncovered, for 45 to 60 minutes.
- Mix in artichoke hearts and top with green onions and parsley.
- Bake an additional 10 minutes.

Serves 8

Note: May substitute chicken broth for wine.

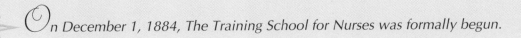

On December 1, 1884, The Training School for Nurses was formally begun.

151

Chicken Carmalane

Olive oil

4-6 boneless, skinless chicken breasts

Seasoned bread crumbs

2 large onions, peeled and sliced into rings

2 (14½ ounce) cans stewed tomatoes

Parmesan cheese

Salt, pepper, and garlic salt to taste

1 (12 ounce) package linguine, cooked
   al dente

- Preheat oven to 325 degrees.
- Coat baking dish with olive oil, then coat chicken in olive oil.
- Dredge both sides of chicken in bread crumbs.
- Layer chicken and onion rings in a 13x9x2 inch baking dish.
- Pour tomatoes over chicken and onions.
- Sprinkle with Parmesan cheese.
- Bake about 45 minutes to 1 hour.
- Sprinkle with salt, pepper, and garlic salt.
- Serve hot over linguine or serve cold with salad.

Serves 4-6

Note: Angel hair pasta can be used instead of linguine.

The Glass Cupola was in the original pavilion for ventilation to reduce transfer of disease. The pavilion/cupola concept was the forerunner of air conditioning.

Chicken Monterey

3 tablespoons extra virgin olive oil

1 (3-4 pound) whole chicken

Bunch fresh basil

8-12 garlic cloves

Salt and freshly ground pepper to taste

2 carrots, peeled

2 stalks celery

1 medium yellow onion

1 cup chicken broth

½ cup fresh orange juice

½ cup crushed tomatoes

Cayenne pepper to taste

2 tablespoons extra virgin olive oil

1 sweet red pepper, julienne cut

½ pound green beans or snow pea pods

- Heat oil in a heavy large skillet.
- Rinse the body cavity of chicken and pat dry.
- Stuff with fresh basil and a handful of whole garlic cloves.
- Sprinkle with salt and pepper.
- Cook chicken gently in oil for 5 minutes.
- Turn and cook other side for another 5 minutes. (Do not attempt to brown the chicken or you will over cook it. It should be pale gold.)
- Remove chicken from the skillet and reserve.
- Chop carrots, celery, onions, and couple cloves of garlic in a food processor until finely minced.
- Add mixture to skillet. Cover and cook about 25 minutes over low heat until vegetables are tender.
- Uncover skillet and add chicken broth, orange juice, and tomatoes.
- Sprinkle with salt and cayenne.
- Simmer, uncovered, for 15 minutes.
- Return chicken to skillet. Cover and simmer about 30 minutes or until chicken is done.
- Baste chicken with sauce occasionally.
- May prepare recipe to this point the day before serving.
- Refrigerate chicken in sauce and reheat gently before proceeding.
- Heat oil in a separate smaller skillet. Sauté peppers and green beans about 5 minutes until crisp-tender.
- Add to chicken and simmer another 5 minutes.

Serves 6

Note: This recipe is easily adaptable to a variety of vegetables. Try yellow squash and /or zucchini, yellow and orange peppers.

Note: A crusty, densely textured French bread is almost a must with this dish. The sauce is really delicious and makes for great plate-mopping with the bread.

Chicken Italiano

¾ **pound boneless, skinless chicken breasts**

¼ **cup light Italian dressing**

1 **(16 ounce) package California-style frozen vegetables, thawed**

½ **cup light Italian dressing**

8 **ounces angel hair pasta, cooked al dente**

Parmesan cheese, grated

- Cut chicken into thin strips.
- In large skillet, combine chicken and Italian dressing.
- Sauté chicken until lightly browned.
- Add vegetables and dressing.
- Cover and simmer for 7 to 9 minutes until vegetables are crisp-tender, stirring frequently.
- Serve over pasta, and sprinkle with Parmesan cheese.

Serves 4

Sherry Chicken in Sour Cream Sauce

6 **boneless, skinless chicken breasts**

1 **(10¾ ounce) can cream of mushroom soup**

1 **(4 ounce) can mushrooms**

1 **cup sour cream**

1 **cup cubed ham**

½ **cup sherry**

1 ½ **cups seedless green grapes**

Paprika to taste

- Preheat oven to 350 degrees.
- Arrange chicken in greased 13x9x2 inch baking dish.
- Combine soup, mushrooms, sour cream, ham, sherry, and grapes. Pour over chicken.
- Sprinkle with paprika.
- Cover and bake for 1 hour to 1 hour, 30 minutes.

Serves 6

St. Luke's was the fourth hospital in the country to operate a nursing school admitting 2 students in the beginning in 1884.

Grandma Helen's Creamed Chicken

¼ **cup chopped onions**

2 tablespoons butter

2-3 teaspoons Hungarian paprika

1 whole chicken, cut up

¼ **cup water**

Salt and pepper to taste

All-purpose flour and milk

1 cup sour cream

1 (12 ounce) package egg noodles, cooked

- Sauté onions in butter in a large stockpot.
- Slowly add paprika.
- Add chicken and water.
- Sprinkle with salt and pepper.
- Cover and cook until tender.
- Remove chicken from sauce.
- Blend flour and milk. Stir into sauce until thickened.
- Stir in sour cream. When blended, decrease heat.
- Do not boil.
- Return chicken pieces and heat thoroughly.
- Serve with noodles.

Serves 4-6

Design of the original St. Luke's pavilion follows the European design endorsed by Florence Nightingale in the book, Note on Hospitals, *1858.*

Chicken Soufflé

⅓ cup chopped onions

⅓ cup diced bell peppers

1 cup diced celery

1 (4 ounce) can mushrooms (optional)

Butter

11 slices white sandwich bread, torn into pieces

4½ cups cooked, diced chicken

3 eggs, beaten

2¼ cups milk

2 (10¾ ounce) cans cream of chicken soup

Shredded Monterey Jack cheese

Paprika to taste

- Prepare the day before serving.
- Sauté onions, peppers, celery, and mushrooms in butter.
- Combine bread cubes, chicken, and vegetable mixture.
- Add eggs and milk. Mix well.
- Pour mixture into greased 13x9x2 inch baking dish.
- Cover and refrigerate overnight.
- Preheat oven to 325 degrees.
- Spread soup on top.
- Sprinkle with cheese.
- Sprinkle paprika on top.
- Bake for 1 hour.
- Cool 5 minutes before serving.

Serves 8-10

Note: May be frozen and served later.

In 1897, St. Luke's Hospital purchased the first horse and buggy ambulance.

Chicken Divan

3 whole chicken breasts

Chopped onions, chopped celery, and chopped carrots

Bay leaf, peppercorns and salt to taste

2 (10¾ ounce) cans cream of chicken soup

1 cup sour cream

1 cup mayonnaise

1 cup shredded sharp Cheddar cheese

1 tablespoon lemon juice

1 teaspoon curry powder to taste

Salt and pepper to taste

1 (10 ounce) package frozen broccoli, cooked and drained

1 cup grated Parmesan cheese

Paprika to taste

Butter

- Preheat oven to 350 degrees.
- Cover chicken in water. Add onions, celery, carrots, bay leaf, peppercorns, and salt. Simmer until cooked.
- Combine soup, sour cream, mayonnaise, Cheddar cheese, lemon juice, curry, salt, and pepper.
- Arrange broccoli in bottom of a 13x9x2 inch baking dish.
- Remove chicken from bone, pulling apart into pieces.
- Spread chicken over broccoli.
- Pour sauce over chicken and broccoli.
- Sprinkle with Parmesan cheese and paprika.
- Dot with butter.
- Bake for 30 to 40 minutes until bubbly and hot.

Serves 6-8

St. Luke's Pavilions were modeled after the original John Hopkins pavilions featured at the Universal Exposition of 1889, Paris, France.

Chicken Wellington

4 boneless, skinless chicken breasts

1 (14 ounce) can chicken broth

1 cup white wine

4 slices Swiss cheese

4 frozen pastry shells, thawed

- Preheat oven to 400 degrees.
- Combine chicken, broth, and wine in a skillet.
- Cover and simmer until tender.
- Cool in liquid.
- Drain and pat dry.
- Cut a pocket into each breast and insert cheese.
- Roll out each pastry shell into a square.
- Wrap each stuffed chicken breast in a pastry shell and seal edges.
- Bake on an ungreased baking sheet for 30 minutes.

Serves 4

During the 1997-1998 fiscal year, St. Luke's hospital provided $18,677,000 in services to charity patients.

Lee's Chicken and Stuffing

Chopped onions to taste

2 stalks celery, diced

Butter

2 boneless, skinless chicken breasts, cooked and cubed

1 cup sour cream

1 (10¾ ounce) can cream of mushroom soup

1 cup chicken broth

1 (6 ounce) package herb-seasoned stuffing mix

- Preheat oven to 350 degrees.
- Sauté onions and celery in butter.
- Add chicken, sour cream, and mushroom soup.
- Pour mixture into an 11x7x2 inch baking dish.
- Mix ½ cup broth with stuffing.
- If too dry, add more broth to moisten stuffing.
- Make enough stuffing completely cover chicken mixture. Spread stuffing evenly.
- Cover with foil.
- Bake for 30 minutes.
- Uncover.
- Increase heat to 375 degrees and bake for 15 minutes.

Serves 4-6

Note: Start with half bag stuffing. Add broth. Add more stuffing if necessary to get right consistency and correct amount to cover chicken mixture.

In 1923 about 60 percent of St. Luke's patients were charity patients.

Chicken Dressing Casserole

1 whole chicken, cooked

1 (10¾ ounce) can cream of chicken soup

1 (10¾ ounce) can cream of celery soup

1 cup milk

1 stick butter, melted

1½ cups chicken broth

1 (6 ounce) package cornbread stuffing

- Preheat oven to 350 degrees.
- Cook chicken in water with seasonings to taste. Cut into pieces.
- Arrange chicken pieces in bottom of 13x9x2 inch baking dish.
- Heat chicken soup, celery soup, and milk in a saucepan.
- Pour over chicken.
- Combine butter, broth, and stuffing mix.
- Spoon stuffing over chicken.
- Bake for 30 minutes.

Serves 4-6

In 1918, the Bethlehem Steel Pavilion was built. The steel company was one of St. Luke's greatest benefactors in the 20th century.

Jean's Chicken Casserole

Chicken

½ cup all-purpose flour

½ teaspoon salt

⅛ teaspoon white pepper

½ teaspoon paprika

2 pounds boneless, skinless chicken breasts, cubed

½ cup vegetable oil

Sauce

1 ½ sticks butter

½ cup chopped fresh mushrooms

⅓ cup finely minced shallots

½ cup finely chopped onions

2 tablespoons minced garlic

2 tablespoons all-purpose flour

½ cup minced ham

½ teaspoon salt

⅛ teaspoon pepper

⅛ teaspoon cayenne pepper

1¾ cups chicken broth

½ cup red Burgundy wine

- Combine flour, salt, pepper, and paprika.
- Dredge chicken in flour mixture.
- Heat oil.
- Brown chicken and place in 2 quart casserole dish. Set aside.
- Preheat oven 350 degrees.
- Melt butter.
- Sauté mushrooms, shallots, onions, and garlic in butter until onions are golden browned.
- Mix in flour.
- Add ham, salt, pepper, and cayenne.
- Brown for 5 minutes.
- Blend in broth and wine.
- Simmer for 30 minutes.
- Pour sauce over chicken.
- Bake for 25 to 30 minutes.

Serves 6

Note: Serve over rice or noodles.

In 1913, St. Luke's was among the first hospitals to have facilities for radiology.

Chicken Tetrazzini

3 tablespoons butter

2 tablespoons all-purpose flour

2 cups chicken broth

Salt and pepper to taste

1 cup heavy cream

3 tablespoons sherry

1 (8 ounce) package thin spaghetti, cooked al dente

3 cups shredded, cooked chicken

1 (8 ounce) package sliced mushrooms, sautéed

1 cup Parmesan cheese

- Preheat oven to 375 degrees.
- Melt butter and stir in flour to make sauce.
- When sauce is smooth, add chicken broth, salt, and pepper.
- Remove from heat.
- Stir in heavy cream and sherry.
- Place spaghetti in bottom of greased 13x9x2 inch baking dish.
- Stir in chicken and mushrooms.
- Pour sauce over chicken mixture.
- Top with Parmesan cheese.
- Bake for about 40 minutes or until lightly browned.

Serves 4-6

In 1919, a motorized ambulance was added to the fleet.

Chicken Fajitas

1 large garlic clove, peeled

3 pickled jalapeño peppers

⅓ cup olive oil

⅓ cup dry sherry

1½ tablespoons chili powder

1 tablespoon ground cumin

2 pounds boneless, skinless chicken breasts

6 flour tortillas

Shredded lettuce, shredded tomatoes, shredded Cheddar cheese, chopped onions, salsa for garnish

- In food processor, chop garlic and jalapeños.
- Add olive oil, sherry, chili powder, and cumin.
- Process about 10 seconds until smooth.
- Pour marinade over chicken.
- Cover with plastic wrap and marinate 1 to 2 hours at room temperature, turning occasionally.
- Drain chicken. Discard marinade.
- Broil on broiler rack or grill for 3 to 4 minutes on each side.
- Slice into strips.
- Serve on warm tortillas with garnishes and salsa.

Serves 6-8

Note: 2 pounds of flank steak is a good substitute. Pierce steak with fork before marinating.

In 1920, the guiding force for 39 years, Dr. William Estes, Sr. retired. His tenure saw the growth from 24 beds to over 200, his legacy, the hospital's devotion to education and compassionate care.

Tender Turkey Burgers

⅔ cup soft whole wheat bread crumbs or Italian bread crumbs

½ cup finely chopped celery

¼ cup finely chopped onions

1 egg or egg substitute

1 tablespoon minced parsley

1 teaspoon Worcestershire sauce

1 teaspoon dried oregano (optional)

½ teaspoon salt

¼ teaspoon pepper or to taste

1 ¼ pounds ground turkey breast

6 whole wheat hamburgers buns

- Combine bread crumbs, celery, onions, egg, Worcestershire sauce, oregano, salt, and pepper.
- Add turkey and mix well.
- Shape mixture into 6 patties.
- Pan fry, grill or broil about 5 minutes per side or until no longer pink.
- Do not overcook.
- Serve on hamburgers buns.

Serves 6

Note: May make mixture into advance and refrigerate or freeze. Add tomato slices and lettuce or spinach for added nutrition.

In the first 50 years St. Luke's Hospital treated 49,448 cases in wards and rooms, and 42,042 cases in its dispensary (emergency room).

Lobster Stuffed Beef Tenderloin

Sauce

½ **cup sliced green onions**

1 **stick butter**

½ **cup dry white wine**

⅛ **teaspoon garlic salt**

Beef

3-4 pound whole beef tenderloin

2 (4 ounce) lobster tails

1 tablespoon butter, melted

1½ **teaspoons lemon juice**

6 slices bacon, partially cooked

- Sauté green onions in butter until tender.
- Add wine and garlic salt.
- Heat thoroughly, stirring constantly.
- Keep sauce warm.
- Preheat oven to 425 degrees.
- Cut tenderloin lengthwise to within ½ inch of bottom.
- Place lobster tails within tenderloin cavity.
- Drizzle with butter and juice.
- Close meat and tie securely. Place on a rack in a roasting pan.
- Roast for 50 to 60 minutes.
- Lay bacon over top and roast an additional 5 minutes.
- Pour sauce into roasting pan and stir to blend with pan juices.
- Spoon sauce over sliced beef.

Serves 6-8

Note: May substitute crabmeat for lobster tails.

In 1931 the Bishopthorpe School, purchased for $50,000, became the new nursing school building at St. Luke's.

Beef with Currant and Black Peppercorn Sauce

2 cups beef broth

1 tablespoon butter

1 tablespoon walnut or vegetable oil

20 ounces center-cut beef tenderloin, cut into 4 (1-inch) thick steaks

¾ cup dry sherry

½ cup currants

1½ tablespoons cracked black peppercorns

1 cup whipping cream

- In small heavy saucepan, boil broth about 15 minutes until reduced to one-half cup.
- Set aside.
- Melt butter with oil over medium-high heat in a large heavy skillet.
- Add steaks and cook about 4 minutes per side for medium rare or to desire degree of doneness.
- Transfer to plates and tent with foil to keep warm.
- Add sherry, currants, and peppercorns to skillet.
- Bring to boil. Cook about 5 minutes, stirring occasionally, until reduced by half.
- Add reserved broth and cream.
- Boil, stirring occasionally, about 8 minutes until thickened to sauce consistency.
- Spoon sauce over steaks.

Serves 4

Note: The cracked peppercorns may be pressed into the tenderloin steaks, creating more of a steak au poive. Mushrooms would make a nice addition to the sauce.

Irene's Brisket

4 pound beef brisket

Salt and pepper to taste

1 onion, sliced

¼ cup ketchup

2 tablespoons brown sugar

5-6 cloves garlic

1 (12 ounce) can beer

2 tablespoons all-purpose flour

½ cup beef broth

- Preheat oven to 300 degrees.
- Sprinkle beef with salt and pepper.
- Place in 13x9x2 inch ovenproof glass baking dish.
- Cover with onions.
- In a small bowl, combine ketchup, brown sugar, garlic, and beer.
- Pour over meat.
- Cover tightly with aluminum foil.
- Bake for 4 hours.
- Remove foil and bake, uncovered, for 40 minutes.
- Remove meat from pan.
- Measure 1 cup of liquid from pan (add water if needed).
- Let brisket cool. Slice against the grain.
- For gravy, combine pan liquid, flour, and beef broth.
- Cook and stir constantly until thickened.
- Place sliced brisket in baking dish and cover with gravy.
- Reheat in oven and serve immediately.

Serves 4-6

In 1940, Bethlehem Steel donated $200,000 for the construction of the 4 story East Wing at St. Luke's Hospital.

Barbecued Boned Short Ribs

1 cup soy sauce

½ cup sesame oil

6 garlic cloves, minced

¼ cup sugar

½ teaspoon white vinegar

½ teaspoon dry mustard

8 large boned short ribs

- Combine soy sauce, oil, garlic, sugar, vinegar, and mustard in a zip-top plastic bag or covered dish.
- Add ribs. Refrigerate at least 1 hour, turning occasionally. May marinate overnight.
- Grill or broil 3 inches from heat source about 6 to 8 minutes per side or to desired degrees of doneness.

Serves 8

Note: Boned short ribs are difficult to find. May substitute New York Strip steaks.

Marinated Flank Steak

½ cup soy sauce

¼ cup packed brown sugar

2 tablespoons canola oil

1 teaspoon ground ginger

¼ teaspoon cracked pepper

2 garlic cloves, minced

1 ½ pounds flank steak

- Mix soy sauce, brown sugar, oil, ginger, pepper, and garlic in blender.
- Pour marinade over steak and refrigerate 4 to 6 hours, turning 2 to 3 times.
- Discard marinade and grill steak.
- Thinly slice diagonally across the grain.

Serves 4-6

Note: Marinade can be used on other meats.

During the second World War, the St. Luke's School of Nursing trained 146 cadet nurses for military service.

Grilled Pesto Skirt Steak with Blue Cheese Fondue

15 wooden skewers

1½ pounds skirt steak, cut lengthwise into ½ inch slices, at room temperature

2 cups pesto

Salt and pepper to taste

1 tablespoon unsalted butter

1½ teaspoons chopped thyme

1 teaspoon minced garlic

2 cups heavy cream

8 ounces crumbled blue cheese

¼ teaspoon pepper

- Soak skewers in cold water for 15 minutes.
- Coat meat with pesto, salt, and pepper.
- Thread meat onto skewers.
- Grill to desired degree of doneness. Keep warm.
- Cook butter, thyme, and garlic for 2 minutes until tender but not browned.
- Add cream and increase heat.
- Simmer until sauce is reduced by one-third. Decrease heat.
- Stir in blue cheese until cheese melts and is smooth.
- Add pepper and pour into fondue pot.

Serves 4

The winter of 1948 brought an ice storm and loss of power to St. Luke's Hospital. Leo Dullenkopf, head electrician, tells us of using the small backup generator, only 100 watts, and of the three man crew sleeping 20 minutes at a time for several days in order to keep the hospital open.

Beef Shish Kabob with Soy Garlic Marinade

Soy Garlic Marinade

¼ **cup vegetable oil**

¼ **cup soy sauce**

2 **tablespoons ketchup**

1 **tablespoon red wine vinegar**

¼ **teaspoon pepper**

2 **teaspoons minced garlic**

Beef

1 **pound beef cubes from rump or sirloin tip roast**

1 **bell pepper, chopped**

1 **(16 ounce) can pineapple chunks, drained**

1 **red onion, quartered and separated**

- Blend oil, soy sauce, ketchup, vinegar, pepper, and garlic.
- Combine beef cubes, pepper, pineapple, and onions.
- Pour marinade over beef. Refrigerate overnight.
- Thread meat, vegetables, and pineapple onto skewers.
- Grill and baste with marinade.

Serves 4

Note: May substitute sweet red or yellow pepper for bell pepper.

In 1944, Bethlehem Steel donated $800,000 for the construction of the North Wing at St. Luke's Hospital.

Yorkie Beef Pudding

3 tablespoons butter

1 small onion, thinly sliced or diced

¾ pound ground beef

½ cup mixed vegetables, cooked

½ teaspoon salt

¼ teaspoon pepper

10 (ounce) can beef gravy

½ cup water

2 eggs, beaten

1 cup milk

1 cup sifted all-purpose flour

½ teaspoon salt

- Preheat oven to 425 degrees.
- Melt 2 tablespoons of butter and pour into a 10 inch quiche dish or pie plate.
- Sauté onions in remaining 1 tablespoon of butter until tender.
- Add meat and cook until done.
- Add vegetables, salt, and pepper.
- Combine gravy and water. Add one-fourth cup gravy to meat and vegetable mixture.
- Whisk together eggs, milk, flour, and salt.
- Pour batter into quiche dish.
- Spread meat and vegetable mixture evenly over batter to within one inch of the edge.
- Bake for 25 to 30 minutes or until browned and puffy.
- Heat remaining gravy to serve with pudding.

Serves 4

William Estes, Jr. retired in 1949 leaving the Estes' Legacy, father and son, the foundation for the ability to provide " Big-city Medicine and Hometown Care" at St. Luke's Hospital.

Beef Stroganoff

1 pound mushrooms, sliced

2 medium onions, sliced

4 tablespoons butter

2½ pounds beef cubes

4 tablespoons butter

2½ teaspoons salt

Pepper to taste

1½ tablespoons all-purpose flour

1 tablespoon tomato paste

1 (8 ounce) container sour cream

¼-½ cup sherry

- Sauté mushrooms and onions in butter.
- Sauté beef in butter in a separate skillet. Add salt and pepper. Set aside.
- Stir flour into mushroom mixture until completely blended.
- Add tomato paste, sour cream, and sherry to mushroom mixture.
- Simmer to combine flavors.
- Add beef. Taste for seasoning.
- Simmer until meat is tender.

Serves 4-6

Note: May add more sour cream or sherry to taste.

In 1950, St. Luke's became the center of polio care in Eastern PA when a treatment facility was established in the Coxe Ward.

Entrées

Swedish Pot Roast

2 tablespoons vegetable oil

3-4 pound rump roast

1 cup thinly sliced onions

1 ¼ cups beef broth

2 tablespoons cider vinegar

2 tablespoons packed brown sugar

1 teaspoon dried dill or 2 tablespoons fresh

1 teaspoon pepper

2 small bay leaves

½ cup plain reduced fat yogurt

3 tablespoons all-purpose flour

- Preheat oven to 325 degrees.
- Heat oil in a Dutch oven over medium heat.
- Add meat and onions.
- Brown meat on all sides and stir onions occasionally.
- Add broth, vinegar, brown sugar, dill, pepper, and bay leaves.
- Cover tightly and bake for 2 hour, 30 minutes to 3 hours until meat in tender.
- Remove meat, cover with foil and let stand 10 to 15 minutes.
- Discard bay leaves.
- Blend yogurt and flour.
- Simmer pan liquid and whisk in flour mixture until smooth and thickened.
- Slice meat across the grain and serve with sauce.

Serves 6-8

In 1952, St. Luke's conducted a fund drive for the first time in its 80 year history with Bethlehem Steel matching 50 cents for each dollar donated by the public.

Sicilian Meat Roll

2 eggs, slightly beaten

¾ cup soft bread crumbs

½ cup tomato juice

2 tablespoons snipped parsley

½ teaspoon dried oregano, crushed

¼ teaspoon salt

¼ teaspoon pepper

1 small garlic clove, minced

2 pounds lean ground beef

6 (1 ounce) slices fully cooked ham

1¾ cups shredded mozzarella cheese

- Preheat oven to 350 degrees.
- Combine eggs, bread crumbs, tomato juice, parsley, oregano, salt, pepper, and garlic.
- Stir in ground beef. Mix well.
- Using a piece of foil, pat meat mixture into a 12x8 inch rectangle.
- Arrange ham slices on top, leaving a ¾ inch border around all edges.
- Sprinkle 1 ½ cups mozzarella cheese over ham.
- Starting from short end, roll up meat using foil to lift meat.
- Press to seal edges and ends.
- Place roll seam side down in a 13x9x2 inch baking dish.
- Bake for 1 hour, 15 minutes or until internal temperature reaches 170 degrees.
- Center of meat roll will be pink due to ham.
- Top with remaining ¼ cup cheese. Bake for an additional 5 minutes until cheese melts.

Serves 8-10

Fireworks exploded and church bells pealed celebrating the successful fundraising campaign of 1953 for St. Luke's Hospital which exceeded its goal of $1 million dollars.

Barbecue

1 pound ground beef

1 medium onion, chopped

Salt and pepper to taste

1 egg

1 cup ketchup

½-1 cup water

1 tablespoon dry mustard

1 tablespoon vinegar

1 tablespoon sugar

1 cup corn flake cereal

- Brown beef with onions, salt, and pepper.
- Stir in egg.
- Add ketchup, water, mustard, vinegar, sugar, and corn flakes.
- Simmer 30 minutes to 1 hour.

Serves 4

To keep the iron lungs in power for the polio patients in 1950, lines were run from other buildings; maintenance crews, doctors and nurses kept 24 hour watch and if a belt broke the bellows would be manually operated. The machines therefore, could continue breathing for the patients.

Awesome Burgers

2 pounds ground beef

¼ cup chopped onions

3 tablespoons Tabasco sauce

2 tablespoons honey

1 tablespoon garlic salt

1 teaspoon crushed red pepper

1 teaspoon black pepper

6 ounces blue cheese, cut into 6 pieces

6 hamburger buns

- Preheat grill to medium-high heat.
- Combine ground beef, onions, Tabasco, honey, garlic salt, red pepper, and pepper.
- Divide mixture into 6 portions.
- Form each portion around a piece of cheese into a patty.
- Grill for 8 to 10 minutes or until done.
- Place on bun and enjoy!

Serves 6

Note: May substitute pepper jack or Cheddar cheese for blue cheese.

Pat's Spaghetti Sauce

1 ½ pounds ground beef

¾ pound bulk sausage

¾ cup chopped celery

½ cup chopped onions

2 (28 ounce) cans Italian tomatoes, chopped

2 (12 ounce) cans tomato paste

¾ pound fresh mushrooms, sliced

4 garlic cloves, sliced

Salt and pepper to taste

- Brown ground beef, sausage, and celery in a greased Dutch oven.
- Add onions and continue browning.
- After meat is browned, add tomatoes.
- Stir in tomato paste and mushrooms.
- Add garlic, salt, and pepper.
- Bring to boil. Reduce heat and simmer for 4 hours.
- Stir about every 30 minutes. After about 2 hours, taste for seasoning.

Serves 8

Burgundy Beef Stew

1 tablespoon all-purpose flour

½ teaspoon salt

½ teaspoon pepper

2 pounds boneless beef chuck, cut into 1½ inch pieces

1 tablespoon olive oil

2 tablespoons butter

2 onions, diced

2 teaspoons minced garlic

2 cups diced carrots

2 cups diced red potatoes

2 teaspoons Dijon mustard or to taste

1 cup red wine

1 cup beef broth

1 tablespoon balsamic vinegar

2 tablespoons dried parsley

2 teaspoons dried thyme

2 tablespoons brown sugar

1 tablespoon butter

½ pound fresh mushrooms, sliced

1 cup frozen green peas, thawed

- Combine flour, salt, and pepper in a large bowl. Add beef and toss to coat. Set aside.
- Heat oil and butter in a Dutch oven. Cook onions and garlic for 2 to 3 minutes over medium heat. Transfer to a plate, using a slotted spoon.
- Brown beef in Dutch oven for 2 to 3 minutes. (May need to do in batches.)
- Return onions and garlic. Stir in carrots, potatoes, mustard, wine, broth, vinegar, parsley, thyme, and brown sugar.
- Bring to boil.
- Reduce heat to medium-low. Cover and simmer for 1 hour, 30 minutes to 2 hours, adding more broth and/or wine if necessary.
- When beef is almost done, melt butter over low heat in a medium skillet.
- Sauté mushrooms, stirring frequently, for 2 minutes over medium heat.
- Add mushrooms and peas to beef mixture. Simmer an additional 3 minutes.
- Serve with noodles or a good bread and a green salad.

Serves 6

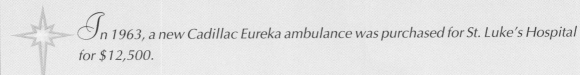

In 1963, a new Cadillac Eureka ambulance was purchased for St. Luke's Hospital for $12,500.

No Peekie Stew

3 pounds lean beef round, cut in 1½ inch cubes, (half round and half chuck)

2 tablespoons all-purpose flour

1 (10¾ ounce) can cream of golden mushroom soup

½ soup can of water

½ soup can sherry or Madeira or beer

1 tablespoon Worcestershire sauce

1 (8 ounce) package sliced mushrooms

Cooked and buttered wide egg noodles

Parsley for garnish

- Preheat oven to 350 degrees.
- Toss beef with flour, coating well.
- Blend soup, water, sherry, and Worcestershire sauce.
- Pour mixture into a 13x9x2 inch baking dish with a lid.
- Add beef and mushrooms. Stir to coat beef with liquids.
- Cover and bake for 3 hours.
- Check at 2 hours, 45 minutes. If very soupy, remove lid for last 15 minutes.
- The stew will thicken as it cools. Stir before serving.
- Serve over buttered noodles.
- Garnish with chopped parsley.

Serves 8-10

In 1960, the hospital had clinical records entered into a central computer pool, once again on the cutting edge of technology.

Tangy Sweet-Sour Beef Stew

1 ½ pounds stew meat, cut into 1 inch
   cubes

2 tablespoons vegetable oil

1 cup chopped carrots

1 cup sliced onions

1 (8 ounce) can tomato sauce

¼ cup packed brown sugar

¼ cup vinegar

1 tablespoon Worcestershire sauce

1 ½ cups water

1 teaspoon salt

4 teaspoons cornstarch

¼ cup cold water

Hot cooked noodles

- Brown meat in oil.
- Add carrots, onions, tomato sauce, brown sugar, vinegar, Worcestershire sauce, water, and salt.
- Cover and simmer 2 hours until meat in tender.
- Blend cornstarch and water. Whisk into stew.
- Cook and stir until thickened and bubbly.
- Serve over noodles.

Serves 4

Note: May substitute mashed potatoes for noodles.

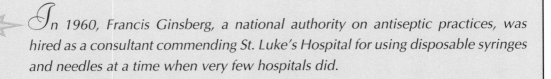

In 1960, Francis Ginsberg, a national authority on antiseptic practices, was hired as a consultant commending St. Luke's Hospital for using disposable syringes and needles at a time when very few hospitals did.

Super Salisbury Steak

1 (10¾ ounce) can condensed cream of mushroom soup, undiluted

1 tablespoon prepared mustard

2 teaspoons Worcestershire sauce

1¼ teaspoons prepared horseradish

1 egg, slightly beaten

¼ cup dry bread crumbs

¼ cup finely chopped onions

½ teaspoon salt

Dash of pepper

1½ pounds ground beef

1-2 tablespoons vegetable oil

½ cup water

- In a small bowl, combine soup, mustard, Worcestershire sauce, and horseradish.
- Mix well and set aside.
- Combine egg, bread crumbs, onions, salt, pepper, and one-fourth cup soup mixture.
- Add beef and mix well.
- Shape mixture into six patties.
- In a large skillet, heat oil over medium-high heat.
- When oil is hot, brown patties on both sides.
- Transfer patties to a plate.
- Drain drippings from skillet and wipe with paper towel.
- Return patties to skillet.
- Blend water with remaining soup mixture.
- Pour soup mixture over patties.
- Cover and simmer for 10 to 15 minutes or until meat is no longer pink.

Serves 6

In 1962, the Department of Nuclear Medicine was established at St. Luke's Hospital.

Stuffed Peppers

1 (29 ounce) can crushed tomatoes

⅛ teaspoon garlic powder

1 tablespoon chopped basil

1 tablespoon sugar

½ teaspoon salt

6 large bell peppers

¾ pound lean ground beef

¼ cup grated cheese

½ cup bread crumbs

½ cup cooked rice

1 egg, slightly beaten

1 tablespoon chopped parsley

⅛ teaspoon garlic powder

- Combine tomatoes, garlic powder, basil, sugar, and salt.
- Simmer for 30 minutes. Set aside.
- Slice top off peppers. Remove seeds. Reserve tops.
- Combine beef, Parmesan cheese, bread crumbs, rice, egg, parsley, garlic powder and ¼ cup tomato sauce.
- Spoon meat mixture into peppers filling three-fourths full. Replace tops.
- Place peppers sideways in a Dutch oven. Pour sauce over peppers.
- Cook about 1 hour, turning peppers occasionally.

Serves 6

Note: May cook in a covered baking dish about 1 hour, turning peppers after 30 minutes.

 In 1965, the first computer was installed at St. Luke's Hospital allowing for more efficient record keeping.

Tamale Pie

Filling

1 (15 ounce) can kidney beans, drained

½ cup chopped onions

½ cup chopped bell peppers

¼ cup chopped black olives

1 cup whole kernel corn

1 garlic clove, minced

1 tomato, chopped

1 teaspoon ground cumin

1-3 teaspoons chili powder

¼ teaspoon dried oregano

½ teaspoon salt

¾ cup shredded Cheddar cheese

½ pound ground beef, cooked and drained

Cornbread

1 cup all-purpose flour

1 cup cornmeal

½ cup sugar

½ cup powdered milk

1 tablespoon baking powder

1 teaspoon salt

2 eggs

½ cup vegetable oil

¼ cup shredded Cheddar cheese

- Combine kidney beans, onions, peppers, olives, corn, garlic, tomatoes, cumin, chili powder, oregano, and salt.
- Simmer for 10 to 15 minutes.
- Stir in cheese and beef. Set aside.
- Blend flour, cornmeal, sugar, powdered milk, baking powder, and salt.
- Mix eggs in a measuring cup. Add water to equal 1 cup.
- Stir in eggs and oil.
- Pour half cornbread mixture into a greased casserole dish. Top with beef mixture.
- Top with remaining cornbread mixture.
- Bake for 425 degrees for 15 minutes.
- Top with cheese and bake an additional 10 minutes.

Serves 6-8

Note: Serve with salsa. May substitute 1 jar salsa for bell peppers and tomatoes. May use 2 packages cornbread mix for cornbread.

Quick and Easy Porcupine Meatballs

1½ **pounds lean ground beef**

¼ **cup uncooked rice**

⅔ **cup milk**

1 **tablespoon instant minced onions or**
    1 **medium onion, grated**

1½ **teaspoons salt**

¼ **teaspoon pepper**

1 **(10½ ounce) can condensed tomato soup**

¾ **cup water**

- Preheat oven to 350 degrees.
- Combine beef, rice, milk, onions, salt, and pepper in large bowl.
- Drop mixture by rounded tablespoons onto a shallow baking dish.
- Combine soup and water.
- Pour over meatballs.
- Cover tightly with foil. Bake for 1 hour.

Serves 4-6

In 1968, another first for St. Luke's was to have a representative of the Ladies' Aid Society on the Board of Trustees.

Mexican Chipotle Meatballs

Sauce

1 (28 ounce) can diced tomatoes, drained and juice reserved

1 (7 ounce) can chipotle chilies in adobo sauce, stemmed, seeded and chopped

1 teaspoon dried Mexican oregano

2 garlic cloves, minced

Meatballs

3 slices bacon, diced

1 garlic clove, peeled

2 large eggs

½ cup bread crumbs or ¾ cup panko

1 teaspoon salt

1½ pounds ground beef or pork

⅓ cup chopped mint leaves

1½ cups chicken broth, warm

- Combine tomatoes, ¼ cup tomato juice, chipotle peppers, 1 tablespoon adobo sauce, oregano, and garlic in a food processor.
- Purée mixture until smooth.
- Preheat oven to 450 degrees.
- In a clean food processor, combine bacon and garlic.
- Process until finely chopped.
- Add eggs, bread crumbs, and salt and process until mixed.
- Add meat and mint.
- Pulse until well mixed but not a paste.
- Transfer mixture to a bowl.
- With wet hands, shape mixture into 12 balls.
- Arrange meatballs in a 13x9x2 inch baking dish.
- Bake for 15 minutes.
- Remove drippings from meatballs.
- Pour tomato sauce over meatballs.
- Bake for an additional 15 to 20 minutes.
- Add warm broth to dish.
- Serve meatballs with sauce.

Serves 4

Note: May serve with cooked rice.

In 1890, the Ladies' Aid Society hosted its first Charity Ball.

Cheddar Cheese Pork Chops

6 center cut pork chops

Garlic powder

3 (10¾ ounce) cans Cheddar cheese soup

Milk

Sliced potatoes and sliced onions (optional)

- Preheat oven to 350 degrees.
- Brown pork chops on both sides with garlic powder.
- Combine soup with three-fourths can of milk.
- Pour some soup mixture on the bottom of a 13x9x2 inch baking dish.
- Place pork chops over soup. Top with potatoes and onions.
- Pour remaining soup mixture over chops and potatoes.
- Cover with foil and bake for 2 hours, 30 minutes or until potatoes are done.

Serves 6

Deviled Pork Chops

⅓ cup soft bread crumbs

½ cup mayonnaise

1 tablespoon prepared mustard

⅛ teaspoon paprika

¼ teaspoon salt

4 pork loin chops

- Combine bread crumbs, mayonnaise, mustard, paprika, and salt.
- Broil pork chops about 8 minutes per side depending on thickness.
- Spread bread crumb mixture over each chop.
- Return to broil for 3 to 5 minutes until bubbly.

Serves 4

In 1803, the construction of the Central Moravian Church was begun. The belfry houses the oldest working tower clock in America.

Orange Glazed Pork Chops

4 pork chops, 1 inch thick

Salt and pepper to taste

2 tablespoons vegetable oil

½ cup orange juice

2 tablespoons packed brown sugar

2½ tablespoons orange marmalade

1 tablespoon vinegar

- Sprinkle chops with salt and pepper.
- Brown pork chops in oil.
- Drain off fat.
- Whisk together orange juice, brown sugar, marmalade, and vinegar. Pour sauce over chops.
- Cover and simmer for 45 to 60 minutes or until done.
- Serve chops with sauce on top.

Serves 4

Saucy Pork Chops

6 pork chops, ½-¾ inches thick

Salt and pepper to taste

2 tablespoons vegetable oil

1 medium onion, thinly sliced

1 (10¾ ounce) can cream of chicken soup

¼ cup ketchup

3 tablespoons Worcestershire sauce

- Sprinkle chops with salt and pepper.
- Brown chops in oil.
- Place onions over chops.
- Blend soup, ketchup, and Worcestershire sauce.
- Pour sauce over chops.
- Cover and simmer for 45 to 50 minutes or until done.
- Transfer chops to a serving platter. Top with warm sauce.

Serves 4-6

In 1947, the Ladies' Aid Society opened a gift shop, now named the Wishing Well Gift Shop and a snack bar called The Oasis.

Pesto-Packed Pork Chops

Filling

3 tablespoons shredded mozzarella cheese
   or crumbled feta cheese

2 tablespoons pesto

1 tablespoon almonds, toasted or pine nuts

Glaze

2 tablespoons jalapeño jelly

3 tablespoons pesto

1 tablespoon balsamic vinegar

4 boneless pork loin chops, 1 ¼ inches
   thick

Rub

1 teaspoon minced garlic

1 teaspoon pepper

½ teaspoon cayenne pepper

½ teaspoon celery seed

½ teaspoon fennel seed, crushed

¼ teaspoon dried thyme, crushed

¼ teaspoon ground cumin

- Blend mozzarella cheese, pesto, and nuts. Set filling aside.
- Melt jelly in a saucepan over low heat.
- Stir in pesto and vinegar. Heat thoroughly. Set glaze aside.
- Slice a pocket in each pork chop, cutting horizontally from fat side to other side.
- Spoon filling into each pocket. Secure opening with a water-soaked toothpick.
- Combine garlic, pepper, cayenne, celery seed, fennel seed, thyme, and cumin.
- Rub mixture evenly onto all sides of chops.
- Grill for 35 to 40 minutes, turning once.
- Brush glaze over chops during last 10 minutes of grilling.
- Remove toothpicks and serve.

Serves 4

On September 8, 1958, an official Department of Volunteer Serves was created. Volunteers work as patient escorts, receptionists, tour guides, and messengers.

Winter Pork Chops with Balsamic Glaze

2 (8 ounce) center cut pork chops, 1½ inches thick

1½ teaspoons lemon pepper

½ teaspoon olive oil

1 teaspoon mined garlic

1 teaspoon dried thyme

2 tablespoons chicken broth

3 tablespoons balsamic vinegar

2 teaspoons butter

- Pat chops dry. Coat with lemon pepper.
- Heat oil over medium high heat.
- Brown chops in oil for 8 minutes.
- Turn over and cook another 7 minutes.
- Transfer chops to a platter and keep warm.
- Add garlic, thyme, broth, and vinegar to skillet.
- Cook and stir about 2 minutes until syrupy.
- Remove from heat. Stir in butter.
- Spoon sauce over chops.
- Serve immediately.

Serves 2

Aunt Sally's Barbequed Leg of Lamb

1 (4-5 pound) leg of lamb, butterfly cut

5 garlic cloves, mashed

2 tablespoons salt

1 teaspoon pepper

⅓ cup chopped pimentos

1 (2 ounce) jar capers

½ teaspoon dried tarragon

½ teaspoon dried oregano

1 cup olive oil

1½ cups wine vinegar

3 tablespoons soy sauce

1 bay leaf, crushed

- Rub lamb with garlic, salt, and pepper.
- Combine pimentos, capers, tarragon, oregano, oil, vinegar, soy sauce, and bay leaf.
- Pour marinade over lamb.
- Cover and refrigerate for 6 to 8 hours or overnight.
- Broil or grill for 10 to 15 minutes, turning once.
- Let rest 15 minutes before carving.
- Boil remaining marinade.
- Serve on the side with lamb.

Serves 6-8

Note: This is an amazing meal served with grilled vegetables, rice pilaf and beautiful salads.

Marinated Butterfly Leg of Lamb

1 (5-6 pound) leg of lamb, butterfly cut

¾ cup vegetable oil

½ cup soy sauce

¼ cup Worcestershire sauce

½ tablespoon dry mustard

½ cup red wine vinegar

⅓ cup lemon juice

2 teaspoons chopped parsley

¼ teaspoon dried oregano

¼ teaspoon dried thyme

½ teaspoon dried basil

½ cup honey

4 garlic cloves, minced

2 medium onions, sliced

- Combine oil, soy sauce, Worcestershire sauce, mustard, vinegar, juice, parsley, oregano, thyme, basil, honey, garlic, and onions.
- Place lamb in a large dish. Pour marinade over top.
- Refrigerate overnight, turning occasionally.
- Discard marinade.
- Grill lamb about 50 minutes, watching carefully to prevent flaming.
- Cool and slice.

Serves 10-12

St. Luke's Cancer Center has some of the most advanced technology available anywhere for the detection and treatment of cancer. The St. Luke's Cancer Center is planning for Trilogy, the first image-guided, intensity-modulated radiation therapy system in the world.

Seattle Salmon with Dijon Sauce

2 pounds salmon fillet

4 tablespoons lemon juice

4 tablespoons Dijon mustard

1 tablespoon olive oil

2 garlic cloves, minced

2 tablespoons fresh chopped dill

¼ teaspoon cayenne pepper

- Preheat oven to 400 degrees.
- Rinse salmon with water and pat dry.
- Place salmon skin side down in a lightly greased 13x9x2 glass baking dish.
- Combine lemon juice, mustard, oil, garlic, dill, and cayenne.
- Spread sauce over salmon.
- Bake for 20 minutes or until fish flakes.

Serves 4-6

Note: This can also be cooked on the outside grill. Preheat grill to 400 degrees and coat both sides of salmon with sauce. Turn once.

Creole Spinach Crab Cakes

1 (6 ounce) package stuffing mix for chicken

1⅔ cups hot water

1 teaspoon lemon juice

1 (10 ounce) package frozen spinach, thawed, drained, and patted dry

1-2 (6 ounce) cans crabmeat, drained and flaked

3 eggs or egg substitute

1 cup grated Parmesan cheese

½ teaspoon cayenne pepper

2 tablespoons butter

- Combine stuffing mix, hot water, and lemon juice in a large bowl.
- Stir in spinach, crabmeat, eggs, Parmesan cheese, and cayenne.
- Shape one-fourth cup mixture into patties, making 15 to 20 patties.
- Cook patties in the butter in large skillet on medium heat for 5 minutes on each side, or until browned and thoroughly heated.

Serves 8-10

Note: Wasabi mayonnaise is a great accompaniment.

Crab and Chicken Roll Ups

3 tablespoons butter

¼ cup all-purpose flour

¾ cup milk

¾ cup chicken broth

⅓ cup dry white wine

¼ cup finely chopped onions

1 tablespoon butter

10 saltine crackers, crushed

12-18 ounces crabmeat

2 tablespoons minced parsley

½ teaspoon salt

Dash of pepper

1 (6½ ounce) can mushroom pieces, drained

4 boneless, skinless chicken breasts (cut out tenderloin), pound between wax paper to flatten

4 slices Swiss cheese

Paprika to taste

- Melt butter in a saucepan. Whisk in flour. Add milk and broth. Cook and stir until bubbly. Add wine. Set sauce aside.
- Sauté onions in butter until tender not browned. Add cracker crumbs, crabmeat, parsley, salt, pepper and 2 tablespoons white sauce.
- Stir in mushrooms.
- Place one-fourth crab mixture at end of each chicken piece. Roll up each chicken and secure with a toothpick.
- Place each roll, seam side down, in a lightly greased 13x9x2 inch baking dish.
- Pour remaining sauce over chicken.
- Cover with foil and bake at 325 degrees for 1 hour.
- Remove, uncover, and place 1 slice of Swiss cheese on each roll.
- Sprinkle with paprika.
- Bake an additional 5 minutes or until cheese melts.

Serves 8

From the Central Moravian belfry, the Trombone Choir, the oldest brass choir in continuous existence in America, announces with significant hymns, the death of members of the congregation, the festivals of the church and significant days of the church year.

Baltimore Crab Cakes

1 pound jumbo lump crabmeat

½ cup Italian seasoned bread crumbs

½ teaspoon baking powder

⅓ cup milk

1 large egg, beaten

¼ cup mayonnaise

2 tablespoons finely chopped green onions

⅛ teaspoon pepper

1 teaspoon chopped parsley

¼ cup all-purpose flour

4 tablespoons butter

- Combine crabmeat, bread crumbs, baking powder, milk, egg, mayonnaise, green onions, pepper, and parsley.
- Do not break up crabmeat.
- Shape mixture into 6 large patties or 8 small patties.
- Wet hands between each patty.
- Coat patties in flour.
- Place on a baking sheet.
- Refrigerate for several hours.
- Cook patties in butter for 4 minutes per side or until is golden browned.
- Serve immediately.

Serves 6-8

Note: Use only fresh crabmeat.

Shrimp with Blue Cheese

2 pounds shrimp, peeled and cleaned

Juice of 1 to 2 limes

1 stick butter

6 ounces cream cheese

2 ounces blue cheese

Parsley for garnish

Cooked pasta or rice

- Preheat oven to 350 degrees.
- Arrange shrimp in the bottom of a casserole dish. Pour lime juice over shrimp.
- In a heavy saucepan, melt butter, cream cheese, and blue cheese.
- Pour mixture over shrimp.
- Bake for 20 minutes.
- Garnish with parsley.
- Serve over pasta or rice.

Serves 6

Crab Cakes

¼ **cup chopped onions**

¼ **cup chopped bell peppers**

1 **tablespoon butter**

1 **pound crabmeat**

2 **eggs, beaten**

½ **cup cracker crumbs or plain bread crumbs**

3 **tablespoons mayonnaise**

1 **teaspoon prepared mustard**

1 **teaspoon Worcestershire sauce**

Dash of Tabasco sauce

Vegetable oil

- Sauté onions and peppers in butter.
- Combine crabmeat, eggs, bread crumbs, mayonnaise, mustard, Worcestershire sauce, and Tabasco sauce.
- Add to onions and peppers.
- Shape mixture into patties and roll in crumbs.
- Cook in oil until golden browned.

Serves 6

Note: You may also bake in oven at 350 degrees for 30 to 40 minutes on a greased baking sheet.

Shrimp Casserole

1 **cup uncooked long grain rice**

1 **stick butter, melted**

1 **bunch green onions, chopped including tops**

1 **(14 ounce) can chicken broth**

1½ **pounds shrimp, shelled and deveined**

½ **(14½ ounce) can diced tomatoes and green chilies**

- Preheat oven to 350 degrees.
- Lightly grease a 13x9x2 inch baking dish.
- Place in order in dish, rice, butter, onions, broth, shrimp, and tomatoes. Cover with foil.
- Bake for 45 minutes.

Serves 4-6

Forty seven patients were treated in the first year of St. Luke's Hospital existence. At the end of the 20th century, 2000 patients per month were being treated.

Fancy Topped Shrimp Casserole

1 cup tomato-vegetable juice cocktail

1 cup mayonnaise

1½-2 pounds cooked shrimp, shelled and deveined

2 cups cooked rice

½ bell pepper, chopped

Salt and pepper to taste

4 tablespoons butter, melted

1 cup bread crumbs

½ cup slivered almonds

- Preheat oven to 375 degrees.
- Blend juice cocktail and mayonnaise until smooth.
- Stir in shrimp, rice, peppers, salt, and pepper.
- Pour mixture into greased 13x9x2 inch baking dish.
- Mix together butter, bread crumbs, and almonds. Sprinkle on top.
- Bake about 45 minutes or until bubbly and browned.

Serves 8

Seafood Casserole

3 pounds sea scallops or lobster

2 pounds shrimp

2 pounds lump crabmeat

6 cups mayonnaise

6 eggs

2¼ tablespoons garlic powder

2¼ tablespoons Old Bay seasoning

½ loaf white sandwich bread, crust removed and cubed

- Preheat oven to 350 degrees.
- Rinse and dry scallops, shrimp, and crabmeat.
- Combine mayonnaise, eggs, garlic powder, and seasoning.
- Add bread cubes to mayonnaise mixture.
- Add seafood.
- Spoon mixture into a greased 13x9x2 inch baking dish.
- Bake for 40 minutes until hot and bubbly.

Serves 8-10

Paula's Scallops

1 ½ pounds fresh sea scallops

Salt and pepper to taste

½ teaspoon garlic powder

¼ teaspoon paprika

¼ cup finely chopped basil

All-purpose flour

Olive oil

¾ cup sherry or dry white wine

1 shallot, finely chopped

1 (8 ounce) package fresh mushrooms, quartered

2 tablespoons butter

3 tablespoons all-purpose flour

Clam juice or chicken broth (if needed)

1 cup grated Gruyère cheese

- Sprinkle scallops with salt, pepper, garlic powder, paprika, and basil.
- Dust scallops with flour.
- Add oil to a greased skillet. Sauté scallops on both sides until browned.
- Remove scallops from pan.
- Add wine, shallots, and mushrooms to drippings.
- Cook for 3 to 4 minutes.
- In separate saucepan, melt butter over medium heat and whisk in flour.
- Mix well and cook 2 minutes, stirring constantly.
- Pour shallots, mushrooms, and liquid into flour mixture. Mix well.
- Add scallops. (If too thick, add clam juice or chicken broth.)
- Transfer to 4 individual baking dishes.
- Top with Gruyère cheese and broil for 1 minute until browned.

Serves 4

Note: Can be served with wild rice.

St. Luke's volunteers help in the Wishing Well Gift Shops, man information desks, help in the surgical waiting room, the mailroom, the print shop, and pharmacy, among other areas. More than 1,000 volunteers — men, women, and juniors — help in many areas across St. Luke's Hospital & Health Network.

Scallop Casserole

1 (12 ounce) package frozen scallops, thawed or 12 ounces fresh scallops

¾ cup light cream

1 cup dry bread crumbs

1 stick butter, melted

2 teaspoons celery seed

1 teaspoon salt

¼ teaspoon pepper

Paprika to taste

- Preheat oven to 375 degrees.
- If scallops are large, cut into 1½ inch pieces.
- Remove any shell particles and wash scallops.
- Arrange scallops in greased 12x8x2 inch or 9x9x2 inch baking dish.
- Pour about half of the light cream over scallops.
- Mix bread crumbs, butter, celery seed, salt, and pepper.
- Sprinkle crumbs over scallops.
- Top with remaining light cream (liquid should come about ¾ of the way up on scallops).
- Sprinkle with paprika.
- Bake, uncovered, for 25 to 30 minutes or until hot and bubbly.

Serves 5

Note: Can double or triple ingredients. Also called Christmas Eve Scallop Casserole. Red paprika makes it festive looking.

Research has shown that laughter makes a difference in the patient recovery rate; St. Luke's Hospital brings the joy of laughter to patients through the not-for-profit organization, Bumper "T" Caring Clowns.

Eggplant Parmesan

2 medium eggplant, peeled and sliced into ¼ inch slices

½ cup olive oil

1 (16 ounce) jar tomato sauce

1 (16 ounce) package mozzarella cheese slices

Grated Parmesan or Romano cheese

Ground pepper to taste

- Preheat oven to broil.
- Arrange eggplant slices on a foil lined baking sheet.
- Lightly brush with oil.
- Broil eggplant until begins to brown and softened.
- Turn slices over and brush with oil.
- Broil eggplant until begins to cook.
- Spread 4 to 5 tablespoons tomato sauce in the bottom of a 13x9x2 inch baking dish.
- Remove eggplant and reset oven to 350 degrees.
- Place a single layer of eggplant slices over sauce.
- Top with a layer of mozzarella cheese slices. Spoon sauce on top. Repeat all layers ending with tomato sauce.
- Cover and bake for 45 minutes.
- Uncover and bake an additional 20 minutes or until golden browned and sauce thickens.
- Cool 5 minutes.
- Top with Parmesan cheese and pepper.

Serves 6-8

Note: May add cooked ground beef, pork, or lamb between layers.

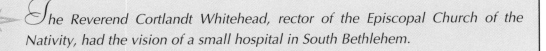

The Reverend Cortlandt Whitehead, rector of the Episcopal Church of the Nativity, had the vision of a small hospital in South Bethlehem.

Desserts

St. Luke's Miners Memorial Hospital
Coaldale • Schuylkill County
Joined Network in 2000

*The land on which St. Luke's Miners Memorial Hospital stands
is on the western perimeter of the Walking Purchase of 1737.*

St. Luke's Miners Memorial Hospital

Coaldale • Schuylkill County
Joined Network in 2000

A new and expanded Emergency Department and a new access road from Route 209 directly to the campus are some of the recent major facility improvements at St. Luke's Miners Memorial Hospital. The Campus has also expanded clinical services, most especially in the area of imaging with the acquisition of a 64-slice CT scanner and in the area of women's health.

Glazed Apricot Nectar Cake

1 (18 ounce) package lemon cake mix

⅓ cup sugar

1 cup apricot nectar

½ cup vegetable oil

4 eggs

1 cup powdered sugar

2 tablespoons lemon juice or juice of
   1 lemon

- Preheat oven to 325 degrees.
- Beat cake mix, sugar, apricot nectar, and oil.
- Add eggs, one at a time, beating well after each addition.
- Pour batter into greased and floured 10 inch tube pan.
- Bake for 1 hour.
- Cool in pan on rack at least 15 minutes. Remove from pan and set aside.
- For glaze, blend powdered sugar and lemon juice until smooth.
- While cake is warm, pour glaze over top and sides of cake.

Serves 8-12

Note: 1 cup orange juice can be substituted for apricot nectar.

The Moravian Apothecary, established in 1743, became known as the oldest drugstore in continuous existence in the United States. It was located in what is now the Moravian Museum.

Apple Cake

3 eggs

1¾ cups sugar

2 cups all-purpose flour

1 teaspoon salt

1 teaspoon baking soda

1 teaspoon cinnamon

1 cup vegetable oil

3 cups thinly sliced apples

1 cup chopped walnuts

- Preheat oven to 350 degrees.
- Cream eggs and sugar.
- In separate mixing bowl, combine flour, salt, baking soda, and cinnamon.
- Add to egg mixture by tablespoonfuls, alternating with oil.
- Stir in apples and walnuts.
- Pour batter into greased and floured 13x9x2 inch baking dish.
- Bake for 35 to 45 minutes or until toothpick comes out clean.

Serves 12-16

Blueberry Cake

1½ cups all-purpose flour

1 teaspoon baking powder

½ teaspoon salt

2 egg whites

2 egg yolks

1 stick butter, softened

1 cup sugar

⅓ cup milk

1 teaspoon lemon juice

2 cups blueberries

- Preheat oven to 350 degrees.
- Combine flour, baking powder, and salt.
- In a separate bowl, beat egg whites until stiff. Set aside.
- Cream egg yolks, butter, and sugar.
- Add flour mixture, alternately with milk, to creamed mixture.
- Fold in egg whites.
- Stir in lemon juice and blueberries.
- Pour batter into a greased and floured Bundt pan.
- Bake for 35 to 40 minutes.
- Sprinkle with additional sugar while cake is still hot.

Serves 12-15

Apple Dapple Cake

Cake

2 cups sugar

1½ cups corn oil

3 eggs

3 cups unsifted all-purpose flour

1 teaspoon baking soda

1 teaspoon salt

3 cups finely diced Granny Smith apples

2 cups chopped pecans

2 teaspoons vanilla

Glaze

1 cup packed dark brown sugar

1 stick butter

½ cup heavy cream

- Preheat oven to 325 degrees.
- Beat together sugar and oil.
- Add eggs, one at a time, beating well after each addition.
- Sift together flour, baking soda, and salt. Stir into egg mixture.
- Beat in apples, pecans, and vanilla.
- Pour batter into a buttered springform pan.
- Bake for 1 hour or until a toothpick comes out clean.
- Combine brown sugar, butter, and cream in a saucepan. Boil for 3 minutes.
- Reserve ⅓ cup of glaze and pour remaining glaze over the cake.
- Cool cake and remove from pan.
- Just before serving, pour reserved warm glaze over cake.

Serves 12-14

In 1985, the Ladies' Aid Society was changed to the St. Luke's Aid Society to indicate its membership also included men, and in 1987, it became The St. Luke's Hospital Auxiliary. In 2006, it was named The Auxiliary of St. Luke's Hospital.

Banana Nut Cake

Cake

2 sticks butter, softened or 1 cup solid vegetable shortening

1½ cups sugar

4 egg yolks

½ cup sour milk

½ teaspoon salt

½ teaspoon vanilla

2 cups finely mashed bananas

3 cups sifted all-purpose flour

1 cup chopped nuts

2 teaspoons baking soda

2 teaspoons baking powder

4 egg whites, stiffly beaten

Icing

1 stick butter, softened

½ cup solid vegetable shortening

¾ cup sugar

7 tablespoons all-purpose flour

½ cup milk

1 teaspoon vanilla

- Preheat oven to 350 degrees.
- Cream butter, sugar, egg yolks, milk, salt, vanilla, and bananas until smooth.
- Stir in flour, nuts, baking soda, and baking powder.
- Fold in egg whites.
- Pour batter into a 13x9x2 inch baking dish or 15x10x1 inch baking sheet.
- Bake for 30 minutes or until done.
- Cream butter, shortening, and sugar until smooth.
- Beat in flour.
- Add milk and vanilla.
- Beat on high for 10 minutes.
- Frost cooled cake.

Serves 12-15

Coconut Cream Cake

1 (18 ounce) package white cake mix with pudding

¾ cup sweetened coconut, flaked

1 (14 ounce) can nonfat sweetened condensed milk

1 teaspoon coconut extract

1 (12 ounce) container nonfat frozen whipped topping, thawed

Coconut for garnish (optional)

- Preheat oven to 350 degrees.
- Prepare cake according to package directions omitting the oil.
- Substitute coconut for oil.
- Pour batter into a greased 13x9x2 inch baking dish.
- Bake for 28 minutes or until done.
- Cool 10 minutes.
- Pierce holes on top of cake.
- Blend milk and coconut extract. Slowly pour over cake, allowing mixture to be absorbed.
- Cool completely.
- Spread whipped topping over top.
- Sprinkle with coconut.
- Cover and refrigerate 4 hours before serving.

Serves 12-15

Note: Freezes well. May bake two cakes and divide milk mixture between two cakes. If unable to find cake mix with pudding, may add 1 (3 ounce) package instant vanilla pudding mix to cake mix.

 Each year the Auxiliary hosts a variety of fundraisers, including the Charity Ball, the Fashion Show and Luncheon, The Classic on the Green Golf Tournament and numerous Special Sales.

Creamsicle Cake

1 (18 ounce) package orange cake mix

1 (3 ounce) package orange flavored gelatin

1 cup hot water

1 cup cold water

1 (3 ounce) package orange flavored gelatin

1 (3 ounce) package instant vanilla pudding mix

1 cup milk

1 teaspoon vanilla

1 (8 ounce) container frozen whipped topping, thawed

- Preheat oven to 350 degrees.
- Prepare cake mix according to package directions.
- Pour batter into a 13x9x2 baking dish.
- When cake is done, pierce holes in top of cake. Cool.
- Dissolve one package gelatin in hot water. Stir in cold water.
- Slowly pour gelatin over cake.
- Refrigerate for 2 to 3 hours.
- Combine remaining package gelatin, pudding mix, milk, and vanilla.
- Beat well.
- Fold in whipped topping.
- Spread topping over cake.
- Store refrigerated.

Serves 12-15

Note: May substitute lemon cake and lemon gelatin or strawberry cake and strawberry gelatin. Cake is light, refreshing and moist.

At one time the silk industry in Bethlehem ranked second as to the number of employees it had. The Bethlehem Silk Company was located on Goepp Street in 1887.

Elite Cake

2 cups all-purpose flour

1½ cups sugar

2 teaspoons baking soda

2 eggs

1 (20 ounce) can crushed pineapple,
    undrained

1 (8 ounce) package cream cheese,
    softened

6 tablespoons butter, softened

1 cup powdered sugar

- Preheat oven to 350 degrees.
- Combine flour, sugar, baking soda, eggs, and pineapple with juice.
- Pour batter into greased 13x9x2 inch glass baking dish.
- Bake for 35 to 40 minutes.
- Cool completely. Remove cake from dish.
- For frosting, blend cream cheese, butter, and sugar.
- Spread frosting over cake.

Serves 15

Lemon Pudding Cake

¾ cup sugar

Dash of salt

3 tablespoons butter, softened

¼ cup sifted all-purpose flour

1 teaspoon lemon zest

¼ cup lemon juice

1¼ cups milk

3 egg yolks, well beaten

3 egg whites, stiffly beaten

- Preheat oven to 350 degrees.
- Combine sugar, salt, butter, flour, zest, juice, milk, and egg yolks. Fold in egg whites.
- Pour batter into an 8x8x2 inch baking dish.
- Place in another pan of hot water, halfway up baking dish for a water dish.
- Bake for 40 minutes or until top is lightly browned.
- Serve warm or chilled.

Serves 6-8

Carrot Cake

Cake

3 cups all-purpose flour

2½ cups sugar

3 tablespoons baking soda

3 tablespoons cinnamon

½ teaspoon salt

4 (4½ ounce) jars strained baby carrots

1⅓ cups vegetable oil

4 eggs, slightly beaten

1 teaspoon vanilla

1 (15 ounce) can crushed pineapple

1 cup chopped walnuts

Cream Cheese Frosting

1 (8 ounce) package cream cheese, softened

1 (3 ounce) package cream cheese, softened

1 stick butter, softened

1 teaspoon vanilla

3-3½ cups powdered sugar

- Preheat oven to 350 degrees.
- Combine flour, sugar, baking soda, cinnamon, and salt until well mixed.
- Add carrots, oil, eggs, and vanilla.
- Mix until thoroughly blended.
- Stir in pineapple and walnuts.
- Pour batter into lightly greased and floured 13x9x2 inch baking dish.
- Bake for 45 minutes or until toothpick comes out clean.
- Cool completely.
- Beat cream cheese, butter, and vanilla until well blended.
- Gradually add powdered sugar and beat until smooth.
- Frost cooled cake.

Serves 15-20

During the groundbreaking for Quakertown Community Hospital on June 29, 1927, C. William Freed, master of ceremony, told the crowd, "This will be a community hospital. We are your servants."

Chocolate Cake with Whipped Cream Topping

Cake

6 tablespoons solid vegetable shortening

2 cups hot black coffee

2 cups all-purpose flour

2 cups sugar

1 cup cocoa powder

2 teaspoons baking powder

2 teaspoons baking soda

Pinch of salt

2 eggs or 3 egg yolks

2 teaspoons vanilla

Icing

¼ cup all-purpose flour

1 cup milk

1 stick butter, softened

½ cup solid vegetable shortening

1 cup sugar

2 teaspoons vanilla

- Preheat oven to 350 degrees.
- Stir shortening into coffee. Set aside to cool.
- Combine flour, sugar, cocoa, baking powder, baking soda, and salt.
- Add coffee mixture and mix well.
- Stir in eggs and vanilla.
- Pour batter into a greased 13x9x2 inch baking dish.
- Bake for 30 minutes.
- Blend flour and milk.
- Microwave for 30 seconds intervals until thickened.
- Cool.
- Cream butter, shortening, sugar, and vanilla.
- Beat at medium/high speed until whipped.
- Add milk mixture. Continue beating until soft peaks form like whipped cream.
- Spread icing over cake.

Serves 12-15

Note: Cake batter will be thin. Coffee mixture should be warm before adding to flour. Do not allow coffee mixture to cool completely. Butter may be substituted for shortening.

In the early 1950s, Quakertown Community Hospital was the only area hospital to accept Blue Cross partial payments without billing patients for the cost difference.

Chocolate Cake

Cake

2 cups sugar

2 cups all-purpose flour

¾ cup cocoa powder

1 teaspoon baking powder

1 ½ teaspoons baking soda

½ teaspoon salt

2 eggs

½ cup vegetable oil

1 cup milk

1 cup hot black coffee

Easy Cream Cheese Icing

1 stick butter, softened

1 (8 ounce) package cream cheese, softened

1 cup powdered sugar

½ teaspoon vanilla

- Preheat oven to 350 degrees.
- Sift together sugar, flour, cocoa, baking powder, baking soda, and salt.
- Add eggs and oil.
- Stir in milk and coffee until well blended.
- Batter will be thin.
- Pour batter into a greased and floured 13x9x2 inch baking dish or two 9 inch round pans.
- Bake for 35 minutes or until toothpick comes out clean.
- Cream butter and cream cheese until light and fluffy.
- Slowly add powdered sugar.
- Stir in vanilla.
- Mix well.
- Frost cooled cake.

Serves 10-12

In 1758, the Moravians built the Old Sun Inn, older than the United States. The Sun Inn was licensed by King George III of England, June 17, 1761. Old registers of the Old Sun Inn list visitors, Martha and George Washington, Lafayette, Franklin, John Adams, Count Pulaski, Baron Von Steuben.

Molten Chocolate Cakes

8 (1 ounce) bittersweet chocolate squares

15 tablespoons unsalted butter

4 large eggs, room temperature

4 large egg yolks, room temperature

½ cup sugar

7 tablespoons all-purpose flour

Ice cream and raspberries for garnish.

- Preheat oven to 325 degrees.
- Melt chocolate and butter in the microwave, stirring until smooth.
- Cool slightly.
- Beat eggs, egg yolks, and sugar for 10 minutes until pale yellow.
- Gradually stir in flour.
- Add chocolate. Beat about 5 minutes until glossy.
- Divide batter among eight buttered and floured 5 ounce ramekins.
- Bake about 12 minutes until edges are set and center appears wet.
- Run a sharp knife around edge and invert onto dessert plates.
- Serve warm with ice cream. Garnish with raspberries.
- Dust edge of plate with cinnamon.

Serves 8

Note: May refrigerate filled ramekins for up to 6 hours. Bake for 18 minutes.

The women of Church of the Nativity responded quickly when asked to help the hospital in 1873. With an endowment from Lehigh Valley Railroad, the women incorporated their organization on August 6, 1874 and call themselves the Ladies' Aid Society of St. Luke's Hospital.

Chocolate Birthday Cake (Ganache Cake)

Cake

Butter for greasing pans

Parchment paper

All-purpose flour for dusting

¾ cup boiling water

½ cup unsweetened cocoa powder (not Dutch process)

1 teaspoon instant espresso granules/ powder

½ cup whole milk

1 teaspoon vanilla

2 cups all-purpose flour

1 ¼ teaspoons baking soda

¼ teaspoon salt

2 sticks unsalted butter, softened

2 cups packed brown sugar

4 large eggs

Ganache

2½ cups heavy cream

20 ounces bittersweet chocolate, finely chopped (not unsweetened)

- Preheat oven to 350 degrees.
- Butter three (7 inch) round cake pans.
- Line bottoms with parchment paper.
- Dust with flour.
- In small bowl, whisk together water, cocoa, and espresso powder until smooth.
- Whisk in milk and vanilla.
- In another small bowl, sift together flour, baking soda, and salt.
- In a large bowl, beat butter and brown sugar with electric mixer on high speed until fluffy.
- Add eggs, one at a time, beating well after each addition.
- Add flour mixture and cocoa mixture in batches to creamed mixture, beginning and ending with flour, mixing at low speed until just combined.
- Divide batter among pans (about 2 ⅓ cups per pan) and smooth tops.
- Place pans in middle of oven.
- Bake for 30 to 35 minutes or until a tester comes out clean.
- Cool in pans on rack for 30 minutes, then invert onto racks.

Patients at the Bethlehem campus enjoy visits from Therapy Dogs.

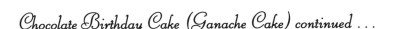

Chocolate Birthday Cake (Ganache Cake) *continued . . .*

- Remove paper and cool completely.
- For icing (ganache), bring cream to a simmer in a 3-4 quart saucepan. Remove from heat.
- Whisk in chocolate until smooth.
- Transfer ganache to a bowl. Cover and refrigerate about 4 hours, stirring occasionally, until thickened, but spreadable. (If ganache becomes too thick, let stand at room temperature until slightly softened.)
- To assemble cake, arrange one cake layer on a cake stand or plate and evenly spread two-thirds cup ganache on top.
- Top with second cake layer and another two-thirds cup ganache, spreading evenly.
- Top with third cake layer.
- Refrigerate cake about 1 hour until ganache is firm.
- Keep remaining ganache at a spreadable consistency, chilling when necessary.

- Spread a thin layer of ganache over top and sides of cake to seal in crumbs.
- Refrigerate 30 minutes.
- Spread remaining ganache evenly over top and sides of cake.
- Store cake covered and refrigerated for 3 days.

Serves 12-16

Note: This cake can also be made in 2 (8 inch) round cake pans. Split layers horizontally and use one-half cup ganache in between layers.

Quakertown Community Hospital joined St. Luke's Hospital & Health Network and was renamed St. Luke's' Quakertown Hospital in August 1995.

Lemon Sponge

1 cup sugar

¼ cup all-purpose flour

⅛ teaspoon salt

2 tablespoons butter, melted

5 tablespoons lemon juice

Zest of 1 lemon

3 egg yolks, well beaten

1½ cups milk

3 egg whites, stiffly beaten

- Preheat oven to 350 degrees.
- Blend sugar, flour, and salt.
- Add to butter.
- Add lemon juice and zest. Blend well.
- Stir in egg yolks and milk.
- Fold in egg whites.
- Divide mixture among eight greased custard cups or into a casserole dish.
- Place in a pan of hot water, half way up baking dish, for a water dish.
- Bake for 45 minutes.

Serves 8

Note: May be served warm or cooled.

Nut and Date Cake

1 cup dates, chopped

¼ cup lukewarm water

1 stick butter, softened

1 cup sugar

1 tablespoon vanilla

3 eggs

1 cup all-purpose flour

1 tablespoon baking powder

Pinch of salt

1 cup nuts, chopped

Powdered sugar

- Preheat oven to 350 degrees.
- Soak dates in lukewarm water.
- Beat butter, sugar, vanilla, and eggs with an electric mixer.
- Add flour, baking powder, and salt.
- Mix in softened dates and nuts.
- Pour batter into a greased and floured 13x9x2 inch baking dish.
- Bake for 25 to 30 minutes.
- Sift powdered sugar over cooled cake.

Serves 10-12

Note: Use an 8x8 square pan for a thicker cake.

Pineapple-Cherry Cake

1 (20 ounce) can crushed pineapple, drained

1 (21 ounce) can cherry pie filling

1 cup shredded coconut (optional)

1 (18 ounce) package yellow cake mix

2 sticks butter, melted

1 cup chopped nuts, walnuts or pecans

- Preheat oven to 300 degrees.
- Spread pineapple on the bottom of a 13x9x2 inch baking dish.
- Top with pie filling, then coconut. Sprinkle cake mix on top.
- Drizzle butter over cake mix.
- Sprinkle with nuts.
- Bake for 1 hour.

Serves 8-10

Note: This is delicious served warm with vanilla ice cream and whipped cream.

Pumpkin Pudding Cake

Cake

1 (29 ounce) can pumpkin

1 cup sugar

3 eggs, beaten

1 (12 ounce) can evaporated milk

1 teaspoon salt

1 teaspoon cinnamon

1 teaspoon ground nutmeg

1 teaspoon ground ginger

Topping

1 (18 ounce) package yellow cake mix

1 cup English walnuts, finely chopped

2 sticks butter, melted

- Preheat oven to 350 degrees.
- Blend pumpkin, sugar, eggs, milk, salt, cinnamon, nutmeg, and ginger.
- Pour batter into a greased 13x9x2 inch baking dish.
- Sprinkle cake mix over batter.
- Sprinkle walnuts over cake mix.
- Drizzle butter over top.
- Bake for 50 to 60 minutes until custard is set.
- Cool and refrigerate.

Serves 12-15

Note: May substitute 3 teaspoons pumpkin pie spice for cinnamon, nutmeg and ginger.

Bourbon Cake

1 (18 ounce) package yellow cake mix

½ cup cornstarch

½ cup sugar

1 cup water

4 eggs

½ cup corn oil

1 ½ teaspoons vanilla

Glaze

1 cup light corn syrup

½ cup sugar

4 tablespoons butter

¾ cup bourbon

- Preheat oven to 350 degrees.
- Combine cake mix, cornstarch, and sugar.
- Beat in water, eggs, oil, and vanilla with electric mixer on low speed.
- Beat for 3 minutes at medium speed.
- Pour batter into a greased and floured 12 cup fluted pan or 10 inch tube pan.
- Bake for 50 to 60 minutes.
- Cool about 15 minutes in pan.
- Combine corn syrup, sugar, and butter in saucepan. Stir over medium heat until smooth.
- Remove and stir in bourbon.
- Remove cake from pan.
- Pierce cake thoroughly with fork or pierce from top to bottom numerous times with a long, thin knife (for more absorption of glaze).
- Brush with one half of glaze.
- Let stand for 1 hour.
- Brush with remaining glaze.
- Store tightly covered for 1 to 3 days.
- To serve, decorate with whipped cream and cherries.

Serves 10-12

Panther Creek Valley Hospital, later known as Coaldale State General Hospital and Miners Memorial Medical Center, joined St. Luke's Hospital & Health Network in June 2000 and was renamed St. Luke's Miners Memorial Hospital.

Inventory Cake Recipe

1 (18 ounce) package chocolate cake mix

1 (3 ounce) package instant chocolate pudding mix

4 eggs

¾ cup sour cream

½ cup canola oil

½ cup water

1 (12 ounce) package miniature semi-sweet chocolate chips

Powdered sugar for dusting

- Preheat oven to 350 degrees.
- Combine cake mix, pudding mix, eggs, sour cream, oil, water, and chocolate chips.
- Beat on medium speed until thoroughly mixed.
- Pour batter into a greased tube cake pan.
- Bake for 40 to 50 minutes.
- Let cake cool 15 minutes.
- Remove from tube pan.
- When cake is cool, dust with powdered sugar.

Serves 12

Note: Moist and delicious.

Chocolate Chess Pie

1 stick butter

2 (1 ounce) squares unsweetened baking chocolate

2 large eggs, beaten

2 tablespoons milk

1 tablespoon vanilla

1 cup sugar

1 (9 inch) pie crust, unbaked

- Preheat oven to 350 degrees.
- Melt butter and chocolate.
- Slowly stir chocolate into eggs.
- Add milk, vanilla, and sugar. Mix well.
- Pour filling into pie crust.
- Bake for 35 minutes.
- Cool before slicing.

Serves 8

Note: May be frozen for up to 2 months covered with foil.

White Cake

½ cup buttermilk

1 teaspoon baking soda

½ cup solid vegetable shortening

2 cups sugar

3 egg yolks

1 egg

1 teaspoon vanilla

2 cups sifted all-purpose flour

½ teaspoon salt

1 teaspoon baking powder

1 cup boiling water

- Preheat oven to 350 degrees.
- Mix together buttermilk with baking soda. Set aside.
- Cream shortening, sugar, egg yolks, egg, and vanilla. Beat well.
- Add buttermilk and baking soda mixture.
- Sift together flour, salt, and baking powder. Add to creamed mixture.
- Add boiling water and mix well.
- Pour batter into a greased and floured 13x9x2 inch baking dish.
- Bake about 35 minutes or until toothpick comes out clean.
- Cool. Frost with favorite icing.

Serves 24

Chocolate Pecan Pie

1 stick butter, melted

1 cup semi-sweet chocolate chips

1 cup chopped pecans

1 teaspoon vanilla

½ cup all-purpose flour

½ cup sugar

½ cup packed brown sugar

2 eggs, beaten

1 (9 inch) pie crust, unbaked

- Preheat oven to 350 degrees.
- Pour warm butter over chocolate and stir until chocolate melts.
- Combine pecans, vanilla, flour, sugar, brown sugar, and eggs. Add to chocolate mixture.
- Pour filling into pie crust.
- Bake for 30 to 40 minutes.
- Do not overbake. Test with a toothpick, which should have some crumbs attached.

Serves 8

Sour Cream Apple Pie

Crust

3 tablespoons milk

½ cup vegetable oil

1½ cups plus 3 tablespoons all-purpose flour

1 tablespoon sugar

½ teaspoon salt

Filling

1 cup sour cream

¾ cup sugar

2 tablespoons all-purpose flour

¼ teaspoon salt

1 teaspoon vanilla

1 egg

3 heaping cups peeled and diced apples

Crumb Topping

1 cup all-purpose flour

½ cup packed light brown sugar

4 tablespoons butter, softened

- Preheat oven to 400 degrees.
- Blend milk and oil until creamy.
- In another bowl, combine flour, sugar, and salt.
- Pour milk mixture over flour mixture and mix well.
- Press dough with a fork or fingers into bottom and up sides of a 10 inch pie plate.
- Combine sour cream, sugar, flour, salt, vanilla, egg, and apples. Mix well.
- Pour filling into crust.
- Bake for 25 minutes.
- Combine flour and brown sugar.
- Cut in butter until crumbly. Shape crumbs into a ball, then crumble mixture up.
- Remove pie from oven and top with crumbs.
- Bake an additional 20 minutes.

Serves 8

The Hotel Bethlehem Corporation was incorporated September 13, 1920. All of the steel used in the Bethlehem Hotel was manufactured by Bethlehem Steel which had the exclusive right to the type of structural steel rolled in one piece, the columns and beams known as "Bethlehem Shapes."

Peanut Butter Pie

1 (8 ounce) package cream cheese, softened

¾ cup sugar

½ cup creamy peanut butter

2 tablespoons milk

1 (9 ounce) container frozen nondairy whipped topping, thawed

1 (9 inch) graham cracker crust

Whipped cream, peanuts or chocolate shavings for garnish

- Blend cream cheese and sugar.
- Mix peanut butter with milk. Add to cream cheese.
- Add whipped topping.
- Pour filling into crust.
- Refrigerate until firm.
- Garnish with whipped cream, peanuts or chocolate shavings.

Serves 10

Note: May be frozen and thawed one hour before serving. May substitute chocolate cookie crust for graham cracker crust.

Pecan Pie

1 stick butter

½ cup sugar

¾ cup light corn syrup

¼ cup maple flavored syrup or 2 tablespoons honey

3 eggs, slightly beaten

1 teaspoon vanilla

1 cup pecans

1 (9 inch) pie crust, unbaked

1 cup pecans

Heavy cream, whipped

- Preheat oven to 350 degrees.
- Cream butter.
- Blend in sugar until light and fluffy.
- Stir in corn syrup, maple syrup, eggs, vanilla, and nuts.
- Pour filling into pie crust.
- Sprinkle nuts on top.
- Bake for 55 minutes.
- Cool.
- Serve small pieces with whipped cream.

Serves 12

Pecan Cheesecake Pie

2 (8 ounce) packages cream cheese, softened

½ teaspoon vanilla

¼ cup sugar

3 eggs

⅓ cup sugar

¾ cup light corn syrup

½ teaspoon lemon juice

½ teaspoon vanilla

1 teaspoon salt

1 tablespoon butter, softened

1 cup chopped pecans

1 (9 inch) deep dish pie crust, baked

1 tablespoon brown sugar

- Preheat oven to 375 degrees.
- Blend cream cheese, vanilla, and sugar until smooth. Set aside.
- Beat together eggs, sugar, corn syrup, lemon juice, vanilla, salt, butter, and pecans.
- Pour cream cheese mixture into pie crust.
- Spread pecan mixture over top.
- Sprinkle with brown sugar.
- Bake for 40 minutes or until center is firm.
- Cool completely before serving.

Serves 8-10

Strawberry Pie

1 ½ cups water

¾ cup sugar

2 tablespoons cornstarch

1 (3 ounce) package strawberry flavored gelatin

2 pints fresh strawberries

1 (9 inch) pie crust, baked

- Combine water, sugar, and cornstarch in saucepan.
- Cook over medium heat, stirring constantly until boil.
- Reduce heat and simmer about 2 minutes.
- Remove from heat and add gelatin.
- Stir until dissolved.
- Arrange strawberries in pie crust. Pour hot glaze over berries.
- Refrigerate.

Serves 6-8

Peach and Blueberry Pie

Crust

½ **cup vegetable oil**

½ **teaspoon salt**

2 **tablespoons sugar**

2 **tablespoons milk**

1 ½ **cups all-purpose flour**

Glaze

1 **cup cold water**

3 **tablespoons cornstarch**

2 **tablespoons light corn syrup**

1 **cup sugar**

2 **tablespoons lemon flavored gelatin**

Filling

2-3 **cups sliced peaches**
  (approximately 4 peaches)

1 **cup blueberries**

- Preheat oven to 350 degrees.
- Blend oil, salt, sugar, milk, and flour with a fork.
- Press mixture into a 9 inch pie plate.
- Pierce crust with a fork and bake about 15 minutes. Do not brown.
- Combine water, cornstarch, corn syrup, and sugar in a saucepan. Cook until thickened and clear.
- Cool slightly and then add lemon gelatin.
- Arrange peaches and blueberries in pie crust. Pour cooked glaze over fruit.
- Refrigerate until ready to serve.

Serves 8

In 1919, the Baby Welfare Association created the Visiting Nurse Association to extend its mission. The two agencies shared one car. The two organizations merged in 1926.

Apple Butter Pumpkin Pie

Filling

1 cup pumpkin

1 cup apple butter

¼ cup packed dark brown sugar

½ teaspoon cinnamon

¼ teaspoon ground ginger

¼ teaspoon ground nutmeg

¼ teaspoon salt

3 eggs, slightly beaten

1 cup evaporated milk

1 (9 inch) frozen deep dish pie crust, thawed and unbaked

Streusel Topping

3 tablespoons butter, softened

½ cup all-purpose flour

¼ cup packed brown sugar

⅓ cup chopped pecans

- Preheat oven to 375 degrees.
- Blend pumpkin, apple butter, brown sugar, cinnamon, ginger, nutmeg, salt, eggs, and milk.
- Pour filling into pie crust.
- Bake for 50 to 60 minutes or until tester comes out clean.
- Mix butter with flour, brown sugar, and pecans until crumbly.
- Sprinkle over filling.
- Bake an additional 15 minutes.

Serves 8

In 1937, the Visiting Nurse Association joined with other agencies to improve conditions for a Mexican labor camp that developed near the Bethlehem Steel coke works.

Pumpkin Pie

Filling

1 (15 ounce) can pumpkin

1 (14 ounce) can sweetened condensed
  milk

1 egg

¾ teaspoon cinnamon

½ teaspoon ground ginger

½ teaspoon ground nutmeg

½ teaspoon salt

1 (6 ounce) graham cracker crust

Topping

¼ cup firmly packed brown sugar

2 tablespoons all-purpose flour

½ teaspoon cinnamon

2 tablespoons cold butter

¾ cup chopped walnuts

- Preheat oven to 425 degrees.
- Blend pumpkin, milk, egg, cinnamon, ginger, nutmeg, and salt.
- Pour filling into crust.
- Bake for 15 minutes.
- Combine brown sugar, flour and cinnamon.
- Cut in butter until crumbly.
- Stir in walnuts.
- Remove pie from oven.
- Reduce temperature to 350 degrees.
- Sprinkle topping over filling.
- Bake an additional 40 minutes until set.
- Serve warm or room temperature.

Serves 8-10

Note: Top with whipped cream.

In 1910, coal miners in the region donated a full day's pay and Lehigh Valley Coal & Navigation Company donated the land and matched the miners' donations to fund the construction of Panther Creek Valley Hospital. (Present day St. Luke's' Miners Memorial Hospital).

Lemon Sponge Pie

2 tablespoons butter, softened

1 cup sugar

3 egg yolks

3 tablespoons all-purpose flour

½ teaspoon salt

Juice of 1 lemon

Zest of 1 lemon

1 ½ cups milk, room temperature

3 egg whites

1 (9 inch) pie crust, unbaked

- Preheat oven to 350 degrees.
- Cream butter.
- Beat in sugar and egg yolks.
- Add flour, salt, juice, zest, and milk.
- Beat egg whites until stiff.
- Fold into lemon mixture.
- Pour filling into pie crust.
- Cover crust edges with aluminum foil.
- Bake for 40 to 45 minutes.

Serves 8

Frozen Pineapple Dessert

1 ½ cups graham cracker crumbs

4 tablespoons butter, melted

1 tablespoon sugar

2 (8 ounce) cans crushed pineapple

1 (12 ounce) can evaporated milk

1 (5 ounce) can evaporated milk

1 (7 ounce) container marshmallow crème

- Combine crumbs, butter, and sugar.
- Press mixture into a pie plate or 8x8x2 inch baking dish.
- Blend pineapple, milk, and marshmallow crème in blender or with electric mixer.
- Pour filling over crust and cover with foil.
- Place in freezer.
- Once frozen, serve and enjoy.

Serves 8-10

Banana Split Dessert

Crust

2 cups graham cracker crumbs

6 tablespoons unsalted butter, melted

Filling

1 stick unsalted butter, softened

2 cups powdered sugar

2 eggs or egg substitute equivalent

1 teaspoon vanilla

Topping

4 large (5 small) bananas, sliced diagonally

2 (16 ounce) cans crushed pineapple, very well drained

1 (8-12 ounce) container frozen nondairy whipped topping, thawed

¾-1 cup chopped walnuts

25-30 maraschino cherries, drained and cut into eighths.

- Preheat oven to 350 degrees.
- Combine crumbs and butter. Press mixture into 13x9x2 inch baking dish.
- Bake for 6 minutes.
- Cool.
- Beat together butter, powdered sugar, eggs, and vanilla until fluffy.
- Spread filling over crust.
- Refrigerate at least 1 hour or freeze 10 to 15 minutes.
- Layer bananas, pineapple, and whipped topping over filling.
- Top with walnuts and cherries.
- Cover and refrigerate at least 1 hour.

Serves 20 or more

Note: Peanuts can be substituted for walnuts.

 The Visiting Nurse Association of Eastern Pennsylvania joined St. Luke's Hospital & Health Network in December 1993 and is now called the Visiting Nurse Association of St. Luke's.

CMP Sundae Cake

⅔ cup chopped peanuts

1 cup all-purpose flour

1 stick butter, melted

½ cup creamy peanut butter

1 (8 ounce) package cream cheese, softened

1 cup powdered sugar

1 cup frozen whipped topping, thawed

1 (3 ounce) package instant chocolate pudding mix

1 (3 ounce) package instant vanilla pudding mix

2¾ cups milk

1 (8 ounce) container frozen whipped topping, thawed

Chocolate shavings and chopped peanuts for garnish

- Preheat oven to 350 degrees.
- Combine peanuts, flour, and butter. Press mixture into a greased 13x9x2 inch baking dish.
- Bake for 20 minutes. Cool.
- Blend peanut butter, cream cheese, powdered sugar, and whipped topping.
- Spread over crust.
- Beat pudding mixes with milk until smooth.
- Spread over cream cheese layer.
- Top with whipped topping.
- Garnish with chocolate and peanuts.

Serves 12-15

St. Luke's Physician Group and St. Luke's Hospital-Bethlehem Campus are the only original members of St. Luke's Hospital & Health Network.

Holiday Cherry Delight

1 ½ cups boiling water

2 (3 ounce) packages cherry flavored gelatin or 1 (6 ounce) package

2 cups ice cubes

1 (21 ounce) can cherry pie filling

4 cups cubed angel food cake or pound cake

1 ½ cups cold milk

1 (3 ounce) package instant vanilla pudding mix

1 (8 ounce) container frozen whipped topping, thawed

Strawberries for garnish

- Stir boiling water with gelatin in large bowl at least 2 minutes until completely dissolved.
- Stir in ice until melted.
- Stir in pie filling.
- Place cake cubes in 3 quart serving bowl.
- Spoon gelatin mixture over cake.
- Refrigerate for 15 minutes or until set but not firm.
- Pour milk into a separate large bowl.
- Whisk in pudding mix for 1 minute.
- Fold in half whipped topping.
- Spoon mixture over gelatin mixture.
- Refrigerate for 3 hours.
- Top with remaining whipped topping.
- Garnish with fresh strawberries.

Serves 16

St. Luke's Singers, founded in 1991, is one of only a few hospital-based choral groups in the United States. The singers have raised more than $120,000 to support various hospital services.

Schaum Torte

¾ **cup egg whites, from 6 eggs**

⅛ **teaspoon salt**

2 cups sugar

1 teaspoon white vinegar

½ **teaspoon vanilla**

2 cups heavy cream

1 pint strawberries, sliced

2 tablespoons slivered toasted almonds

- Preheat oven to 275 degrees.
- Beat egg whites and salt at high speed until frothy.
- Add sugar, 2 tablespoons at a time, beating well after each addition.
- Add vinegar and vanilla and beat 10 minutes.
- Cut two 9 inch circles from brown paper.
- Divide meringue in half and spread onto each paper circle.
- Place on baking sheet.
- Bake for 1 hour until delicately firm.
- Cool in oven.
- When cool, store in covered container.
- Twenty minutes before serving, whip cream.
- Place one meringue layer on a plate and top with half whipped cream and half strawberries.
- Place second meringue on top and spread remaining whipped cream and strawberries.
- Top with almonds.

Serves 8-10

Note: The whipped cream must be sweetened.

More than 70 singers from 14 communities, as well as St. Luke's employees, volunteers, nurses and physicians, comprise the St. Luke's Singers.

Coconut Almond Macaroon Torte

Cake

6 large eggs, separated and at room temperature

½ cup packed light brown sugar

½ teaspoon salt

1 ⅓ cups finely ground almonds

1 cup shredded coconut

¼ teaspoon orange zest

Filling and Topping

½ cup red raspberry preserves

2 tablespoons butter

¼ cup semi-sweet chocolate chips

1 tablespoon cocoa powder

1 tablespoon powdered sugar

¼ teaspoon orange zest

- Preheat oven to 350 degrees.
- Butter only the bottom of a 10 inch springform pan.
- Separate eggs into two bowls. Allow to come to room temperature.
- Beat egg whites until stiff.
- Without washing beaters, beat egg yolks, gradually adding brown sugar and salt.
- Beat 2 minutes at high speed.
- Stir almonds and coconut into yolk mixture.
- Add orange zest.
- Mix well.
- Fold egg whites into yolk mixture, carefully and quickly.
- Pour batter into prepared pan.
- Bake for 30 minutes.
- Cool completely.
- Remove cake from pan. Cut in half, using a serrated knife and a gentle sawing motion.
- Spread raspberry preserves over the bottom half.
- Replace with the top half.
- Melt butter and chocolate chips in the top of a double boiler.
- Sift in cocoa and powdered sugar.
- Stir in orange zest.
- Spread warm topping over top of cake, just to the edge.

Serves 10-12

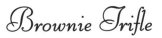
Brownie Trifle

1 (20 ounce) package fudge brownie mix

½ cup vegetable oil

¼ cup water

2 eggs

½ cup coffee-flavored liqueur

1 (3 ounce) package instant chocolate pudding mix

10 snack size chocolate-coated caramel-peanut nougat bars, chopped

1 (8 ounce) container frozen whipped topping, thawed

Chocolate shavings

- Prepare brownie mix, oil, water, and eggs according to package directions.
- Bake in a 13x9x2 inch baking dish, according to package directions.
- Pierce top of warm brownies at 1 inch intervals.
- Brush with liqueur.
- Cool. Crumble into small pieces.
- Prepare pudding mix according to package directions. Do not refrigerate.
- Place half brownie crumbs in a 3 quart bowl.
- Top with half each of the pudding, chocolate pieces, and whipped topping.
- Repeat layers of brownies, pudding, chocolate, and whipped topping.
- Top with chocolate shavings.
- Cover and refrigerate at least 8 hours.

Serves 12-14

The first heart catheterization unit in the Lehigh Valley was installed at St. Luke's in 1957, donated by Bethlehem Steel.

Black Bottom Cherry Dessert

⅔ cup powdered sugar

½ teaspoon almond extract

1 egg

1 (3 ounce) package cream cheese, softened

1¾ cups biscuit baking mix

⅔ cup miniature semi-sweet chocolate chips

1 (21 ounce) can cherry pie filling

¼ cup white chocolate chips

2 teaspoons solid vegetable shortening

- Preheat oven to 400 degrees.
- Combine powdered sugar, almond extract, egg, and cream cheese in medium bowl.
- Stir in biscuit baking mix.
- Roll or pat dough into a 12 inch circle on an ungreased baking sheet.
- Flute edge if desired.
- Bake 8 to 10 minutes or until crust is lightly browned.
- Sprinkle chocolate chips over hot crust.
- Bake about 1 minute or until chips melt. Spread chocolate evenly.
- Cool 5 minutes. Gently loosen from baking sheet and transfer to a serving plate.
- Spread pie filling over chocolate.
- Heat white baking chips and shortening over low heat, stirring frequently until smooth.
- With a fork, drizzle melted white chocolate over pie filling.

Serves 8

On the occasion of the 100th year celebration Executive Vice President Richard Suck said, "We confidently open the door to a new century in the history of St. Luke's Hospital."

Apple Crisp

8 apples, peeled and sliced

1 cup all-purpose flour

1 cup sugar

1 teaspoon salt

1 teaspoon baking powder

1 egg

1 stick butter, melted

1 teaspoon cinnamon

- Preheat oven to 375 degrees.
- Arrange apples on the bottom of 10x6x2 inch greased glass baking dish.
- Combine flour, sugar, salt, baking powder, and egg with a fork.
- Spread mixture over apples.
- Pour butter over apples and crumb mixture.
- Sprinkle cinnamon on top.
- Bake for 40 minutes.

Serves 6-8

Old Fashioned Apple Crisp

3-4 medium apples, peeled and sliced

¾ cup quick-cooking oats

¾ cup packed brown sugar

½ cup all-purpose flour

1 teaspoon cinnamon

1 stick butter

- Preheat oven to 350 degrees.
- Arrange apples in a greased 8 or 9 inch square baking dish.
- Combine oats, brown sugar, flour, and cinnamon.
- Cut in butter with pastry blender to make coarse crumbs.
- Sprinkle crumbs over apples.
- Bake for 35 to 40 minutes or until apples are soft.

Serves 4-6

Note: Serve warm with ice cream or whipped cream.

Apple Crisp

¾ cup packed brown sugar

½ cup all-purpose flour

1 stick butter, softened

Cinnamon and ground nutmeg to taste

4 cups mixed apples, cored, peeled, and
sliced medium thin

- Preheat oven to 375 degrees.
- Combine brown sugar, flour, butter, cinnamon, and nutmeg until crumbly.
- Arrange apples in a 10 inch glass pie pan.
- Cover with topping.
- Bake for 35 to 40 minutes or until browned and crunchy.
- Best served warm, topped with ice cream, whipped cream or the sauce from Pears in Burgundy recipe.

Serves 6

Note: Best made with Granny Smith, Macoun, Braeburn, or Fortune apples.

Pears in Burgundy

1 (16 ounce) can pear halves

½ cup dry red wine

½ cup orange juice

½ teaspoon ground cinnamon

¼ teaspoon ground cloves

¼ teaspoon lemon or orange zest

3 tablespoons sugar

- Drain pear juice into small saucepan. Reserve pears.
- Add wine, orange juice, cinnamon, cloves, zest, and sugar.
- Bring to boil. Reduce heat and simmer uncovered until liquid is reduced by half.
- Arrange pears in 4 stemmed glasses.
- Pour warm liquid over pears.
- Refrigerate before serving.

Serves 4

I Can't Believe It's Not Apple Crisp

4 cups peeled and sliced zucchini

⅓ cup lemon juice

½ cup packed brown sugar

½ teaspoon cinnamon

¼ teaspoon ground nutmeg

1¾ cups all-purpose flour

½ cup sugar

¼ teaspoon salt

1 stick butter

- Combine zucchini and lemon juice.
- Simmer for 15 minutes.
- Add brown sugar, cinnamon, and nutmeg. Cook an additional 5 minutes.
- Preheat oven to 350 degrees.
- Combine flour, sugar, and salt.
- Cut in butter until crumbly.
- Add ⅓ cup crumb mixture to zucchini mixture.
- Press half remaining crumb mixture in the bottom of a greased 9x9x2 inch baking dish.
- Pour zucchini mixture on top. Sprinkle with remaining crumb mixture.
- Bake for 40 to 45 minutes.

Serves 7-9

Note: Recipe may be doubled and baked in a 13x8x2 inch baking dish.

Butter Balls

2 cups all-purpose flour

¼ cup sugar

½ teaspoon salt

2 sticks butter, softened

2 teaspoons vanilla

2 cups chopped nuts (walnuts, pecans, hazelnuts)

½ cup granulated or powdered sugar

- Preheat oven to 325 degrees.
- Combine flour, sugar, and salt.
- Cut in butter and add vanilla.
- Add nuts and mix well.
- Roll dough into walnut size balls. Place on an ungreased baking sheet.
- Bake for 40 to 45 minutes or until slightly browned on edges.
- Roll in granulated or powdered sugar when cool.

Makes 2½ dozen balls

Blackberry Peach Cobbler

10 ripe peaches, peeled, pitted and
   chopped

1 vanilla bean, split lengthwise

½ cup sugar

1½ cups all-purpose flour

½ cup sugar

½ teaspoon baking powder

½ teaspoon salt

1½ sticks unsalted butter, softened

⅓ cup buttermilk

1½ pints blackberries

- Combine peaches, vanilla bean, and sugar.
- Cover and refrigerate 8 hours or overnight.
- Preheat oven to 350 degrees.
- Combine flour, sugar, baking powder, and salt.
- Add butter and beat until crumbly.
- Stir in buttermilk.
- Remove vanilla bean from peaches.
- Fill eight ramekins with peaches and blackberries.
- Top with batter.
- Bake for 35 minutes or until golden browned and fruit is bubbly.
- Cool on wire racks.

Serves 8

Note: Recipe uses 8 (5 inch) ramekins. This is delicious served warm with vanilla ice cream.

In 1978, St. Luke's Hospital opened the first vascular laboratory in the Lehigh Valley, one of the first in the United States, Canada and Puerto Rico to receive accreditation.

Beth's Brown Butter Peach Tart

Crust

7 tablespoons butter (No substitutions!), melted

⅓ cup sugar

¼ teaspoon vanilla

1 cup all-purpose flour

Pinch of salt

Filling

½ cup sugar

2 large eggs

¼ cup all-purpose flour

1 stick butter (No substitutions!)

3 medium peaches, peeled and thinly sliced

Powdered sugar

- Preheat oven to 375 degrees.
- Combine butter, sugar, and vanilla.
- Stir in flour and salt until dough just begins to come together.
- Press dough into a 9 inch tart pan.
- Bake crust for 15 minutes or until golden browned.
- In small bowl, beat sugar and eggs until well mixed.
- Beat in flour until blended. Set aside.
- In small saucepan, melt butter over medium heat.
- Cook and stir butter occasionally for about 5 minutes until a dark, nutty brown color. (Be careful not to burn butter.)
- Pour hot butter in a steady stream into egg mixture until blended.
- Arrange peach slices on warm tart shell.
- Pour hot butter mixture over peaches.
- Bake tart for 45 minutes or until puffed and golden browned.
- Cool completely on wire rack.
- Refrigerate.
- Dust with powdered sugar before serving.

Serves 8-10

The South Wing, opened March 25, 1995, a 235,000 square-foot building, is one of St. Luke's single greatest achievements during the 1990's.

Boston Cream Cheesecake

1 (9 ounce) package yellow cake mix (one layer size)

2 (8 ounce) packages cream cheese, softened

½ cup sugar

1 teaspoon vanilla

2 eggs

⅓ cup sour cream

2 (1 ounce) unsweetened chocolate squares

3 tablespoons butter

2 tablespoons boiling water

1 cup powdered sugar

1 teaspoon vanilla

- Preheat oven to 350 degrees.
- Prepare cake mix according to package directions.
- Pour batter evenly into greased 9 inch springform pan.
- Bake for 20 minutes.
- Beat cream cheese, sugar, and vanilla at medium speed until well blended.
- Add eggs, one at a time, mixing at low speed after each addition.
- Blend in sour cream.
- Pour filling over cake layer and bake for 35 minutes.
- Run knife around rim of pan to loosen cake.
- Cool before removing rim.
- For topping, melt chocolate and butter in small saucepan over low heat, stirring until smooth.
- Remove from heat.
- Add boiling water, powdered sugar, and vanilla and mix well.
- Spread over cooled cheesecake.

Serves 12

June 10, 1983 Dr. Terrill Theman performed the first open-heart surgery at St. Luke's Hospital. Today, more than 750 open-heart surgeries are performed each year.

Coconut Cream Cheesecake

Crust

⅔ cup all-purpose flour

1 tablespoon sugar

5 tablespoons butter, well chilled and cut into pieces

Filling

3 (8 ounce) packages cream cheese, softened

1 ½ cups sugar

4 eggs

2 egg yolks

2 cups coconut

1 teaspoon lemon juice

½ teaspoon vanilla

½ teaspoon almond extract

1 cup heavy cream

1 cup toasted coconut

- Preheat oven to 325 degrees.
- Combine flour and sugar.
- Cut in butter until crumbly.
- Gather dough into a ball. Wrap in plastic wrap.
- Refrigerate 15 minutes.
- Press dough into the bottom of a 10 inch springform pan.
- Bake for 15 to 20 minutes and cool.
- Beat cream cheese and sugar until smooth.
- Beat in eggs and egg yolks, one at a time, beating well after each addition.
- Mix in coconut, lemon juice, vanilla, almond extract, and cream.
- Pour filling into cooled crust.
- Bake at 300 degrees for 1 hour, 10 minutes.
- Cool.
- Top with toasted coconut.

Serves 8-12

 In the 1990's St. Luke's Hospital transitioned from a hospital to an integrated, regional, cost-effective health care delivery system.

Chocolate Raspberry Truffle Cheesecake

1 ½ cups finely crushed cream filled chocolate cookies (approximately 18)

2 tablespoons butter, melted

3 (8 ounce) packages cream cheese, softened

1 ¼ cups sugar

3 eggs

1 cup sour cream

1 teaspoon vanilla

1 (8 ounce) package cream cheese, softened

1 (6 ounce) package semi-sweet chocolate chips, melted

⅓ cup seedless raspberry preserves

1 (6 ounce) package semi-sweet chocolate chips

¼ cup whipping cream

- Preheat oven to 325 degrees.
- Combine cookie crumbs and butter.
- Press mixture into bottom of 9 inch springform pan.
- Beat cream cheese and sugar in medium bowl on medium speed until fluffy.
- Add eggs, one at a time, beating well after each addition.
- Blend in sour cream and vanilla.
- Pour batter over crust.
- In medium bowl, combine cream cheese and chocolate. Mix well.
- Add preserves and mix well.
- Drop rounded tablespoons of chocolate mixture over plain cream cheese batter.
- Do not swirl.
- Bake for 1 hour, 20 minutes.
- Loosen cake from pan rim, but allow to cool before removing rim.
- Melt chocolate chips with whipping cream over low heat, stirring until smooth.
- Spread over cheesecake.

Serves 10-12

Nut Butter Cookies

4 sticks butter, softened

2½ cups sugar

3 eggs

1 tablespoon molasses

1 teaspoon vanilla

1 teaspoon salt

1 teaspoon baking soda

5½ cups all-purpose flour

1 cup crushed walnuts

- Cream butter and sugar.
- Beat in eggs until well mixed.
- Add molasses and vanilla.
- Combine salt, baking soda, and flour.
- Add dry ingredients to creamed mixture.
- Mix in walnuts.
- Shape dough into logs about 1 ½ inches in diameter.
- Wrap in wax paper.
- Refrigerate overnight.
- Preheat oven to 350 degrees.
- Slice and bake for 8 to 10 minutes.

Makes 120 cookies

Note: Recipe can be halved. Unbaked rolls may be frozen or kept in refrigerator for up to 1 week before baking.

St. Luke's Hospital took a giant technological leap, June 2, 1994, when cardiologists began using the Rotoblator system to remove plaque blocking coronary arteries. St. Luke's Hospital was the first hospital in the region to offer the Rotoblator system.

Cranberry Oatmeal Cookies

1 ½ cups all-purpose flour

1 teaspoon baking soda

1 teaspoon cinnamon

½ teaspoon salt

1 cup packed brown sugar

½ cup sugar

2 sticks butter, softened

2 eggs

1 ¼ teaspoons vanilla

3 cups quick-cooking oats

1 (6 ounce) package dried cranberries

1 cup chopped pecans

- Preheat oven to 350 degrees.
- Combine flour, baking soda, cinnamon, and salt. Set aside.
- Beat brown sugar, sugar, and butter in a separate mixing bowl until creamy.
- Add eggs and vanilla and beat until smooth.
- Beat in flour mixture.
- Stir in oats, cranberries, and pecans.
- Drop dough by rounded teaspoonfuls onto an ungreased baking sheet.
- Bake for 9 to 10 minutes until golden browned.
- Remove to a wire rack to cool completely.

Makes 4 dozen cookies

Note: To prepare for future use, drop the dough by tablespoonfuls onto a baking sheet and freeze. Remove frozen cookies and seal in a freezer bag. Keep frozen until just before baking.

 St. Luke's Hospital has a 36,000 square-foot education center, The Priscilla Payne Hurd Education Center.

Snickerdoodle Cookies

1 cup solid vegetable shortening

2 eggs

1 ½ cups sugar

2¾ cups all-purpose flour

1 teaspoon baking soda

2 teaspoons cream of tartar

½ teaspoon salt

2 tablespoons sugar

2 teaspoons cinnamon

- Combine shortening, eggs, and sugar.
- Sift together flour, baking soda, cream of tartar, and salt.
- Stir into egg mixture.
- Refrigerate dough 1 hour.
- Preheat oven to 400 degrees.
- Roll dough into teaspoon size balls.
- Mix sugar and cinnamon together.
- Roll dough balls into sugar mixture.
- Place balls 2 inches apart on ungreased baking sheet.
- Bake for 8 to 10 minutes or until lightly browned but still soft.

Makes 5 dozen cookies

Peanut Drop Cookies

2 cups packed brown sugar

2 eggs

1 ¼ cups solid vegetable shortening

1 teaspoon vanilla

½ cup water

4 cups sifted all-purpose flour

1 teaspoon baking soda

1 teaspoon salt

Chunky peanut butter

- Preheat oven to 350 degrees.
- Cream brown sugar, eggs, and shortening.
- Add vanilla and water.
- Combine flour, baking soda, and salt. Add to creamed mixture.
- Drop dough by teaspoonfuls onto a greased baking sheet.
- Top with one-half teaspoon peanut butter. Spoon another one-half teaspoon of dough as top layer.
- Bake for 12 to 14 minutes.

Makes 5 dozen cookies

Grandmother Martha's Shortbread

2 sticks butter, softened

½ cup sugar

2 cups all-purpose flour

1 egg yolk

1 teaspoon vanilla

Dash of salt

- Preheat oven to 350 degrees.
- Cream butter and sugar.
- Add flour and mix.
- Add egg yolk, vanilla, and salt. Mix well.
- Press mixture into 13x9x2 inch baking dish.
- With a sharp knife, cut into squares and pierce each square with a fork.
- Bake for 25 to 30 minutes.
- Cool for about 5 minutes.
- Cut into squares and remove from pan.

Serves 10-12

Note: May top with sprinkles, colored according to the current holiday, before baking. May also use a smaller pan to produce thicker pieces.

In a Pinch Chocolate Cookies

1 (18 ounce) package Betty Crocker
  Devil's Food cake mix (brand sensitive)

½ cup vegetable oil

2 eggs

Chocolate chips, nuts, or coconut
  (your choice)

- Preheat oven to 350 degrees.
- Combine cake mix, oil, and eggs by hand until well blended.
- Batter will be thick.
- Add half bag chocolate chips or handful of nuts or coconut.
- Drop dough by teaspoonfuls onto baking sheet.
- Bake for 8 to 10 minutes.

Makes 36 cookies

Note: Peanut butter chips work well.

Desserts

Snow Covered Almond Crescents

2 sticks butter, softened

¾ cup powdered sugar

½ teaspoon almond extract

1¾ cups all-purpose flour

¼ teaspoon salt

1 cup quick-cooking oats

½ cup finely chopped almonds

Powdered sugar

- Preheat oven to 325 degrees.
- Beat butter, powdered sugar, and almond extract until well blended.
- Add flour and salt.
- Stir in oats and almonds.
- Using level measuring tablespoon, shape dough into crescents.
- Bake on an ungreased baking sheet for 14 to 17 minutes until bottoms are lightly browned.
- Cool on wire rack.
- Sift powdered sugar and sprinkle over cookies.

Makes 3 dozen cookies

Note: A combination of 1 teaspoon almond extract and 1 teaspoon vanilla may be used.

In 1995, Priscilla Payne Hurd received the first and only honorary diploma and nursing pin ever conferred by the St. Luke's School of Nursing. When the honors were conferred on her, Mrs. Hurd remarked, "You have given me a great gift. You have placed my name into the keeping of a healing hospital and its School of Nursing."

Crème De Menthe Squares

Cake

1 cup sugar

1 stick butter, softened

4 eggs, beaten

1 cup all-purpose flour

½ teaspoon salt

½ teaspoon vanilla

1 (16 ounce) can chocolate syrup

Mint

2 cups powdered sugar

¼ cup crème de menthe liqueur

1 stick butter, softened

Glaze

1 (6 ounce) package semi-sweet chocolate chips

6 tablespoons butter

- Preheat oven to 350 degrees.
- Combine sugar, butter, eggs, flour, salt, vanilla, and chocolate syrup.
- Pour batter into a lightly greased 13x9x2 inch baking dish.
- Bake for 30 minutes.
- Cool.
- Blend powdered sugar, liqueur, and butter.
- Spread over cooled cake.
- Melt chocolate chips and butter in a saucepan.
- Cool slightly and spread over mint layer.
- Refrigerate 3 hours or overnight.
- Cut into squares.

Serves about 20

Over $10.5 million was raised during the three-year fund raising campaign for St. Luke's Hospital in the 1990's. St. Luke's Hospital Auxiliary pledged $1 million to the campaign and remarkably fulfilled the pledge in only five years.

Brutzel Bars

1 sleeve saltine or club crackers

2 sticks butter

1 cup sugar

1 cup semi-sweet chocolate chips

Finely chopped walnuts

- Preheat oven to 350 degrees.
- Line a baking sheet with foil. Spray with cooking spray.
- Arrange crackers on sheet, pushing edges together.
- Melt butter and sugar in a saucepan. Bring to boil.
- Reduce heat to a gentle boil. (Brutzel stage.)
- Pour sugar mixture over crackers. Spread immediately.
- Bake for 10 minutes or until lightly golden browned.
- Remove from oven. Rearrange crackers if necessary.
- Top with chocolate chips. Allow to melt for 3 minutes.
- Spread chocolate over crackers. Top with walnuts immediately.
- Refrigerate.
- When firm, break into pieces and serve.

Serves 8-10

St. Luke's success was nationally recognized on January 8, 1998 with the announcement that St. Luke's Hospital and Health Network had been chosen as one of the nation's best-performing hospitals.

No Mix Bars

1 stick butter

1 cup graham cracker crumbs

1 cup flaked coconut

1 (6 ounce) package semi-sweet chocolate chips

1 (6 ounce) package butterscotch chips

1 cup chopped walnuts

1 (14 ounce) can sweetened condensed milk

- Preheat oven to 350 degrees.
- Place butter in 13x9x2 inch baking dish.
- Place in oven to melt butter.
- Remove from oven.
- Sprinkle in order the cracker crumbs, coconut, chocolate chips, butterscotch chips, and walnuts.
- Spoon milk over layers.
- Do not mix.
- Bake for 30 minutes.
- Cool and cut into bars.

Serves 12-15

Note: Easy for children to make!

Apricot Squares

2 sticks plus 4 tablespoons butter

1½ cups sugar

3 cups all-purpose flour

¾ teaspoon baking soda

¾ cup walnuts, chopped

1 cup coconut

2 (18 ounce) jars apricot preserves

- Preheat oven to 350 degrees.
- In large bowl, cream butter.
- Stir in sugar, flour, and baking soda with wooden spoon until crumbly.
- Add nuts and coconut.
- Press 4 cups of crumb mixture into a greased and floured jelly roll pan.
- Bake for 15 minutes.
- Spread preserves over crust.
- Sprinkle with remaining crumbs.
- Bake for 20 to 25 minutes or until golden browned. Check after 15 minutes. Do not over cook.

Makes 20 squares

Marbled Brownies

1 cup all-purpose flour

¼ teaspoon baking powder

¼ teaspoon salt

1 stick butter, softened

1 ½ cups sugar

2 eggs

1 teaspoon vanilla

2 (1 ounce) unsweetened chocolate squares, melted

1 cup nuts (optional)

- Preheat oven to 350 degrees.
- Sift together flour, baking powder, and salt. Set aside.
- Beat butter, sugar, eggs, and vanilla until light and fluffy.
- Stir in flour mixture and nuts until well combined.
- Divide batter in half.
- Stir chocolate into one half of batter.
- Spoon plain and chocolate batter alternately into a 9x9x2 inch baking dish.
- Swirl with a knife.
- Bake for 25 to 30 minutes.
- Cool for 10 minutes.

Serves 8

Note: May grease pan with cooking spray. Easily doubled using a 13x8x2 inch baking dish to serve 18.

Peanut Butter Yummies

1 (16 ounce) package powdered sugar

½ cup creamy peanut butter

1 egg, beaten

1 tablespoon butter, softened

½ teaspoon vanilla

½ cup chopped pecans

- Combine powdered sugar, peanut butter, egg, butter, vanilla, and pecans.
- Shape mixture into balls.
- Refrigerate for 4 to 5 hours.

Serves 20

Double Chocolate Brownies

5⅓ tablespoons butter

¾ cup sugar

2 tablespoons water

1 (12 ounce) package semi-sweet
   chocolate chips

1 teaspoon vanilla

2 eggs

¾ cup all-purpose flour

¼ teaspoon baking soda

¼ teaspoon salt

- Preheat oven to 325 degrees.
- Combine butter, sugar, and water in a saucepan.
- Bring to boil.
- Remove from heat.
- Add half chocolate chips and vanilla.
- Stir until chocolate melts and is smooth.
- Transfer to a bowl.
- Add eggs, one at a time, beating well after each addition.
- In a separate bowl, combine flour, baking soda, and salt.
- Gradually add flour mixture to chocolate mixture.
- Stir in remaining chocolate chips.
- Spread batter into 9x9x2 inch square baking dish.
- Bake for 30 to 35 minutes.

Makes 16 brownies

In 1997, 100 Top Hospitals Benchmarks for Success: "It is St. Luke's cost effectiveness coupled with outstanding clinical outcomes that resulted in St. Luke's being named one of the best hospitals in the United States."

Marble Squares

1 (8 ounce) package cream cheese, softened

⅓ cup sugar

1 egg

1 stick butter

¾ cup water

5 tablespoons cocoa powder

1½ tablespoons vegetable oil

2 cups all-purpose flour

2 cups sugar

2 eggs

½ cup sour cream

1 teaspoon baking soda

½ teaspoon salt

1 (6 ounce) package semi-sweet chocolate chips

- Preheat oven to 375 degrees.
- Blend cream cheese and sugar.
- Add egg and mix well. Set aside.
- Combine butter, water, cocoa, and oil in a saucepan.
- Bring to boil and remove from heat.
- Stir in flour, sugar, and eggs, mixing well.
- Add sour cream, baking soda, and salt. Mix well.
- Pour batter onto greased and floured jelly roll pan.
- Dot cream cheese mixture on top. Swirl with a knife to marbleize.
- Sprinkle with chocolate chips.
- Bake for 25 to 35 minutes.

Serves 24

On March 31, 1998, St. Luke's dispatched HealthStar, a 35 feet long and 11 feet high mobile health clinic offering preventive health services to almost any neighborhood.

Peanut Butter Fudge

1 (12 ounce) jar creamy peanut butter

1 (7 ounce) jar marshmallow crème

1 (16 ounce) package powdered sugar

4 tablespoons butter, softened

½ cup milk

- Cream peanut butter and marshmallow crème until smooth.
- Combine powdered sugar, butter, and milk in a saucepan.
- Bring to boil. Boil and stir for 2 minutes.
- Immediately beat into peanut butter mixture until creamy.
- Immediately pour into an 8x8x2 or 10x8x2 inch baking dish.
- Cover with plastic wrap. Refrigerate.
- Cut when firm.

Serves 10-12

Mint Meringue Kisses

2 egg whites

⅔ cup sugar

2 drops green food coloring

1 teaspoon peppermint extract

1 (12 ounce) package miniature semi-sweet chocolate chips

- Preheat oven to 350 degrees.
- Beat egg whites and sugar until stiff.
- Stir in coloring, peppermint extract, and chocolate chips.
- Drop batter by teaspoonfuls onto an ungreased baking sheet.
- Place in preheated oven.
- Immediately turn off oven and leave overnight. Do not open oven.

Makes about 40 (1 inch) round kisses

Fudge Frosting or Fudge

½ **cup cocoa powder**

2 cups sugar

1 cup milk

Butter the size of a walnut

1 teaspoon vanilla

- Combine cocoa, sugar, milk, and butter.
- Bring to boil. Boil for 8 minutes.
- Remove from heat and add vanilla.
- Beat with a mixer until cold and a spreading consistency.

Makes frosting for one cake

Note: To make fudge, boil for 12 minutes and test for soft ball stage consistency.

Coconut Ice Cream

2 cups whole milk

1 ½ cups sweetened coconut cream

1 ½ teaspoons rum

- In a large saucepan, bring milk to a boil over high heat. Do not allow to boil over.
- Immediately stir in coconut cream and remove from heat.
- Pass mixture through fine sieve into a bowl.
- Stir in rum.
- Cool completely in refrigerator over a bowl of ice cubes for at least 30 minutes.
- Transfer to an ice cream maker and follow manufacturers directions.
- Makes about 1 quart.

Serves 4-6

Note: Coconut cream can be found with drink mixes.

Strawberry Ice Cream

1 (16 ounce) package frozen strawberries
   in syrup, thawed

2 tablespoons lemon juice

½ cup sugar

1 cup sour cream

- Crush strawberries in large mixing bowl.
- Add lemon juice, sugar, and sour cream.
- Mix well.
- Pour mixture into 2 freezer containers and cover.
- Freeze 2 or more hours, stirring twice during freezing process.

Serves 4-6

Note: This is a tart, easy dessert from the 1920's.

Lemon Ice Cream

½ cup lemon juice

4 teaspoons lemon zest

2 cups sugar

1 quart light cream

- Combine juice, zest and sugar.
- Slowly stir in light cream.
- Pour mixture into two shallow and wide freezer containers.
- Cover.
- Freeze quickly at coldest setting for 3 hours.
- Do not stir while freezing.

Serves 6-8

Of significant importance was the decision of University of Pennsylvania Health System to partner with St. Luke's Hospital in the area of medical education.

Celebrities & Chefs

St. Luke's Diploma School of Nursing

Located on the Bethlehem Campus
Founded in 1884

The Auxiliary of St. Luke's Hospital
has raised more than $500,000 in support of nursing scholarships,
faculty research, endowment and a computer center.

St. Luke's Diploma School of Nursing

Located on the Bethlehem Campus
Founded in 1884

The gazebo shown on the front of this page is located in the Bishop Thorpe Garden on the School's Campus. It was fashioned from ornate ironwork salvaged and restored from the Bishop Thorpe Manor, once used as a residence hall and classrooms for the nursing students.

St. Luke's Diploma School of Nursing is the nation's oldest, continuously operating, hospital-based diploma school of nursing. Fully accredited, the school has graduated more than 3,700 professional nurses. Since June 1998, St. Luke's and Moravian College have partnered to provide an accredited baccalaureate degree in nursing.

Potato Lasagna of Wild Mushrooms with Herb Sauce

Courtesy of Inn of the Falcon, Bethlehem, PA

4 large russet potatoes, peeled and sliced into 3x1½ inch rectangles (16 slices)

2 tablespoons butter

3 ounces shiitake mushrooms, chopped

3 ounces oyster mushrooms, chopped

3 ounces white mushrooms, chopped

3 ounces chanterelle mushrooms, chopped (optional)

2 tablespoons butter

1 large shallot, finely chopped

¾ cup court bouillon or celery broth

4 tablespoons butter

½ bunch parsley, minced

Roma tomatoes, diced

- Preheat oven to 350 degrees.
- Arrange potato slices in single layer on a buttered baking sheet, and top slices with butter.
- Bake until potatoes are soft.
- Sauté all mushrooms in butter. Add shallots.
- Cover mushrooms and keep warm.
- In saucepan, reduce court bouillon by one-fourth.
- Transfer court bouillon to blender and add remaining butter. Blend to emulsify.
- Stir in parsley. Reserve sauce and keep warm.
- To assemble each serving, place one potato slice at bottom of deep soup plate. Alternately layer mushroom mixture and the three additional potato slices per plate, finishing with potato on top.
- Drizzle sauce over each plate and garnish with tomatoes.

Serves 4

*I*n July 1865, the announcement went forth that the Hon. Asa Packer proposed to crown his successful enterprise and public benefits in the Lehigh Valley by founding, "in Bethlehem South", a great polytechnic institute: to devote $500,000 and fifty-seven acres of land and to call it the Lehigh University. Ground was broken for Lehigh University, July 1866 for the original building, Packer Hall.

Shiitake Mushroom Pâté

Courtesy of Inn of the Falcon, Bethlehem, PA

2 pounds shiitake mushrooms, stems removed

1 tablespoon clarified butter

1 medium onion, finely diced

1 teaspoon salt or to taste

1 teaspoon pepper or to taste

3 tablespoons brandy

1 cup dry white wine

1 (10 ounce) package fresh spinach, rinsed

1 teaspoon fresh minced tarragon

1 teaspoon minced garlic

1 (8 ounce) package cream cheese, softened

3 eggs

¼ cup toasted walnuts, chopped

1 tablespoon clarified butter

- Clean mushrooms and chop in a food processor.
- Heat 1 tablespoon clarified butter in a 5 quart saucepan over medium heat.
- When butter is hot, add onions, salt, and pepper. Sauté for 2 minutes.
- Add mushrooms and sauté for 3 to 4 minutes.
- Add brandy and simmer for 2 minutes.
- Stir in white wine. Simmer for 12 to 15 minutes, stirring frequently.
- Add spinach, tarragon, and garlic and cook for an additional 3 minutes.
- Remove from heat and transfer mixture to a stainless steel bowl.
- Cool at room temperature for 15 minutes. Refrigerate about 30 to 40 minutes until the mixture is cold.
- Transfer to a colander to drain any excess liquid.
- Return mushroom mixture to the stainless steel bowl.
- In a food processor fitted with a metal blade, blend cream cheese and eggs to a smooth paste.
- Fold cream cheese paste and chopped walnuts into mushroom mixture. Add salt and pepper to taste.

In 1996, the Coxe Pavilion at St. Luke's Bethlehem, the last remaining original hospital pavilion was returned to the original exterior condition.

Shiitake Mushroom Pâté, continued . . .

- Preheat oven to 350 degrees.
- Lightly coat a 9x5 inch loaf pan with clarified butter. Line with parchment paper and coat again with clarified butter.
- Spread mushroom mixture evenly into pan.
- Cover with foil.
- Place pan in a roasting pan half filled with hot water.
- Bake about 1 hour, 30 minutes or until internal temperature reaches 160 degrees.
- Remove loaf pan from roasting pan. Cool at room temperature for 30 minutes before removing the foil.

- Invert pâté onto a baking sheet covered with plastic wrap.
- Remove pan and parchment paper. Cover pâté with plastic wrap.
- Refrigerate for 12 hours before serving.
- Slice chilled pâté and serve 1 to 2 slices per person with warm toasted walnut bread.

Serves 12-15

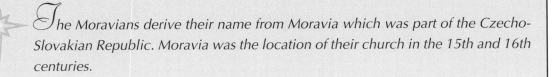

The Moravians derive their name from Moravia which was part of the Czecho-Slovakian Republic. Moravia was the location of their church in the 15th and 16th centuries.

Chocolate Terrine

Courtesy of Inn of the Falcon, Bethlehem, PA

Mousse

2 (12 ounce) packages semi-sweet chocolate chips

1½ sticks butter

12 egg yolks

16 egg whites

6 tablespoons sugar

Pastry

⅔ cup ground hazelnuts

½ cup all-purpose flour

2 tablespoons sugar

5 tablespoons butter

1 egg yolk

3 teaspoons heavy cream

Glaze

1 (6 ounce) package semi-sweet chocolate chips

4 tablespoons butter

1 tablespoon light corn syrup

⅔ cup heavy cream

¼ cup brandy

- Melt chocolate and butter in the top of a double boiler.
- Cool. Beat in egg yolks, one at a time.
- Beat egg whites with sugar. Fold into chocolate mixture until blended.
- Pour mixture into a 13½x4x3¾ inch wax paper lined terrine mold.
- Freeze for 12 hours.
- Preheat oven to 350 degrees.
- Combine nuts, flour, and sugar.
- Cut in butter. Add egg yolk and enough cream to form a dough ball.
- Roll out dough on a baking sheet into a flat rectangle slightly larger than the terrine pan.
- Cover with plastic wrap and refrigerate until firm.
- Bake until golden browned.
- Invert frozen terrine on top of crust. Remove terrine pan and waxed paper. (If the pan is difficult to remove a quick plunge into hot water may help.) Cut off excess crust.
- Melt chocolate chips with butter.
- Add corn syrup, cream, and brandy.
- Brush glaze onto crust and terrine. Freeze until firm.

Serves 12-15

Spa Cucumber and Dill Vinaigrette

Courtesy of Inn of the Falcon, Bethlehem, PA

1 cup English cucumber, peeled and diced into ¼ inch pieces

2 tablespoons shallots, peeled and finely chopped

1 teaspoon minced garlic

2 tablespoons honey mustard

1 cup herb-flavored olive oil

½ cup rice wine vinegar

½ cup orange juice

1 tablespoon finely chopped fresh dill

1 tablespoon finely chopped fresh thyme

1 tablespoon finely chopped fresh chives

Salt and pepper to taste

1 cup sparkling raspberry water

- In a bowl, combine cucumbers, shallots, garlic, mustard, oil, vinegar, orange juice, dill, thyme, and chives. Stir lightly.
- Using a bar blender, blend mixture 2 cups at a time, until it is very smooth.
- Add salt and pepper.
- Stir in sparkling water and serve.

Makes 1 quart

Note: The stems of herbs may be used to flavor an oil by placing them in the oil bottle.

Bobotie (South African Lamb and Custard Casserole)

Courtesy of Inn of the Falcon, Bethlehem, PA

Lamb

1 slice homemade-type white bread, torn into pieces

1 cup milk

1 cup minced onions

2 tablespoons olive oil or peanut oil

1 teaspoon curry powder or to taste

2 tablespoons apricot preserves

2 pounds boneless lamb shoulder, trimmed and finely chopped

1 large egg

¼ cup coarsely chopped blanched almonds

2 tablespoons fresh lemon juice or to taste

5 lemon or lime leaves, (optional) (available in West African or Asian markets)

Custard

1 ½ cups milk

3 large eggs

Salt and pepper to taste

Yellow rice and fruit chutney as a side dish

- Preheat oven to 325 degrees.
- Soak bread in milk, mashing it up.
- In a heavy pot, cook onions in oil over moderately low heat until softened.
- Add curry and preserves. Cook and stir for 1 minute.
- Add lamb and cook and stir mixture over moderate heat until lamb is no longer pink.
- Stir in egg, almonds, lemon juice, and bread mixture.
- Spoon mixture into the buttered 8x8x2 inch baking dish. Arrange lemon or lime leaves on top.
- Bake for 15 minutes.
- In a bowl, whisk together milk, eggs, salt, and pepper.
- Pour egg mixture evenly over lamb mixture and bake another 30 to 35 minutes or until the custard is just set.
- Serve Bobotie with yellow rice and chutney.

Serves 6-8

In 1741, the Moravians left Philadelphia and settled in the area where the Monocacy Creek joins the Lehigh River.

Chilled Strawberry Soup in Melon Bowls

Courtesy of Inn of the Falcon, Bethlehem, PA

2 pints fresh strawberries, washed and hulled

1 cup orange juice

1 ¼ teaspoons instant tapioca

⅛ teaspoon ground allspice

⅛ teaspoon cinnamon

½ cup sugar

1 teaspoon grated lemon zest or to taste

1 tablespoon lemon juice or to taste

1 cup buttermilk

2 chilled cantaloupes

4 paper-thin lemon slices

- Reserve 6 strawberries.
- Purée remaining berries in food processor or blender.
- Strain into 4 quart saucepan and add orange juice.
- In a small bowl, mix tapioca with one-fourth cup of strawberry purée.
- Add tapioca mixture to saucepan. Stir in allspice and cinnamon.
- Heat, stirring constantly, until mixture comes to a boil.
- Cook for 1 minute or until thickened.
- Remove from heat and pour soup into a large bowl.
- Add sugar, lemon zest, lemon juice, and buttermilk. Blend well.
- Slice reserved strawberries and fold into soup.
- Cover and refrigerate at least 8 hours.
- Cut melons in half, making saw tooth edges.
- Scoop out seeds and turn melon halves upside down on paper towels to drain.
- Cover with plastic wrap and refrigerate until ready to serve.
- Fill melons with soup and float a lemon slice on each.

Serves 4

The Moravians strong love of music is evidenced in the Bach Choir drawing music-lovers from all over the United States to Bethlehem each year for the Bach Festival.

Lemongrass Soup

Courtesy of Inn of the Falcon, Bethlehem, PA

5 cups unsweetened coconut milk

1 cup dry white wine

¼ cup plus 2 tablespoons fresh lemon juice

4 stalks fresh lemongrass, tops trimmed and bulb crushed

½ pound fresh ginger, peeled and minced

1 stalk celery, coarsely chopped

¼ cup minced fresh cilantro

1 tablespoon minced garlic

½ teaspoon salt

½ teaspoon freshly ground pepper

1½ pound live lobster

1 tablespoon olive oil

1 medium onion, halved lengthwise and thinly sliced

1 medium carrot, thinly sliced

1 small leek, white and tender green only, halved lengthwise and thinly sliced crosswise

10 medium shiitake mushrooms, caps only, minced

3 ounces thin French green beans, cut into 1 inch pieces

¼ cup coarsely chopped fresh basil

2 tablespoons finely chopped chives

1 large tomato, peeled, seeded, and cut into ⅓ inch dice

Salt and pepper to taste

- In a large nonreactive casserole dish, combine coconut milk, wine, lemon juice, lemongrass, ginger, celery, cilantro, garlic, salt, and pepper.
- Bring to boil over moderately high heat.
- Add lobster, cover, and cook for 10 minutes.
- Remove from heat, transfer lobster to a platter and let cool.
- Strain cooking liquid and reserve.
- Twist off lobster tail. Using shears, cut along the underside of the tail shell, separate shell, and remove the meat.
- Twist off claws, crack them, and remove the meat.
- Cut the lobster meat in ½ inch pieces and set aside.
- In a large stockpot, heat oil over moderately high heat.
- Add onions, carrots, leeks, and mushrooms. Cook, stirring, for 2 minutes.
- Add reserved coconut milk broth and green beans. Bring to boil.
- Reduce heat to moderately low and simmer gently about 5 minutes until the vegetables are tender.
- The soup may be prepared to this point up to 1 day ahead. Let cool, cover, and refrigerate overnight. Wrap the lobster meat and refrigerate separately. Reheat soup over moderate heat before continuing.
- Stir in lobster meat, basil, chives, and tomatoes.
- Bring to boil over moderately high heat.
- Add salt and pepper and serve immediately.

Serves 6-8

Tiramisu

Courtesy of Inn of the Falcon, Bethlehem, PA

3 large eggs yolks

⅔ cup powdered sugar

10 ounces (about 1 ¼ cups) mascarpone cheese

¼ cup dark rum

3 egg whites, room temperature

Pinch of salt

1 (7 ounce) package savoiardi (crisp Italian ladyfingers)

⅓ cup strong brewed coffee, room temperature

2 tablespoons grated bittersweet chocolate

- Beat together egg yolks and powdered sugar until pale and thickened.
- Add mascarpone and rum. Beat mixture until smooth.
- In another bowl, beat egg whites with salt into stiff peaks.
- Gently but thoroughly fold egg whites into mascarpone mixture.
- Arrange ladyfingers in a shallow 1 ½ quart serving dish. Drizzle coffee over ladyfingers.
- Spread mascarpone mixture over ladyfingers, smoothing the top.
- Sprinkle with chocolate. Cover and refrigerate for at least 6 hours or overnight.

Serves 6-8

Tinsley Jeter, a developer, named the streets in Fountain Hill, the area in which St. Luke's Bethlehem is located, keeping the Indian names, such as Mohican, Seneca, Delaware and using the names of people connected to the locality, examples, Freytag, Fiot, and Schoenen.

Crostini, Salsa Di Alicia

Courtesy of Cooking Cottage, Sellersville, PA

Crostini

1 (16 ounce) loaf Italian bread, cut into 2 inch cubes

1 pound Swiss cheese, cut into 1 inch cubes

8 (6 inch) branches of rosemary, with or without leaves (optional)

1 stick butter, melted

½ teaspoon dried oregano

Sauce

1 (2 ounce) can anchovies, drained, chopped, and mashed

½ cup olive oil

2 garlic cloves, finely chopped

2 tablespoons chopped parsley

¼ cup red wine vinegar

- Preheat oven to 350 degrees.
- Beginning and ending with bread, alternate threading bread and cheese onto skewers or rosemary branches.
- Lay skewers or branches in a buttered 13x9x2 inch baking dish.
- Combine butter and oregano. Brush generously over bread and cheese.
- Bake about 10 to 15 minutes or until browned and cheese melts.
- Combine anchovies, oil, garlic, parsley, and vinegar in a saucepan.
- Bring to boil, stirring constantly.
- Slide the bread and cheese off the skewers onto a platter. (Rosemary branches may remain on the platter.)
- Pour sauce over top and serve.

Serves 8-10

"*The Pennsylvania Dutch are not Dutch but originate in the racial stocks of South Germany. The odd dialect spoken by these Dutch descendants, neither German nor English, is known as Pennsylvania Dutch.*"

No Bake Fudge Cookies

Courtesy of Nicole Brewer, Miss Pennsylvania 2005-2006

2 cups sugar

½ cup milk

1 stick butter

¾ cup creamy peanut butter

6 tablespoons cocoa powder

1 teaspoon vanilla

3 cups quick-cooking oats

- Combine sugar, milk, and butter in a large Dutch oven.
- Boil for 1 minute over medium heat.
- Add peanut butter and cocoa.
- Mix well with wire whisk.
- Remove from heat and stir in vanilla.
- Stir in oats until mixture holds its shape.
- Drop batter by teaspoonfuls or cookie scoop onto a wax paper lined baking sheet.
- Cool before serving.

Makes 48 cookies

Note: You may need to increase the amount of oats by as much as ½ cup depending on altitude and humidity.

With the growth of industry, thousands of people from Europe, Hungarian, Lithuanian, Polish, Bohemian, Bulgarian and Russian, came to this area with their languages and churches and customs.

Baked Macaroni and Cheese

Courtesy of Nicole Brewer, Miss Pennsylvania 2005-2006

Macaroni

1 (8 ounce) package macaroni

3 tablespoons butter

1 packet powdered cheese sauce mix, from macaroni

3 cups milk

½ cup chopped onions

1 large egg, beaten

1 ½ cups shredded sharp Cheddar cheese

1 ½ cups shredded mozzarella cheese

½ cup shredded Parmesan cheese

1 teaspoon salt

Fresh black pepper to taste

Topping

4 tablespoons butter

1 cup bread crumbs

- Preheat oven to 350 degrees.
- Cook pasta in salted boiling water until al dente. Drain well.
- Melt butter in a saucepan. Whisk in cheese mix. Stir about 3 minutes or until smooth.
- Stir in milk and onions.
- Slowly add egg. Do not cook egg.
- Stir in three-fourths Cheddar, mozzarella, and Parmesan cheese.
- Add salt and pepper.
- Fold in macaroni. Pour mixture into a 2 quart casserole dish.
- Top with remaining Cheddar, mozzarella, and Parmesan cheese.
- Melt butter in a saucepan. Add bread crumbs and toss to coat.
- Sprinkle over macaroni.
- Bake for 30 minutes.
- Remove from oven and let stand 5 minutes before serving.

Serves 4-6

Bethlehem Steel and Lehigh University on the South side merged the interests of the two towns. In 1917, South and West Bethlehem merged into one city. The Hill-to-Hill Bridge opened in1923.

Bananas Foster

Courtesy of Brennan's Restaurant, New Orleans, Louisiana

4 tablespoons butter

1 cup packed brown sugar

½ teaspoon cinnamon

¼ cup banana liqueur

4 bananas, cut in half lengthwise, then halved again

¼ cup dark rum

4 scoops vanilla ice cream

- Combine butter, brown sugar, cinnamon, and banana liqueur in a flambé pan or skillet.
- Place pan over low heat on an alcohol burner or on top of the stove. Cook, stirring, until the sugar dissolves.
- Stir in bananas.
- When bananas soften and begin to brown, carefully add rum.
- Continue to cook sauce until the rum is hot, then tip the pan slightly and ignite rum.
- When flames subside, lift bananas out of pan and place four banana pieces over each ice cream portion.
- Generously spoon warm sauce over top of ice cream and serve immediately.

Serves 4

Note: Since New Orleans was the major port of entry for bananas shipped from Central and South America in the 1950's, Owen Edward Brennan challenged his head chef, Paul Blange to include bananas in a new creation. In 1951, Chef Paul created Bananas Foster, named after Richard Foster, who was Chairman of and served with Owen on the New Orleans Crime Commission, a civic effort to clean up the French Quarter. Richard Foster, who owned Foster Awning company, was a good friend of Owen and a frequent restaurant customer. Since Bananas Foster was introduced, it became the most requested item on the restaurant's menu. Thirty-five thousand pounds of bananas are flamed each year at the restaurant in preparation of the world famous dessert!

Neiman Marcus Chicken Salad

Courtesy of Neiman Marcus

1 ½ **pounds chicken breasts, cooked and refrigerated**

1 **tablespoon cider vinegar**

½ **cup finely diced celery**

1 **cup mayonnaise**

6 **tablespoons heavy cream**

1 ½ **teaspoons salt or to taste**

⅛ **teaspoon white pepper or to taste**

- Cut chicken into one-inch pieces.
- Sprinkle with cider vinegar.
- Add celery.
- Combine mayonnaise and cream.
- Fold in diced chicken and celery.
- Add salt and pepper.
- Refrigerate until ready to serve.

Serves 4

Filet Chesapeake

Courtesy of Marblehead Grille and Chowder House, Easton, PA

1 **stick butter**

4 **slices sweet red pepper**

4 **slices bell pepper**

4 **ounces crabmeat**

Pinch or two of Old Bay seasoning

2 **(6 ounce) filet mignons**

2 **slices Monterey Jack cheese**

- Melt and slightly brown butter in a skillet.
- Sauté red and bell peppers until tender.
- Add crabmeat and seasoning.
- Grill filets to desired degree of doneness.
- Melt cheese on top of each filet.
- Divide crabmeat topping among each filet.

Serves 2

Note: May substitute boneless chicken breast halves for filet mignon.

Orange Soufflé

Courtesy of Neiman Marcus

2 (1 ounce) envelopes unflavored gelatin

½ cup orange juice

2 cups sugar

4 egg yolks

1 cup orange juice

3 tablespoons fresh lemon juice

1 cup orange juice

2 cups heavy cream, whipped to soft peaks

1 cup Mandarin oranges

- Soften gelatin in orange juice. Set aside.
- Combine sugar, egg yolks, and orange juice.
- Cook over low heat until mixture is steaming and slightly thickened. Do not boil.
- Add gelatin, lemon juice, and orange juice.
- Transfer custard to a clean mixing bowl.
- Immerse the bowl into a larger bowl filled with ice and water. Cool custard, stirring occasionally, until syrupy.
- Gently fold whipped cream into custard mixture, until no streaks remain.
- Place oranges in the bottom of a 2 quart ring mold or in 12 individual molds.
- Pour custard into molds.
- Refrigerate about 2 hours or until firm.

Serves 12

Note: This soufflé is served with the Neiman Marcus Chicken Salad. Lemon or banana bread slices accompany this soufflé.

Moravian Seminary was the first girl's boarding school in America, founded in 1742 by Countess Benigna Zinzendorf.

Curried Tuna in Endive Sheaves

Courtesy of Soho Charcuterie Restaurant in Manhattan

Curried Mayonnaise

1 egg

2 egg yolks

¼ cup curry powder

1½ tablespoons chutney

1½ tablespoons tarragon vinegar

1 teaspoon freshly squeezed lemon juice

¼ teaspoon salt (optional)

¼ teaspoon freshly ground black pepper

1¾ cups light vegetable oil (approximately)

Tuna

½ cup finely diced apples

¼ cup finely diced celery

1 packed tablespoon currants

¾ cup green onions, sliced into ¼ inch
   rounds

1 tablespoon minced red onions

2 level tablespoons blanched toasted
   almonds, sliced

1 (7½ ounce) can solid or chunk tuna in
   water, drained

2 large Belgian endives

- Blend egg, egg yolks, curry, chutney, vinegar, lemon juice, salt, and pepper in a food processor or mixing bowl.
- If mixing by hand, chop chutney into small pieces.
- Process or whisk while very, very slowly adding oil to reach desired mayonnaise consistency.
- Salt and pepper to taste. Set aside. Makes 2 cups mayonnaise.
- Combine apples, celery, currants, green onions, red onions, and almonds in a mixing bowl.
- Add tuna and enough curried mayonnaise to bind.
- Stir well and refrigerate at least one hour. Separate endive leaves and rinse each in cold water.
- Drain and dry well on paper towel.
- Just before serving, spoon a tablespoon of tuna mixture into the hollows of endive spears.
- Arrange on a platter.

Serves 8-10

Fudge Tart

Courtesy of Apollo Grill, Bethlehem, PA

Crust

1¾ cups all-purpose flour

1½ sticks butter, softened

⅓ cup cocoa powder

¼ cup sugar

Dash of salt

¼-½ cup ice-cold coffee

Filling

24 ounces bittersweet chocolate

1⅓ cups sugar

⅓ cup coffee-flavored liqueur

4 tablespoons butter, softened

¼ cup heavy cream

5 eggs, beaten

- Blend flour, butter, cocoa, sugar, and salt in a food processor until small pea size balls form.
- Gradually add coffee until mixture forms into dough.
- Divide dough into two balls.
- Cover and refrigerate 1 hour.
- Roll out dough and line two 9 inch tart pans.
- Preheat oven to 350 degrees.
- Combine chocolate, sugar, liqueur, butter, and heavy cream.
- Microwave on high at 2 minute intervals, stirring until chocolate melts and is the consistency of grainy wet sand.
- Blend eggs into chocolate mixture.
- Divide filling between two tart pans.
- Bake for 30 to 40 minutes or until set.

Serves 12-16

Note: To serve, microwave each slice 30 seconds and top with vanilla bean ice cream.

The Moravian Church was established by Count Nicholas Zinzendorf in 1740. During a candle service on Christmas Eve, Count Zinzendorf named the town Bethlehem.

Thai Shrimp

Courtesy of Apollo Grill, Bethlehem, PA

1 cup soy sauce

1 cup vegetable oil

½ cup sesame oil

¼ cup sugar

3 tablespoons rice vinegar

2 tablespoons water

2 tablespoons sweet chili sauce

1 tablespoon minced garlic

1 teaspoon grated ginger

1 teaspoon Chinese five spice powder

⅛ teaspoon curry powder

4 pounds raw shrimp, peeled and deveined

Black and white sesame seeds

- Combine soy sauce, vegetable oil, sesame oil, sugar, vinegar, water, chili sauce, garlic, ginger, spice powder, and curry.
- Add shrimp to marinade. Marinate for 25 minutes.
- Sprinkle shrimp lightly with black and white sesame seeds.
- Sauté shrimp on medium high heat approximately 3 minutes on each side.
- Spoon shrimp into serving dish and sprinkle lightly with more black and white sesame seeds.

Serves 8-10

Note: Serve with sweet chili sauce and wasabi.

St. Luke's Hospital (Bethlehem, Allentown) was designated a General Electric Healthcare Global Show Site in 2002, bringing the world's leading-edge imaging technology to the hospital. There are only five such sites in the world.

Moravian Sugar Cake - Southern Style

Courtesy of Gordon and Mary Mowrer, Former Bethlehem Mayor

2-3 small potatoes, enough to make 1 cup mashed

1 ½ envelopes active dry yeast

1 cup potato cooking water

1 cup sugar

½ cup solid vegetable shortening

1 teaspoon salt

2 eggs

4 cups all-purpose flour

Butter

Light brown sugar, cinnamon, and ground nutmeg to taste

- Boil potatoes and mash. Reserve water.
- Dissolve yeast in water.
- Cream sugar, shortening, and salt.
- Add eggs, one at a time, mixing well after each addition.
- Stir in 1 cup mashed potatoes.
- Gradually stir in 2 cups flour until combined. Add remaining flour. Do not mix.
- Pour yeast mixture over flour. Blend with hands. Dough will be sticky.
- Press dough into 2 or 3 greased 9 inch round pans or one 9 inch pan and a 13x9x2 inch baking dish.
- Dough should be ¾ inch thick.
- Let rise in a warm place for 3 to 4 hours.
- Dot with butter.
- Sprinkle heavily with brown sugar, cinnamon, and nutmeg.
- Bake at 350 degrees for 10 to 12 minutes or until golden browned.
- Serve warm.

Serves 15-20

The first water works in the country was constructed in the valley of the Monocacy Creek in Bethlehem.

Bouillabaisse

Courtesy of Manor House Inn, Center Valley, PA

Shrimp

8 large shrimp, peeled and deveined, save shells

Olive oil

Mirepoix

1 cup coarsely chopped carrots

1 cup coarsely chopped celery

1 cup coarsely chopped onions

1 cup coarsely chopped leeks

1 quart seafood broth

1 quart tomato juice

1 quart clam juice

2 bulbs fennel

1 large carrot, chopped

1 large onion, chopped

6 garlic cloves, chopped

White wine

½ cup tomato paste

4 bay leaves

½ tablespoon Old Bay seasoning

Zest of 2 lemons

Juice of 2 lemons

1 large pinch of saffron

Salt and pepper to taste

Seafood

6 large sea scallops

12 mussels

8 ounces lobster meat

8 ounces lump crabmeat

8 clams, in shell

4-6 portions firm, mild fish

Saffron Aïoli

6 egg yolks

1 tablespoon chopped garlic

1 large pinch of saffron

Salt and pepper to taste

Olive oil

French bread croutons

Bouillabaisse, continued . . .

- Sauté shrimp shells in oil with carrots, celery, onions, and leeks in a large stockpot.
- Add seafood broth, tomato juice, and clam juice.
- Cook until liquid is reduced by half. Strain broth and set aside.
- In same stockpot, sauté fennel, carrots, onions, and garlic until softened.
- Deglaze with wine. Return strained broth to pot.
- Stir in tomato paste, bay leaves, seasoning, zest, lemon juice, saffron, salt, and pepper.
- Add shrimp, scallops, mussels, lobster, crabmeat, clams, and fish.
- Boil until mussels and clams open.

- Blend egg yolks, garlic, and saffron in a food processor.
- Add salt and pepper.
- While blending, add oil until mixture reaches a mayonnaise consistency.
- To serve, place a dollop of aïoli and croutons in a large soup bowl. Ladle soup on top with an assortment of seafood.

Serves 4-6

In 1997, St. Luke's and the University of Pennsylvania Health System (UPHS) established the first and only UPHS strategic partnership with a hospital in the Greater Lehigh Valley. St. Luke's and UPHS have successful cooperative agreements in trauma, cancer and medical education.

Coquilles St. Jacques

Courtesy of Manor House Inn, Center Valley, PA

Scallops

16-20 jumbo sea scallops

Butter

Whole peppercorns

White wine

1 cup chopped green onions

1 cup heavy cream

Sauce

3 cups shiitake mushrooms, sliced

3 tablespoons shallots, chopped

Vegetable oil

Dash of truffle oil

- Sear sea scallops in a hot pan with butter and peppercorns.
- Deglaze pan with white wine.
- Add green onions and heavy cream.
- For the sauce, sauté mushrooms and shallots in vegetable oil. Add truffle oil.
- Pour mushroom sauce on a platter. Arrange scallops over mushroom sauce.
- Lightly drizzle with additional truffle oil.

Serves 4-6

The Coxe Pavilion was built as a Nightingale Ward, a European design endorsed by Florence Nightingale. It was her belief that patients would recover faster with direct exposure to sunlight and fresh air. The glass cupola at the top of the building was created as a means of ventilation to reduce the transfer of disease. The St. Luke's pavilions were modeled after the original Johns Hopkins pavilions and were featured at the Universal Exposition of 1889 in Paris.

Pâté En Terrine

Courtesy of Manor House Inn, Center Valley, PA

1 pound ground veal

1 pound ground pork

½ pound fatback

3 eggs

1 teaspoon salt

1 teaspoon pepper

1 teaspoon dried basil

1 teaspoon ground thyme

1 teaspoon garlic

1 teaspoon minced shallots

Dash of horseradish

Dash of white wine

1 cup whole pistachios, shelled

Bacon slices

Garnishes with mixed greens, cornichons, capers, diced red onions, lingonberry sauce, whole grain mustard and crackers

- Preheat oven to 350 degrees.
- Purée veal, pork, fatback, eggs, salt, pepper, basil, thyme, garlic, shallots, horseradish, and wine in a food processor.
- Add whole pistachios.
- Spoon mixture into bacon-lined 9x5x2 inch loaf pan.
- Cover in plastic wrap. Cover with a weight.
- Bake in water bath for 1 hour, 30 minutes to 2 hours.
- Drain off fat. Refrigerate.
- Cut into ½ inch slices and arrange on a platter.
- Garnish with greens, cornichons, capers, onions, sauce, mustard and serve with crackers.

Serves 6-8

The Coxe Pavilion was later used for medical/surgical patients and as an isolation ward. In the 1970's, the building was converted to office space and was used by various departments until it was closed in 1994. The renovation of the building to its original look was completed in 1999. The Fowler Family Museum, which chronicles the history of St. Luke's Hospital and the St. Luke's School of Nursing, is housed in the Coxe Pavilion.

Pan Seared Duck Breast with Green Onion Risotto

Courtesy of Saucon Valley Country Club

Duck Breast

4 (4 ounce) duck breast

1 tablespoon olive oil

Green Onion Risotto

6 cups water

1 cup Arborio rice

1 tablespoon butter

1 tablespoon olive oil

¼ cup minced shallots

⅔ cup dry red wine

2 cups low sodium chicken broth

2 tablespoons Parmesan cheese

1 tablespoon butter

Salt and pepper to taste

1 cup chopped green onions

Smoked Tomato Coulis

3 ripe plum tomatoes, halved, seeded, and
    chopped

¼ cup extra virgin olive oil

3 tablespoons balsamic vinegar

1 teaspoon liquid smoke

Salt and pepper to taste

Chive Oil

1 bunch fresh chives

½ cup extra virgin olive oil

- Score the fat on each duck breast in a criss-cross pattern, to prevent curling while cooking.
- Heat sauté pan on medium until hot. Add olive oil.
- When oil just begins to smoke, place duck breast in pan fat side down.
- Sear for 4 to 5 minutes, until fat looks crisp. Turn carefully and cook 1 to 1 ½ minutes or until desired doneness.
- Remove from pan and keep warm.
- For risotto, bring water to boil in a medium saucepan.
- Add rice and simmer about 20 minutes.
- Drain in strainer and rinse.
- In same saucepan, melt butter with oil over medium heat.
- Add shallots and sauté for 1 minute. Return rice and add wine. Simmer about 4 minutes until almost all the liquid evaporates, stirring frequently.
- Add broth, one cup at a time, stirring frequently, until broth is absorbed and rice becomes tender. Process could take 12 to 14 minutes.
- When rice is tender, stir in cheese, butter, salt, and pepper.
- For coulis, blend tomatoes in food processor until almost smooth.

Pan Seared Duck Breast with Green Onion Risotto, continued . . .

- Slowly add oil, then vinegar, and liquid smoke.
- Process until smooth. Add salt and pepper. (May be made up to 8 hours ahead.)
- For chive oil, have a bowl of ice water ready. Blanch chives in boiling water. Drain through sieve and immediately place in ice water until chilled. Remove from water and squeeze excess water out. Drain on paper towels.
- Chop chives and place in blender. Purée with olive oil until smooth.

- Cover and refrigerate up to 8 hours before serving. Strain chive mixture through sieve, pressing on solids, before serving.
- To serve, scoop desired amount of risotto onto plate. Place whole or sliced duck breast on top.
- Drizzle smoked tomato coulis around the outside of risotto. Drizzle chive oil over coulis for extra color.

Serves 4

A press conference and national media tour were held in December 2002 at St. Luke's to introduce the GE Innova 4100, interventional radiology equipment used in vascular procedures, the first of its kind in the world. Clinical trials for the Innova 4100 were held at St. Luke's Hospital. With the images created by the Innova 4100, physicians can better treat a variety of blood vessel disorders, uterine fibroids and other conditions without major surgery. With these precise images, physicians are able to see clearly inside a patient's blood vessels while guiding catheters and other medical devices to areas of the vessel needing treatment.

Jackson Salad

Courtesy of Saucon Valley Country Club

Salad

1 head crisp Romaine lettuce, cut, rinsed and dried

1 beefsteak tomato, sliced

3 slices red onion

2 tablespoons blue cheese, crumbled

1 tablespoon bacon bits

½ cup artichoke hearts

½ cup seasoned croutons

Dressing

1 egg

1 teaspoon English mustard

¼ teaspoon kosher salt

⅛ teaspoon white pepper

½ cup canola oil

¼ cup tarragon vinegar

- Place lettuce in a salad bowl. Add tomatoes, onions, blue cheese, bacon bits, artichoke hearts, and croutons.
- For the dressing, beat egg and add mustard, salt, pepper, and tarragon vinegar. Blend well.
- Slowly add oil until completely blended.
- Taste dressing and adjust any seasonings to taste.
- Add dressing to salad, toss and serve.

Serves 2-4

St. Luke's was first named one of the nation's best heart hospitals by U.S. News & World Report in 1999. St. Luke's would eventually receive this national recognition for seven consecutive years — an unprecedented achievement among Pennsylvania heart hospitals. In 2003, St. Luke's was the highest ranked heart hospital in Pennsylvania.

Maryland Crab Cakes

Courtesy of Saucon Valley Country Club

3 large eggs

1 cup mayonnaise

1 tablespoon Dijon mustard

1 teaspoon Old Bay seasoning

2 tablespoons crushed cracker crumbs

1 tablespoon chopped parsley

¼ cup fresh lemon juice

1 pound jumbo lump crabmeat

1 pound lump crabmeat

Melted butter (optional)

Paprika to taste (optional)

Tartar sauce, Rémoulade sauce, cocktail
    sauce or lemons

- Beat eggs to a smooth consistency.
- Add mayonnaise, mustard, seasoning, cracker crumbs, parsley, and lemon juice.
- Beat until thoroughly mixed.
- In a separate bowl, combine jumbo crabmeat and crabmeat.
- Fold mayonnaise mixture into crabmeat.
- Refrigerate for about 30 minutes.
- Preheat oven to 425 degrees.
- Remove crab mixture from refrigerator and gently mix again.
- Using an ice cream scoop, spoon crab mixture onto a large, greased baking sheet.
- Drizzle with butter and sprinkle with paprika.
- Bake for 15 minutes or until golden browned.
- Serve with tartar sauce, Rémoulade sauce, cocktail sauce, or fresh lemons.

Serves 8-10

In 2002, St. Luke's became the first hospital in Pennsylvania to use the da Vinci robotically assisted surgery system. Subsequently, St. Luke's became the first hospital in the region to offer robotically assisted heart surgery (2003) and the first in the state to provide robotically assisted prostatectomy (2004). Today, St. Luke's has the most experienced robotically assisted surgical team in Pennsylvania.

Sautéed Bay Scallops and Shiitake Mushrooms in a Sherry Cream Sauce

Courtesy of Chef Tim Widrick, Edge Restaurant, Bethlehem, PA

1 pound dry bay scallops

¼ pound diced shiitake mushrooms

¼ cup sherry wine

¼ cup heavy cream

¼ teaspoon fresh chopped garlic

Salt and pepper to taste

Precooked puff pastry

- In a hot skillet, sauté scallops and shiitake mushrooms.
- Cook for 1 minute then add sherry.
- Reduce sauce by half.
- Add cream, garlic, salt, and pepper.
- Reduce to desired thickness.
- Serve on a precooked puff pastry.

Serves 4

Greek Horiatiki Salad

Courtesy of Gus's Crossroads Inn, Bethlehem, PA

4 red skin potatoes

Feta cheese, crumbled

Tomatoes, diced

Cucumber, sliced

Kalamata olives

Capers

Olive oil and red wine to taste

- Boil potatoes until soft.
- Drain potatoes, cool, and remove outer skin.
- Slice potatoes about ⅛ inch thick and place in large bowl.
- Add feta cheese, tomatoes, cucumbers, olives, and capers.
- Add oil and wine. Toss to coat.
- Serve cool.

Serves 2

Whole Baby Flounder or Red Snapper

Courtesy of Gus's Crossroads Inn, Bethlehem, PA

1 whole flounder or red snapper

Extra virgin olive oil

Freshly squeezed lemon juice

Dried oregano

- Place cleaned whole fish in a broiler pan. (Head may be removed, if preferred.)
- Slice diagonally across fish 3 times with a sharp knife.
- In a bowl, whisk together oil, lemon juice, and oregano. Pour over entire fish.
- Broil for 10 to 15 minutes, depending on the size of fish.
- Serve with fresh Dandelion greens or spinach sautéed in olive oil and fresh garlic.

Serves 4

Note: A pleasant ending to this wonderful meal is a mixture of fresh yogurt mixed with honey and crushed walnuts.

Crossroads Chicken

Courtesy of Gus's Crossroads Inn, Bethlehem, PA

2 boneless, skinless chicken breast halves

Extra virgin olive oil

¼ cup balsamic vinegar

2 tablespoons honey

Fresh whole leaf spinach, rinsed

Sliced mushrooms

2 slices of Swiss cheese

- Sauté chicken in small amount of oil.
- When chicken is cooked thoroughly, add vinegar, honey, spinach, and mushrooms.
- Simmer until spinach wilts and mushrooms are soft.
- Top with Swiss cheese. Cover pan until cheese melts.
- Serve with pan juices ladled over the top.

Serves 2

Southwestern Corn and Red Pepper Chowder

Courtesy of Rob Vaughn, Anchor, WFMZ-TV

2 ½ slices thick-sliced bacon

1 cup chopped onions

1 ½ cups diced sweet red peppers

2 cups frozen corn

2 large tomatoes, diced

2 chicken bouillon cubes

2 cups water

1 (14 ounce) can evaporated milk

- Slice bacon into narrow strips.
- Brown bacon in a large saucepan until crispy.
- Add onions and cook until soft.
- Add peppers and cook until soft.
- Add corn, tomatoes, bouillon, and water.
- Simmer until thoroughly cooked.
- Add evaporated milk and heat thoroughly.

Serves 10-12

Sour Cream Pound Cake

Courtesy of Rob Vaughn, Anchor, WFMZ-TV

2 ¼ cups all-purpose flour

2 cups sugar

1 teaspoon vanilla

1 (8 ounce) container sour cream

½ teaspoon salt

½ teaspoon baking soda

2 sticks butter, softened

3 large eggs, room temperature

- Preheat oven to 325 degrees.
- Combine flour, sugar, vanilla, sour cream, salt, baking soda, butter, and eggs in a large mixing bowl.
- Blend at low speed to moisten.
- Beat 3 minutes at medium speed.
- Pour batter into greased and floured 10 inch tube pan.
- Bake for 60 to 70 minutes or until center springs back when touched lightly.
- Cool 15 minutes.
- Remove from pan and allow to cool completely.

Serves 10-12

Note: This pound cake can also be made in layers or a 13x8x2 inch baking dish. It can be served plain, with powdered sugar sprinkled on top, or iced.

Kibbee

Courtesy of Ed Hanna, Chief Meteorologist, WFMZ-TV

1 cup bulgur wheat

½ cup pine nuts

4 medium onions, minced

1½ pounds lean ground beef

1 teaspoon pepper

1 teaspoon salt

⅛ teaspoon ground allspice

3 tablespoons butter, melted

- Soak bulgur wheat for 1 hour. Squeeze to drain.
- Sauté pine nuts and onions until lightly browned.
- Combine wheat, beef, pepper, salt and allspice.
- Mix and knead for about 10 minutes. Divide in half.
- Press one half into the bottom of a buttered 8x8x2 inch baking dish.
- Spread onion mixture on top.
- Press remaining meat mixture over onions, pressing down and smoothing top.
- Run a spatula along outer edges, forming a ridge.
- Dip spatula in cold water and slice lengthwise down the pan. Slice crosswise forming diamond shaped pieces.
- Brush top with butter.
- Bake at 400 degrees for 20 to 30 minutes or until browned.

Serves 6-8

When the Men's Pavilion of St. Luke's Hospital opened in 1881, the present management was established and has continued ever since. St. Luke's was the pioneer in establishing the modern system of hospital management, namely, placing the whole care and responsibility of the management and treatment of patients under one head and director. This system has been taken up and followed by the best hospitals in the country.

Chef Donovan's White Chocolate Cheesecake

Courtesy of Chef Brian Donovan

Crust

2 cups graham cracker crumbs

¼ teaspoon ground cinnamon

1 stick butter, melted

½ cup sugar

Filling

1¼ pounds white chocolate, broken into pieces

1¼ cups heavy cream

2 (8 ounce) packages cream cheese, softened

1 (3 ounce) package cream cheese, softened

1 cup sugar

4 eggs

1½ cups sour cream

¼ teaspoon salt

2 tablespoons vanilla

- Preheat oven to 325 degrees.
- Combine crumbs, cinnamon, butter, and sugar. Mixture will be sticky.
- Butter the bottom and sides of a 9 inch springform pan.
- Press mixture into the bottom and up the sides, evenly distributed and all the way to the top.
- Set aside.
- Combine white chocolate and cream in a metal or heatproof bowl. Set it over, but not touching boiling water.
- Cook and stir until chocolate melts and is smooth. Remove from heat. Do not allow chocolate to cook more than enough to blend with the cream.
- With a paddle attachment on an electric mixer, as opposed to a whip, beat cream cheese until smooth.
- Add sugar and beat until smooth and aerated.
- While mixing on medium speed, slowly pour in chocolate mixture. Blend well.
- Add eggs, sour cream, salt, and vanilla. Blend only until smooth trying to avoid the whip and the sides.
- Pour filling into crust, avoid spilling on the edge.
- Wrap entire pan in two layers of heavy duty foil. Wrap right up to the top edge of the pan, but then fan it out so when the cheesecake rises, it does not touch.
- Place wrapped cheesecake pan into a water bath filled with boiling water, at least ½ inch deep.
- Bake for 1 hour, 15 minutes or until top hasn't lost its shimmer.
- Remove from water bath. Cool at room temperature.
- Refrigerate at least 6 hours.

Serves 12-16

Index

Index

Index

When You Cook Upon A Star

The Auxiliary of St. Luke's Hospital
801 Ostrum Street
Bethlehem, PA 18015
Phone: 610-954-3393 • Email: www.auxiliary@slhn.org

Please send me _____ copies of *When You Cook Upon A Star* @ $25.00 each_____
(Tax included for Pennsylvania residents)

Postage and Handling ($5.00 for first book; $3.00 each for additional
books to same address)   _____

TOTAL: $ _____

Name _____

Address _____

City _____ State_____Zip _____

Daytime phone number _____ Email _____

Make checks payable to: The Auxiliary of St. Luke's Hospital

- -

When You Cook Upon A Star

The Auxiliary of St. Luke's Hospital
801 Ostrum Street
Bethlehem, PA 18015
Phone: 610-954-3393 • Email: www.auxiliary@slhn.org

Please send me _____ copies of *When You Cook Upon A Star* @ $25.00 each_____
(Tax included for Pennsylvania residents)

Postage and Handling ($5.00 for first book; $3.00 each for additional
books to same address)   _____

TOTAL: $ _____

Name _____

Address _____

City _____ State_____Zip _____

Daytime phone number _____ Email _____

Make checks payable to: The Auxiliary of St. Luke's Hospital